*Dreaming in Russian*

# Dreaming in Russian

## THE CUBAN SOVIET IMAGINARY

*by Jacqueline Loss*

University of Texas Press     *Austin*

Requests for permission to reproduce material from this work should be sent to:
Permissions
University of Texas Press
P.O. Box 7819
Austin, TX 78713-7819
utpress.utexas.edu/index.php/rp-form

⊗ The paper used in this book meets the minimum requirements of
ANSI/NISO Z39.48-1992 (R1997) (Permanence of Paper).

LIBRARY OF CONGRESS CATALOGING-IN-PUBLICATION DATA
Loss, Jacqueline.
Dreaming in Russian : the Cuban Soviet imaginary / by Jacqueline Loss. —
First edition.
    p.    cm.
Includes bibliographical references and index.
ISBN 978-0-292-76203-9
1. Cuba—Relations—Soviet Union.   2. Soviet Union—Relations—Cuba.
3. Cuba—Civilization—1959-   4. Imagination—Political aspects—Cuba.
5. Imagination—Social aspects—Cuba.   6. Popular culture—Cuba.
7. Collective memory—Cuba.   I. Title.
F1776.3.S65L67   2013
327.7291047—dc23                                                    2012042788

doi:10.7560/745292

First paperback edition, 2014

# Contents

*Acknowledgments*

$T$o talk about what one believes to be hers is difficult, let alone pretending to know anything about another. My readings of what constitute "dreaming in Russian" are themselves phantasmagoric, to borrow a word from Chapter 5's title — "Phantasmagoric Sputnik" — a title that in many ways is an equally accurate assessment of this book. They may be characterized by a vague yet strong generational affinity with the Muñequitos Rusos generation, those who came of age in the 1980s and who were raised on Soviet Bloc cartoons. And this from someone who hardly knows any cartoons but the *Flintstones*, but who is affectively informed by a world that was once rendered as split in two and momentarily delivered as "one."

This book is the product of over ten years of discussions. My steady and remarkable group of interlocutors has dialogued with me closely, helped introduce me to old and new stories, artwork, personal collections, and people. Ernesto René Rodríguez's musings on the 1980s in Cuba were irresistible. Raúl Aguiar, Carmen Berenguer Hernández, Yana Elsa Brugal, Víctor Fowler Calzada, Jorge Miralles, Antonio José Ponte, and Reina María Rodríguez have elaborately shaped my understanding of what their pasts — experienced through a Soviet lens — felt like. Raúl Aguiar's generosity, not only with his own childhood Rusophillic archive but also with his vast awareness of Cuban fiction today, has been immense. Initial conversations with Jorge Fornet confirmed to me that I could be onto something. Caridad Tamayo has been an amazing friend and colleague whose assistance at every step of the way has been essential. Desiderio Navarro's exceptional relationship to the Soviet Bloc would require a lifetime to begin to understand; I thank him for translating for me aspects of it. Pedro Manuel González Reinoso, Oneyda González, Polina Martínez Shvietsova, Gustavo Pérez, Dmitri Prieto Samsonov, Anna Lidia Vega Serova, and Yoss have also helped make this project a labor of love. Artists Gertrudis Rivalta, Tonel, and Jorge Luis Marrero have lingered with me, especially through e-mails, about their own investments in the topic. Most of these names will re-appear in the succeeding chapters, reminding me how fortunate I have been to collaborate with these thinkers and creators. That my readings do not always collude with theirs is to be expected, but I hope that they sometimes do, and at least create productive discrepancies.

Anke Birkenmaier, Esther Allen, Naomi Lindstrom, Odette Casamayor-Cisneros, Ariana Hernández Reguant, Marta Hernández Salván, Osvaldo Pardo, Rachel Price, José Manuel Prieto, Laura Redruello, Andrew Rubin, César Salgado, Rainer Schultz, and Armando Suárez Cobián all have engaged with this project; I thank them. The hard work and reliability of teaching assistant Jorge Castillo have allowed me to get to this point. It is nearly impossible to imagine the fruits of my effort without Esther Whitfield's collaboration. I thank Mervyn J. Bain for keeping me abreast of this topic from an entirely distinct disciplinary perspective. For the readings of José Quiroga and Elzbieta Sklodowska, I am indebted. My colleagues in Spanish; the Department of Literatures, Cultures and Languages; and the Research Foundation at the University of Connecticut have helped me sustain the kind of long-term research that this project has entailed.

My father, Calvin Loss, my mother, Barbara Rosenberg Loss, my brother, Daniel Loss, and my aunts, Florence Preiser and Madeleine Buchsbaum, have offered a degree of belief in me that has propelled me forth.

I am grateful to Mary Taveras and Sue Carter for their careful editing of my book, to Casey Kittrell for his introduction to the University of Texas Press, to Molly R. Frisinger, Victoria A. Davis, and especially, to Theresa May, for helping me bring this book to fruition.

*Dreaming in Russian*

*Introduction*

his book emerged from the sort of conversation that often has
the greatest impact on me—the sort that doesn't include me.
It took place in 2001 when I accompanied a Cuban colleague who lived in the
United States and his Spanish-speaking Russian wife to the Old Havana home
of two of his friends who remained on the island: a theater critic and a painter.
After a bit of rum, the linguistic world switched to Russian, and in the last thirty
or so minutes of the dinner, I was left out. There was laughter and little translation. All four eventually reconciled their behavior, explaining to me that they
had in common this phenomenon of longing for certain elements of the Soviet
Union, where they had all studied some years before. It was becoming clear to
me that although Russian was no longer the principal language of international
affairs, it did function as a foil in my presence. For these Cubans, who were
born in the 1940s and 1950s and who had studied in the Soviet Union, the Russian language—at least for that evening—continued to defend Cuba against
the Americans.

Around that same time something else occurred. I was wandering around
Havana in a manner that I envision to be similar to the way *flâneurs* wandered
around Paris, although I was under the impression (at least back then) that I
was reflecting on something other than the aura of urban ruins, something that
seduced me as much and was at once frivolous and crucial. Accompanying me
was my accomplice in the streets, who delivered a speech on why he preferred
that his sexual partners sport simple, childish, cotton underwear instead of, say,
Victoria's Secret or even Spain's answer to it, Women's Secret—both brands
that "regular" Cubans can hardly access as purchasing consumers. From what I
gathered, he was not making excuses for a Lolita-like perversion; rather, he explained that this plain cotton underwear was evocative of another period, the
period of his youth, when almost everyone donned the same kind of bloom-

ers. It was the time when Cubans acquired their clothing primarily by way of the Soviet Bloc—not China, Venezuela, the United States, Western Europe, or through tourist transactions.

Then other hearsay corroborated. My friend's fancy was not exactly a rarity. A year or two later, the award-winning Cuban writer Wendy Guerra (born in 1970) told me that her future book would be entitled "Bloomers," and although it was later renamed *Ropa interior*, a standard term for undergarments, both the new and revised titles similarly flash back to the 1980s, when Cubans shared the same style of underwear with a vast number of folks from far away.

*Dreaming in Russian: The Soviet Cuban Imaginary* demonstrates that while the Soviet Bloc no longer exists as Cuba's political ally, it has left significant and complex remnants within the island's contemporary cultural production. Drawing on interviews with Cuban artists, functionaries, and intellectuals; and cinematographic and bibliographic archives from the 1960s, 1970s, and 1980s; as well as theory on postmodernism, postcolonialism, and post-Soviet culture, this book illustrates that Cuba is in the unusual position of remembering its own interactions with the Soviet Union at the same time that Cuba's political and social order is perceived by some as a relic of the Cold War.

In the wake of the Soviet Union's disintegration in 1991, food, electricity, and gasoline became scarce. In order to survive without its greatest ally, Cuba faced the necessity of revising legal, cultural, and economic paradigms. In 1992, the Cuban Constitution was modified; references to Marx and Lenin were accompanied by newly added references to the Cuban national hero José Martí, and the phrase "fraternity with the Soviet Union" was deleted. In 1993, the legalization of the dollar as a form of exchange signaled the beginning of a dual economy. Amid this social upheaval, it is not surprising that almost immediately after the Soviet Union's dissolution, many Cubans claimed to have inherited next to nothing from the Soviets and even blamed the Revolution's most repressive measures on Soviet influence. Nevertheless, as *Dreaming in Russian* attests, cultural production since the mid-1990s does account for the Soviet impact, via interpretive approaches that range from naïve nostalgia to parody. Cuban artists often implement a "defensive memory" as a mode of catharsis and as a manner of combating fear about their nation's unknown future. The "Russian" of this book's title refers to the ambiguous ways in which Cubans utilize the term "*rusos*," to refer to all those people and things from the Soviet Union, and at times, even from other parts of the Soviet Bloc. In addition, in some instances, "*ruso*" was utilized against the officially ordained "Soviet." Today, these ambiguities and conscious misidentifications remain in effect.

Toward the end of the 1990s and into the twenty-first century, nostalgia for the Soviet Bloc and more specifically for East Germany has been a force with which artists, politicians, social scientists, and cultural critics have contended.

That phenomenon, known by the German term "*Ostalgie,*" achieved international attention in 2003 with Wolfgang Becker's ironic, pop-cultural *Good Bye, Lenin!*—a film that tragicomically depicts a son's efforts to preserve the memories of his convalescing Socialist mother in the face of a burgeoning capitalism in Berlin. A more somber cinematographic portrayal of life in East Germany is represented in Florian Henckel von Donnersmarck's fraught melodrama *The Lives of Others* (2006). Such films chronicle contemporary currents and excavate recent history; at the same time, Socialist politics have made a real comeback, not only in the former Soviet Bloc but also throughout many regions in Latin America. These processes have numerous implications for the study of contemporary Cuban cultural politics.

In fact, both films have elicited vivid and direct comparisons by Cubans. The former screened for crowds at a small German film festival in 2003 in Havana and inspired Asori Soto's short 2005 documentary about Soviet Bloc cartoons, entitled *Good Bye, Lolek.* The fact that *The Lives of Others,* a film showing the evildoings of the Stasi and the involvement of the German people in everyday espionage, was, in fact, also shown in Cuba in 2007 might suggest that the Cuban government was not fearful of any comparisons between East German and Cuban history. However, the film was screened only for a limited time and to a select group of people in a fashion that secured both a distance and a lack of complicity for Cubans on the island—the precariousness of which is obvious in Cubans playfully calling the film "La vida de nosotros" (Our Lives) rather than its title in Spanish, *La vida de los otros.*

In 1997, the same year that Abel Prieto became minister of culture in Cuba, he published *El humor de Misha: La crisis del "socialismo real" en el chiste político* (Misha's Humor: The Crisis of "Real Socialism" in Political Jokes), a fascinating account of Socialist humor involving the Soviets. By directly addressing this theme, it is as if Prieto were ensuring his readers that Cubans are onlookers, rather than direct victims—that they are far removed from the sort of oppressive experience that evoked such a humoristic response. Prieto identifies jokes related to the internationalist notion of "la amistad entre los pueblos" (friendship among peoples) and explains that they emerged from the "colonial perception of relations between the USSR and other countries from the Bloc"—a perception that cannot be compared to Cubans' experience of the Soviets, since, according to Prieto, Cubans placed themselves in a position that was aesthetically and sentimentally superior to them.[1]

With respect to the term "*bolos,*" which Cubans use to refer to the Soviets, Prieto asserts:

> It was more a benevolent, pardoning parody, without rancor or bile.
> This expression separates us radically from every Plattist mechanism of

subordination. It places Cubans in a superior, almost paternal position, and they contemplate the *bolo* as someone who came from the rudimentary world. There is not the Plattist admiration for the foreigner, nor the envy, nor the eagerness to imitate, nor the hate that is generated as the inverse of Plattism against the colonizer.[2]

The contrast that Prieto draws between the Soviet impact in Cuba and the expansion of the United States' sphere of influence on the island at the turn of the twentieth century through the Platt Amendment relies on the notion that the Soviet Union is not a colonizer, like the United States.[3] If the Revolution, as Roberto Fernández Retamar advised in his groundbreaking 1971 essay "Calibán," was to move forward on the right footing, Cubans needed to embrace the Shakespearian figure of Caliban as the rebellious hybrid voice of the new Americas, rather than hold on to the voice of the colonizer represented by Ariel, the Europeanized, bourgeois intellectual. Prieto's analysis of the Soviet impact in Cuba, on the other hand, would seem to say that the Revolution does not have to bother with reforming the "Yuris" (after Yuri Gagarin) of "Generation Y," who were born in the 1970s (many of whom were given Russian names), when the Soviets were most influential.

During the December 2000 visit of Vladimir Putin to Cuba—the first Russian president to visit the island since the Soviet disintegration—a Cuban on the streets told Reuter's correspondent Isabel García-Zarza what she thought about the Russian/Soviet presence: "No quedó nada, no bailamos como los rusos, no comemos como los rusos, y ni siquiera bebemos vodka" (Nothing remained, we don't dance like Russians, we don't eat like Russians, and we don't even drink vodka). A Russian who had lived in Cuba for thirteen years stated that "cubanos y rusos son pueblos con una cultura y una idiosincracia tan diferentes que la fusión era imposible y la influencia mínima" (Cubans and Russians are peoples whose cultures and idiosyncracies are so different that their fusion was impossible and the influence, minimal).[4] The presence of Russian names on the island, good deals at Russian stores, and Putin's recollections of speaking in his native tongue with Cubans counteracted these expressions of disunion.

The troubled union is recalled stereotypically in the 2005 slapstick Spanish/Cuban co-production *Un rey en la Habana* (A King in Havana), directed by the Cuban Alexis Valdés. This film is one of numerous examples illustrating that Cubans on the island and in the diaspora often remember the Soviets similarly—though, as we shall see, the ramifications of these memories may be distinct. In the film, dwellers of a tenement house (known in Cuba as a *solar*) plot to swindle a Spaniard who has died of an overdose of "sex pills." So that his beautiful young Cuban girlfriend can collect the Spaniard's foreign assets, her neighbors incinerate his corpse and stage her marriage to a dummy made up to look like the deceased. The dummy is prepared by the same makeup artist who—we are told—transformed the award-winning Cuban actor Mario Balmaseda into Lenin in Nikolai Pogodin's *The Chimes of the Kremlin* for the 1980 theatrical production. This detail might have gone unnoticed if it were not for numerous jokes about the Soviet period from the very start, most of which relate to the machinery it supplied Cuba. "Love's like a Russian TV. While it works, great, but when it breaks, shit!"

In order for the hoax to be carried out, the body is brought to the "Cuba-USSR Friendship" incinerator, but alas, it is not functioning. Guarding the incinerator is Gerardo, an aging stalwart who was introduced to viewers earlier in the film when he was looking for "[his] Capital," which his son tells us is "of course the one by Karl Marx." The old Communist explains that the incinerator is not working because they are waiting for a part from the Soviet Union, and when he is told that the country itself no longer exists, he is unalarmed. "So what? People wait for Santa Claus every year. In life, expectation is what matters. The spare part is a metaphor." *Un rey en la Habana* suggests that comical metaphors like these not only existed in Cuba during the Soviet period itself, but also sustained the island throughout the Special Period in times of peace — a time of material dearth and little ideological renewal after the Soviet Union's collapse.

Susan Buck-Morss's analysis of political philosophy and the arts in the Soviet Union during and immediately after Perestroika helps to explain the post-Soviet period in Cuba; the term "Perestroika" itself is for many Cubans problematic, since it detracts from the autochthony that they needed to uphold, particularly in the wake of the crisis of the disintegration of the Soviet Union in 1991.

> In the last days of the Soviet regime, dissident artists within the Soviet Union represented its past history as a dreamworld, depicting the crumbling of the Soviet era before it occurred in fact. For this generation, the moment of awakening replaced that of revolutionary rupture as the defining phenomenological experience. Exemplary is a 1983 painting of Aleksandr Kosolapov, *The Manifesto*, in which, against a martial red sky and amidst ruins that include a bust of Lenin, three putti try to decipher a surviving copy of Marx's *Communist Manifesto*. The dreamer who is still inside the dream of history accepts its logic as inexorable. But at the moment of awakening, when the dream's coherence dissipates, all that is left are scattered images. The compelling nature of their connection has been shattered.[5]

Identification and analysis of scattered images of the Soviet Union and, to a lesser extent, the Soviet Bloc within contemporary Cuban culture is what this book sets out to do, a project that is particularly complex since within Cuba, the dreamer, as *Un rey en la Habana* implies, is still inside of the dream of history, even though it may be narrated in a slightly different way.

More than any other artistic piece, the 1995 *nueva trova* song "Konchalovski hace rato que no monta en Lada" (Konchalovsky Hasn't Ridden a Lada in a While), by the well-known Cuban singer Frank Delgado, captures what it feels like to inhabit the remains of the Soviet Bloc in the Caribbean.[6] Born in 1960, Delgado was fed, as the song recounts, a Soviet-Cuban cultural diet typical of the 1970s and came of age in the 1980s with a broad familiarity of Soviet culture, like many of the artists whose works I examine in this book. The laughter and sighs of the listeners heard in Delgado's live recording of the song suggest that in the aftermath of the Soviets' impositions, Cubans experienced some longing for certain aspects of the diet, but felt even more relief over their ability to express their taste concerning ideological matters related to the Soviet Bloc. Delgado's ballad revels in that ability to have an opinion about Karl Marx. The song's repeated question and answer—"Someone asked me if I'd read *Capital.* / Yes, but I didn't like it, since the heroine dies in the end"—marks the conversion of Marxism-Leninism from being the singular master narrative to becoming just another ideology or minor fiction up for critique. Even for Gerardo of Valdés's comedy, *Capital* is a work of literature.

Subjects struggling to find their place in the new world disorder is a characteristic Cuban response to the Soviet disappearance from the island in the early 1990s. The construct of the "Special Period" was built upon Cubans not feeling the failure of the utopian fantasy through the passionate assertion of rhetorical difference from the failed international narrative. Buck-Morss's observation brilliantly describes artistic reactions to the obligatory sentimental numbing. "Precisely because these socialist dreamworlds entered into the utopian fantasy of childhood, they acquired a critical power, as memory, in adults."[7] The very same statement is relevant to the experience of those who came of age in a dreamworld composed of the replication of Soviet greatness in Cuba. They may have witnessed it at the massive 1976 exhibition in Cuba's capital building, called Logros de la ciencia y la técnica soviética (Accomplishments in Soviet Science and Technology), or they may have watched Arnaldo Tamayo, the first Cuban cosmonaut, lift into outer space with Soyuz 38 from the Baikonur Cosmodrome in 1980. The greatness of such machinery "balanced out" adults' complaints regarding the drabness of Soviet material products, cartoons, and cinema, and their distrust of having to regularly assume the rhetoric of that faraway nation as their own.

The sarcasm of Delgado's lyrics was echoed across Cuban society, especially in the last decade of the second millennium and in the first few years of the third one. About the decade of the 1990s, the Cuban philosopher Jorge Luis Acanda remarked: "We demystify all those cultural products that make up this ideological complex that we can denominate as the *Soviet*, from Socialist realism to Russian cartoons to the quality of the technology *made in USSR* and the so-called omnisapience of the PCUS [Communist Party of the Soviet Union] leaders."[8] The characteristic of "omnisapience," or all-wisdom, most frequently used to refer to God, is here applied to the Soviets, implying the extent to which Soviets were an almost invisible force with superhuman power. Within the process of desacralization, "made in USSR" is deprived of its use value and is in the process of becoming a relic. Yet, relics too can have their prestige.

How was that omnisapience construed? Víctor Fowler Calzada, a Cuban writer, scholar, and librarian, once conveyed to me that it was as if every discipline was approached and every structure of knowledge was attained through the Soviet lens. One of Fowler Calzada's many anecdotes illustrating this concept was that of a colleague who, having studied the Soviet Bibliothecal-Bibliographic Classification system (the BBK) between 1986 and 1989, proposed its adoption in Cuba just as the Berlin Wall was coming down. This seemingly minor story is emblematic of an approach to not only knowledge and its dissemination through pedagogy at all levels and in every discipline, but also to entertainment originating in an entirely different context. As might be expected, ideology (as it is everywhere in distinct variations) was disseminated to children in joint publishing projects—USSR and Cuba—through books such as *A los niños sobre Lenin* (To the Children about Lenin), the back cover of which features children exotic to the Cuban scene on a troika with Lenin in a kind of grandfather role.

Children's books were often based on popular stories, such as *Mashenka y el oso* (Mashenka and the Bear), first published in Spanish by the Soviet publisher Malysh in the 1970s. Those with animated versions were even more well known. While some books were produced in collaboration with Soviet publishers, others were published in the German Democratic Republic, Czechoslovakia, and other countries of the former Socialist Bloc.

Another good example of the Soviet omnipresence is found in the work of Lázaro Saavedra (born in 1964 in Havana), who often recontextualizes present-day or historical paraphernalia within his work with the slightest artistic authorship. *Del diario de observaciones* (From the Diary of Observations) presents an emblematic page from a 1979 workbook that sought to inscribe children within the Socialist imaginary through typical ideologically framed questions about Socialist holidays and the geography of the Socialist world. Cubans were interpellated into the Soviet consciousness through the domestic rehearsal of the Soviet family. See, for example, how the Soviet domestic sphere was represented in the children's pop-up book *La gallinita pinta* (The Hen Paints), by

*Back cover of* A los niños sobre Lenin *(To the children about Lenin), compiled by A. Kravchenko, designed by N. Liamin, translated by Nina Vasílieva. Moscow: Malysh, 1980. Edition by Gladys Valdés. Havana: Gente Nueva. Copyright 1979 by Malysh.*

L. Mayorova, which elucidates the felicity and sustainability of the amorous union between Cuba and the USSR with the words "En una casa muy linda vivían el abuelo y la abuela" (In a very pretty house lived the grandfather and grandmother). The image provides a sentimental texture for the prescribed admiration of Soviet culture and its penetration in Cuba.

Many Cubans didn't work with Soviets, or travel to the Soviet Union, or be-

Mashenka y el oso *front cover illustration,
by Evgenii Rachev, 1979. Moscow: Malysh,
1981. Courtesy of Vladimir Turkov.*

Mashenka y el oso *landscape 1 illustration,
by Evgenii Rachev, 1979. Moscow: Malysh,
1981. Courtesy of Vladimir Turkov.*

Mashenka y el oso *landscape 2 illustration,
by Evgenii Rachev, 1979. Moscow: Malysh,
1981. Courtesy of Vladimir Turkov.*

Mashenka y el oso *back cover illustration,
by Evgenii Rachev, 1979. Moscow: Malysh,
1981. Courtesy of Vladimir Turkov.*

El 1° de Mayo celebramos la fiesta de los ...............................

Los países socialistas celebran esta fiesta con gran alegría

porque están gobernados por los propios ...............................

El primer país socialista del mundo fue la ...............................

Circula con una línea roja la parte que corresponde a la
Unión Soviética.

Cuba es el primer país socialista de ...............................

Otros países socialistas que conoces son: ...............................

40

*Lázaro Saavedra, "Del diario de observaciones" (from a 1979 elementary-school workbook), circulated on Internet around 2007.*

long to a professional echelon that relied on Soviet formation, and so are less aware of having had "real" experiences with them than of having had "real" experiences with products made by them. In this way the phenomenon that I am describing as "dreaming in Russian" is not one that the masses are necessarily conscious of having affected them; rather, it is composed of diverse currents that are inscribed within contemporary Cuban culture and society and that continue to have actual effects on the way that the nation envisions its present, past, and future. Prior to 1989, the Soviets were criticized in private; public criticism — even of the sort comedian Enrique Arredondo offered when in the 1970s his character Bernabé said to his grandchild, "Si no te portas bien, te voy a castigar viendo los muñequitos rusos" (If you don't behave, I'll punish you by making you watch the Russian cartoons) on the television show *Detrás de la fachada* — could lead to punishment. Then, immediately after the Soviet disintegration, the Soviets were publicly criticized and, sometimes, privately yearned for. Already, in the second half of the first decade of the millennium, they are being re-exhibited, with different, discrepant objectives in mind.

Until now, the question of how Cubans process their country's relationship with the Soviet Bloc has been examined tangentially, even though for nearly three decades the Soviet Union subsidized the island economically, intervened in military matters, and exported distinct pedagogical and cultural models to the island.[9] The rapid creation between 2007 and 2011 of "sites of memory" by different official and sub-official groups has skewed the process of recollection. For Pierre Nora, such "sites of memory" are created when history has deteriorated the process of spontaneous memory. In 2010, for example, the International Book Fair of Cuba was dedicated to Russia. With this commemoration in mind, Cuban publications such as *El cuentero* and *La gaceta de Cuba*, among numerous others across the island and in different disciplines, dedicated special issues to the Soviet Union and Russia. When I began this project, it would have been impossible to envision Russia's new economic, political, cultural, and even religious investments in Cuba, which include plans to drill for oil off the coast of Cuba, a new partnership pact signed by Raúl Castro and Dmitry Medvedev in 2009, more scholarly exchanges for Cubans in Russia as of 2010, and the consecration of the Russian Orthodox Church in Havana in 2008. Some of the luckier Cuban artists and scholars, who were already fleshing out their relationships to the previous "friendship," utilized the fair as a venue to promote their works.

This fortune depends on several factors—happenstance, economics, and felicitous interactions with the right people. Not all of the production that emerged around the book fair restored happy memories. For Svetlana Boym, "Restorative nostalgia puts emphasis on *nostos* and proposes to rebuild the lost

*"En una casa muy linda vivían el abuelo y la abuela." Page from* La gallinita pinta, *by L. Mayorova, adapted by Sonia Pérez Tobella, translated by Edgar Timor, published in the USSR, 1970.*

home and patch up the memory gaps. . . . [Restorative] nostalgics do not think of themselves as nostalgic; they believe that their project is about truth. . . . Restorative nostalgia manifests itself in total reconstructions of monuments of the past."[10] "Restorative nostalgia" is constitutive of distinct bents within contemporary Cuban rhetoric. In "De lo efímero, lo temporal y lo permanente" (About the Ephemeral, the Temporal, and the Permanent), Fernando Rojas, the current vice-minister of culture and the former editor of *El caimán barbudo*, the official publication for Cuban youth, defends the Cuban Revolution's Leninism and its Socialist survival in a post-Soviet world. Furthermore, the anthology compiled by Enrique Ubieta Gómez, in which Rojas's article appears, speaks in favor of those Cubans "that do not look for the outside and after . . . they play out life on the inside and now."[11] In a section of his essay appropriately entitled "Requiem por el lácteo y otras reminscencias" (Requiem for Milk and Other Reminiscences), Ubieta Gómez yearns for an imaginary, whole Cuba, and it is in this vein that Rojas recollects his childhood experiences of drinking cheap milk in the early 1960s in a recently inaugurated Parque Lenin. The significance of the economic disinheritance from the Soviet Union can only be understood if we take into account that in 1985, at the height of commercial relations, commercial exchanges reached nearly 10 billion pesos.[12]

Memory becomes the point of departure for linking the early years of the Cuban Revolution to its future. Fernando Rojas writes: "The unknown Leninist tradition recognized the priority of a politics of absolute solidarity with national liberation movements, and something of that remained . . . within the heart of the Soviet bureaucracy, and most of all, in the people of that tremendous country."[13] According to Rojas, however, Cubans developed that aspect of the tradition even further than the Soviets. In "El triunfo de Stalin" (The Triumph of Stalin), published in *El caimán barbudo* in 2004, Rojas evokes a similar phrase. Speaking of the USSR in the 1930s, he states: "The paradox resides in the very excesses of principles of the decade that helped that great country resist and conquer."[14] Allow me to take Rojas's words, and especially the phrases "that tremendous country" and "that great country," a step further. If, in fact, such a Leninist tradition was unknown, it is difficult to envision how it left its mark on the Cuban people and government, both cited by Rojas as under its influence. Taking Lenin Park to be the founding myth for a narrative that refuses to see Cuba's alliance with the Soviet Bloc as a failure, Rojas also bitterly rejects the notion that Cuba was a pawn of the Soviets and affirms that Cuba sustained its alliance with them on shared ideological grounds.

An especially controversial moment within Rojas's reflections on the Soviet Union occurs when, in "¿Por qué cayó el socialismo en Europa oriental?" (Why Did Eastern European Socialism Fall?), a debate published in *Temas* in December 2004, Rojas ponders the extent to which the Soviets could have defended themselves against the Nazis "without the forced industrialization, without the agricultural cooperativization, and without the unity of the nationalities."[15] When the journal's editor, Rafael Hernández, asks whether Rojas is suggesting that the Soviet Union could not have withstood the Nazi invasion without Stalin's authoritarianism, Rojas warns against conflating those programs with Stalin, but confesses his own quandary over this period. Rojas is not the only Cuban thinker who has turned to Lenin for rethinking Cuba's future. By returning to the October Revolution of 1917, and especially to important Socialists cast aside by the Revolution, some Cubans, such as Celia Hart, Ariel Dacal, and Francisco Brown Infante, invested in rescuing Socialism from bureaucratization.[16] In "La bandera de Coyoacan" (The Flag of Coyoacan), Hart urges Cubans and internationalists alike to embrace the tradition of Leon Trotsky. The daughter of Cuban revolutionaries Armando Hart and Haydée Santamaría, Hart distinguishes Trotskyism from the horrors of Stalinism. While Fernando Rojas's tone is defensively nationalistic and hardly admits errors, referring to the 1960s as "the epoch of the best Havana nights [that] almost completely banished the squalor that shows, for instance, in scenes of *P.M.*,"[17] Hart is critical of Cubans having silenced particular thinkers. Yet, both Rojas and Hart insist upon capturing distinct "lost" moments in order to sustain the future of the Cuban Revolution.

In light of such recuperations and more recent memorializations, it is essential for the more rebarbative dimensions of the history of the Soviet-Cuban relationship to be explored. Many Cuban memories can be connected to the Soviet legacy, but one in particular is worth keeping in mind because it speaks to multiple legacies. The 2007 appearance of Luis Pavón Tamayo, president of the Consejo Nacional de Cultura (National Council on Culture) between 1971 and 1976 (arguably the most repressive period of the Cuban Revolution), on the television show *Impronta*, which was dedicated to those Cubans who left important marks within the cultural realm, sparked contentious debates on the Sovietized past and Cuban present on the island and abroad. During Pavón's era, not heeding the Revolution's prescriptions of treating art as its own weapon was considered ideological deviation. The degree of artistic and intellectual repression in the Gray Period of the 1970s, epitomized by Pavón, is often blamed on Stalinist tactics that were exported from the Soviet Union, along with its petroleum and machinery.

Of the many powerful and immediate responses to the Pavón scandal, one that is particularly illustrative is that of Reina María Rodríguez (born in Havana in 1952), who contested the homage to the Gray Period with another dimension of Russian and Soviet inheritance that also penetrated the island's intellectuals and artists in "unofficial ways." The following passage conveys the degree to which contestatory voices on the island were made up not only of those fighting against imperialistic and colonial situations, but also of those fighting against authoritarianism and totalitarianism in the Socialist Bloc. In "Carta para no ser un espíritu prisionero" (Letter so as not to Be a Captive Spirit), originally published on the website of *Cubaencuentro*, Rodríguez writes: "About four years ago I read a book called *A Captive Spirit* published by Galaxia Gutenberg and translated from Russian by Selma Ancira—compiled texts by Marina Tsvetaeva (fragments of her diary, stories, and poems). There also appeared, at the end of the book, documents extracted from the archives of the KGB." *A Captive Spirit* has an introduction that states: "Russian writers, who were raised in spaces where liberty has not abounded, have always felt themselves to be carriers of this liberty; because of this, their luck has always been fateful. The early death of Pushkin and Lermontov, the madness of Gogol, the captivity of Dostoevsky, the censorship, the faithful companion to all who studied carefully the work of Tolstoy and Chekhov, are some examples from the past." And it continues: "This tradition has been perfected in the Soviet epoch: years of praises, chants, and also of silences, prisons, and exterminations."

> Let's remember, I'm thinking about Mandelstam, Pasternak, the Akhmatova, who didn't even have a cemetery. I can't, after having read these authors and knowing how they lived and died (Mayakovsky, for example, and Marina Tsvetaeva , who hung herself in Yelabuga), sit idly by something that seems to me, at a distance from those events, and in this island at the center of the Caribbean, a tragedy for the Cuban nation, which already experienced expulsions and censorship in the 1970s and still continues to experience them.[18]

Rodríguez upholds beacons of truth within environments that proved to be hostile to free thinking and creation. In her evocation of Soviet critical literary forces, Rodríguez demands that Cuban civil society recognize that it remains indebted not only to some of the ugliest aspects of the Soviet system, but also to a bounty of dissenting Russian and Soviet thinkers.

The term "transition" generally focuses on Cuba in relation to its future—a future in which the United States occupies a central position. However, we need to be asking other questions in order to more deeply understand the past, present, and future: How do collective/artistic memories of the Soviet-Cuban relationship evolve in a society whose government remains Socialist? How are Cubans documenting this inheritance within distinct cultural venues? How does this particular experience of hybridity, wherein imperialism and leftist politics converge, challenge existing frameworks of identity politics within and outside of Cuba? How does the current memorialization of the Soviet Bloc in Cuba complicate the notion of transition to capitalism? Rafael Hernández, founder and editor-in-chief of the Cuban journal *Temas*, argued in a 2009 University of Chicago speech entitled "The Cuban Transition: Imagined and Actual" that "debates in Cuba" have stirred for "half a century about transition" and that since the mid-1990s, Cuba has undergone immense changes in the realms of social diversity, race relations, economic changes, and religious differences. His point of view contrasts with what is generally said about the Cuban transition from the outside, which generally sees "what should happen" as "something that is going to happen when Fidel Castro dies," something that is similar to the "radical transformation that happened in Chile, in Spain, when authoritarian regimes failed and in Eastern Europe and in the Soviet Union when socialism collapsed." Hernández also notes that to imagine the future "Cuban transition" as a time when Cuban exiles reconcile with those on the island is also flawed, since these encounters exist in the here and now.[19]

*Dreaming in Russian* was conceived around the turn of the twenty-first century, when the rhetoric of the transition seemed especially monolithic and Cuba saw itself as isolated, without the economic and ideological support of Venezuela, which it has today, and without the support of other Socialist brethren throughout Latin America. The focus on the "transition," as a monolithic category, overlooks Cuba's past relationship with the Soviet Bloc, as well as Russia and Cuba's current fascination with each other, especially in the arts. This investigation, in contrast, examines artistic and intellectual reflections on a failed international solidarity and an unknown future, and renders for posterity the traces of that solidarity, taking the form of parody and "petite monument making."

This book is not a historical account. It is structured like a jigsaw puzzle that pieces together Cubans' diverse feelings toward, reactions to, and re-creations of the Soviets. The book thus evokes impulses to remember that occur throughout the 1990s and the new millennium. They take us, for the most part, back to the 1960s, 1970s, and 1980s, but sometimes even further into the past.

There is an abundance of cultural production in the post-Soviet period that confronts how to reckon with this queer dimension of Cuba's past that was tied to such a faraway cultural and political sphere. In order to address the extent to which the post-Soviet situation in Cuba evokes a postmodern, individualistic, unleashed logic, I sort through hypotheses of first-rate researchers: Esther Whitfield, who has theorized the commodification of culture of the Special Period; José Quiroga, who has analyzed different memory sites that inform Cuba's post–Cold War realities; and Rafael Rojas, who has retrieved the Cuban-Soviet library. My argument about the points of comparison between the "post" in "post-Soviet" and the "post" in "postcolonial" echoes Kwame Anthony Appiah's articulation of the relationship between postmodernity and postcoloniality and David Chioni Moore's analysis of Sovietization as colonization. Lawrence La Fountain-Stokes's conceptualization of the *transloca* in Latin America sheds light on the challenge to the nation's narrative of solidarity put forth by drag performance and queer *bildungsroman* in post–Cold War Cuba. The discussions of mourning for Communism in the post-Soviet world, in general, and the more specific German phenomenon of *Ostalgie* (the nostalgia felt for the German Democratic Republic), ground the significance of remembering the Soviet Bloc in Cuba today.

Chapter 1, "Koniec," examines biculturalism in the anthropological, literary, and visual production of the children of mixed marriages (Cubans and persons from the former Soviet Bloc)—a group that Ernesto Hernández Busto once said was ignored due to *criollo* chauvinism—as well as the visual documentation of them and their families by filmmakers and photographers. I examine the process through which artists such as Polina Martínez Shvietsova, Dmitri Prieto Samsonov, and Anna Lidia Vega Serova interrogate the viability of Fernando Ortiz's term *"ajiaco,"* the characteristic Cuban stew which is now a long-established metaphor for the country's cultural mixing, to explain their particular experiences of biculturalism as well as the overall aesthetic, social, and political implications of these experiences. In addition to auto-ethnographic pursuits, artists' interest in Soviet immigration and biculturalism in Cuba also stands for a sentimental and even ideological emblem, as can be seen within the 2006 documentary *Todas iban a ser reinas* (They Were All Going to Be Queens), by the Cubans Gustavo Pérez and Oneyda González, and the 2009 photographs *Érase una vez . . . una matrioshka* (Once upon a Time There Was a Matrioshka), by the Cuban Lissette Solórzano.

Chapter 2, "Crossed Destinies," examines the social and psychological hysteria rendered by the Soviet-Cuban relationship by focusing on the performance of "La Rusa Roxana Rojo" (the Red Russian Roxana), by Pedro González Reinoso. La Rusa's parodic performance is paradigmatic not only of the iconography and new histories of the Soviet Bloc, but also of what La Fountain-Stokes "nicknamed *transloca* because of their exploration of homosexuality, transvestism, and spatial displacement."[20] Performing the *transloca* has different connotations for Puerto Rico and Cuba, given the two islands' distinct social and political histories. However, the post-Soviet period in Cuba has produced economic conditions of migration, of back-and-forthness that can be compared to what Luis Rafael Sánchez termed Puerto Rico's *"guagua aérea"* (air bus). While the performance of "La Rusa Roxana Rojo" was born in 1992, the character's biography goes back to the 1930s, when Roxana escaped with her mother from the horrors of the Nazi concentration camps and Stalin's gulags. La Rusa hardly renders a Western diva, but rather plays with distinct layers of the Soviet inheritance in Cuba. With references to Soviet and Russian literature and film, along with popular culture from the Soviet Bloc and the Americas, La Rusa, an exemplary *transloca*, sheds light on the notion of progress and masculinity posited by the Cuban-Soviet relationship. Moreover, the phantasmagoric mood in which many characters inhabit the present in works of fiction by Adelaida Fernández de Juan, Jorge Miralles, Ernesto Pérez Castillo, and Ulises Rodríguez Febles suggests that Cubans project their own disillusionment and yearning onto the Russians, who already experienced the collapse of their nation's system.

Chapter 3, "Cuban Intermediaries," analyzes fictitious and pictorial travelogues to the Soviet Union and Russia in the 1980s, 1990s, and into the twenty-first century, examining what they convey about paradigms of race, aesthetics, and economics; the commensurability of experiences; and Cubans' relationship to Perestroika. In much of the writing by José Manuel Prieto, Jesús Díaz, Antonio Armenteros, Emilio García Montiel, and Antonio Álvarez Gil, from the 1980s to the present, Cuban protagonists transported to the Soviet Union and Russia become the living proof of influence. Stories by Cubans who traveled to the Soviet Bloc and documented their journeys date these publications. The at-home sentiment conveyed by Samuel Feijóo's travelogue of his 1964 journey to the Soviet Union, published in his Santa Clara journal *Islas*, contrasts sharply with Roberto Fandiño's sixteen-minute 1963 documentary *Gente de Moscú* (People of Moscow), with its definitively outsider perspective. These diverse Cuban eyewitnesses to the Soviet Bloc in the early years of the Cuban Revolution serve as a backdrop to this chapter's engagement with contemporary and often less idealistic prose, poetry, and visual arts.

It is certain that Cubans traditionally, socially, and culturally identify with the West, but this chapter addresses the extent to which Cubans' vision of the so-called West is, in fact, altered when they travel to the so-called East, actually or metaphorically. Iván de la Nuez coined the term "Eastern" to refer to a post-Soviet genre that "explodes around 1989" and is crafted by writers from the former Socialist Bloc and by others who decisively position themselves through the post-Soviet gaze. As is the case with my own investigation, de la Nuez includes José Manuel Prieto, Cuban novelist and scholar, and Desiderio Navarro, editor-in-chief of the journal *Criterios*, within this grouping, on account of their vast cosmopolitan and Soviet formation, to which their current intellectual projects are indebted. By including these thinkers within the category, de la Nuez similarly challenges Cubans' identification with the West and admits to a more complicated definition of the so-called transition.

> The "Eastern" would cover, then, the not-so-casual passage between the societies based on manual labor—the dictatorships of the proletariat— and the societies of computer science and Internet: the passage from one PC (Partido Comunista/Communist Party) to another PC (Per-

sonal Computer). An itinerary that covers twenty years that are slipped in between the crisis of Communism and today's crisis of Capitalism . . .

This Occidental world has been the mirror — and the mirage — in which those countries looked at each other to overthrow their respective tyrannies. Also because there is one thing, among many others, that the Occident can do: learn. To focus on some artists from the East whose work functioned, under Communism, as a detector of repression, artists who today, in the new world, do not limit themselves to dwelling on the censorship of times past. On the contrary, they have continued to train their critical eye so as to be able to perceive other authoritarian forms, not always evident, that are renewed in the post-Communist present.[21]

The narrators of José Manuel Prieto's Russian trilogy — *Enciclopedia de una vida en Rusia* (Encyclopedia of a Life in Russia), *Livadia* (Nocturnal Butterflies of the Russian Empire), and *Rex* — for instance, are relics of the former Soviet-Cuban solidarity in post-Soviet Russia, yielding a cosmopolitan subjectivity wherein letters, dollars, and spaces converge, borders are transgressed, and authenticity is questioned. But many more authors can be analyzed in de la Nuez's category. The trajectories of the protagonists' lives in Alejandro Aguilar's *Casa de cambio* (Currency Exchange Agency) and Jesús Díaz's *Las cuatro fugas de Manuel* (Manuel's Four Escapes) are determined by their having been in Hungary and the Soviet Union at the time of Perestroika and Glasnost. As Rafael Rojas remarks in "Souvenirs de un Caribe soviético" about another work, Emilio García Montiel's book of poems *Cartas desde Rusia* (Letters from Russia), Cuban subjectivity is informed by more than just the Soviet ideological prescription; it is also informed by those beautiful things that survived in spite of that system, things that existed prior to it. Antonio Álvarez Gil, for example, like José Manuel Prieto, was sent to the Soviet Union to study engineering. His highly realist writing in *Unos y otros* (These and Those) and in *Del tiempo y las cosas* (Of Time and Things) captures the negotiations and expectations that Cubans and other foreigners realized in the Soviet Union, while his *Callejones de Arbat* (Alleys of Arbat) is a writhing tale about the transfer of systematic repression from the Soviet Union to Cuba. Chapter 3 also shows Cubans forecasting their future by taking measure of the chaotic, post-imperial, eclectic, decentralizing East.[22]

Chapter 4, "Made in USSR," explores the production of the Muñequitos Rusos generation, referring to the children who grew up with Soviet Bloc animation and popular culture. As children, few were as conscious of this inheritance as Raúl Aguiar, a Cuban writer born in Havana in 1962 who has become known especially for his award-winning contributions to science fiction, a

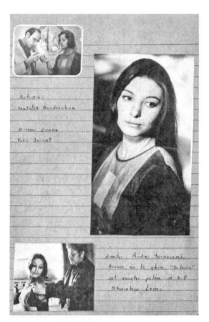
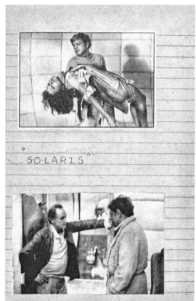

From Raúl Aguiar's personal scrapbook, circa 1978–1988.

genre in Cuba that recognizes its debt to the Soviets. Aguiar not only regularly voyaged to the Soviet Union in his imagination, but also documented that travel through an elaborate scrapbook dedicated to Soviet science fiction films, such as *Solaris*, featured in the figures above. He additionally guarded that inheritance by preserving filmstrips made in the Soviet Union of cartoons and by amassing a collection of Soviet magazines. While his peers may not have been such childhood Russophiles as he, their artistic production reveals a contact zone through intertextualities and parodies that respond not only to animation but also to cinema (by directors such as Andrei Tarkovsky), poster art, and even popular television shows from the Soviet Bloc. Many of their works signal them suffering the same fate as the cartoons; that is, the sense that they are relics. The Cuban science fiction writer Yoss (José Miguel Sánchez, born in 1969) was the first to render this preoccupation in his article "Lo que dejaron los rusos" (What the Russians Left Behind), published in the Cuban journal *Temas* in 2004. Wendy Guerra, Ena Lucía Portela, Rubén Rodríguez, Ricardo Alberto Pérez, Ernesto René Rodríguez, and the musical group Porno para Ricardo — all more or less Yoss's contemporaries — engage the Soviets in their texts to convey particularities of a Cuban childhood and present that were oddly fractured by their Sovietized past. However, according to Yoani Sánchez, who refers to that age group as Generation Y (the title of her controversial blog), Cuba's solidarity with the East hardly impacted her generation's identity. A central question of this chapter concerns the role that the Internet plays in determining the velocity of creating and circulating narratives of nostalgia today as both artistic and sociological strategies.

Chapter 5, "The Phantasmagoric Sputnik," examines how Cubans today represent, archive, and exhibit Soviet definitions of progress. No analysis of the Soviets' scientific advancements can ignore their massive 1976 exhibition Logros de la ciencia y la técnica soviética, nor the fact that a bit more than a decade later their culture seemed to be on its way toward extinction, and as such, blocked from Cuba's sight. This chapter explores the consequences of such shocking transformations on sentimental and critical levels within the visual art of Tonel, Jorge Luis Marrero, Tessio Barba, Hamlet Lavastida, Alejandro Campins, and Gertrudis Rivalta; the music of Nacional Electrónica; and the writing of Ramón Fernández Larrea, all of which render the Soviet fall from grace with dismay, anger, and a sense of absurdity.

With the demise of the Soviets, Cubans immediately disconnected from them publicly, and it became permissible to critique them; however, once artists demonstrated ways in which the Cuban present is married to the Soviet past, tensions surfaced of the sort that beg the question of whether, in fact, the systems of discipline and punishment are also transculturated aspects of Cuban society. One cannot interpret Esteban Insausti's documentary *Existen* (They Exist), about the insane inhabiting Havana's streets, or even Antonio José Ponte's "Corazón de Skitalietz" (Heart of Skitalietz), about post-Soviet wanderers, without considering this possibility.

The Pavón crisis was just one of the many immediate struggles related to control over historical narrative that informed the Cuba-USSR and the Post-Soviet Experience symposium that took place in February 2007 at the University of Connecticut, co-organized by José Manuel Prieto and myself. What was both emotionally and intellectually provocative was the range of affect elicited by the presentations. Taste, tone, and humor were perhaps the most tangible dimensions of the discussion—all categories that are crucial to unveiling the significance of Sovietization, not only on the island but also elsewhere in the Socialist Bloc. To reflect upon the Cuban-Soviet solidarity is to create a parenthesis within the notion of transition. It is a broad parenthesis that allows for many other groups—Cubans on the island and off, Fidelistas and anti-Fidelistas, Cubans and non-Cubans, former citizens of the Soviet Bloc, and so on—to participate in the discussion, on both official and unofficial levels.

*Dreaming in Russian* suggests that memories are evoked when other realities—tourism, the dollar, the euro, the *Cristina* show, Hollywood films—occupy spaces that previously were occupied by *pesos*, *libretas*, visits to the Soviet Bloc, and Russian cartoons. On the island, as recently as ten years ago, it would have been impossible to imagine that November 2007 would see not only the controversial visual arts exhibition Vostok, but also the launch of a "Taller Permanente," that is, a permanent workshop: "Revolución Bolchevique: Historia de la URSS y Cuba, Análisis crítico socialista desde el siglo XXI" (The Bolshevik Revolution: History of the USSR and Cuba, Critical Socialist Analysis from the Twenty-First Century). That in 2008 the renowned filmmaker Enrique Colina would make a documentary entitled *Los rusos en Cuba* (Russians in Cuba) or that in 2010 the book fair in Havana would be dedicated to Russia would have been inconceivable. What these discussions will mean in light of the new phases of social, cultural, political, and economic coquetry is provocative. These analyses illustrate tendencies toward "restorative nostalgia" and critical debate.

The cultural analyses realized in this book do not project onto Cuba a facile nostalgia for the ideologies of the Soviet Union. The pain and consternation that result from the Cuban experience of disinheritance, evident within contemporary culture, demand that we question the degree to which Cuba may be involved in a teleological passage toward capitalism.

Just how late the Soviets and the rest of the Eastern Bloc arrived to the *ajiaco* is debatable. Whether or not the importation of Soviet commodities also meant the transplantation of practices of thought and worldviews from the Soviet Bloc to Cuba needs to be a central question within Cuban studies because on it rests Cubans' conceptualization of the nationalistic nature of the Revolution and of the Cubanness of every aspect of their lives.

CHAPTER ONE

# *Koniec*

> *Her name is Carmen. This is a name for a Russian girl? ... Actually it's an interesting mix, Russian and Cuban. Very precocious, a little of the exhibitionist.*
>
> MARTIN CRUZ SMITH, *HAVANA BAY*

> *La rusita era linda y estaba consciente de ello. La mezcla de sangre la había favorecido mucho. Tenía a un tiempo la enigmática belleza de las mujeres rusas y la salsa ... de las chicas cubanas.*
>
> *The little Russian girl was pretty and conscious of it. The mix of blood had favored her a lot. At the same time she had the enigmatic beauty of Russian women and the salsa ... of Cuban girls.*
>
> ANTONIO ÁLVAREZ GIL, *NAUFRAGIOS*

These epigraphs undoubtedly tell us more about the authors' fantasies than about the Russian-Cuban young ladies themselves. What the offspring of the distant entities from the former Soviet Bloc and Cuba might look like is a question that has gripped my interlocutors over the years. With such characteristic projections in mind, this chapter seeks to (1) examine the communitarian project of the children of mixed marriages, (2) explore the adult artistic creations of these children, (3) analyze the symbolic function of their "Russian" mothers in a recent documentary and photo-essay, and (4) interpret the role of the binational in contemporary fiction.

To the question of what remains of the Soviet-Cuban relationship, the renowned Cuban intellectual Jesús Díaz answered: the children of mixed marriages—the very *polovinas* that Ernesto Hernández Busto claims have been neglected on account of *criollo* chauvinism. What Hernández Busto does not take into account is that as adults, these children are now speaking out for themselves, and the symbolic weight of their dialogue goes beyond that of ethnic identity.

From the 1960s to the 1980s, many Cubans traveled to the Soviet Bloc to work, to study, and for vacation (usually earned as a bonus from work as "national heroes"). Mervyn J. Bain estimates that by the mid-1980s, eight thousand Cubans were studying in Soviet universities yearly.[1] Some Cubans even found themselves in the Soviet Union after winning the grand prize of the popular 1980s television show *9550*, a Sunday quiz show hosted by Yiqui Quintana whose title referred to the number of kilometers between Havana and Moscow. Others were able to travel there as winners of prestigious literary prizes. One complex instance of the latter is the case of Heberto Padilla, who, as José Manuel Prieto describes in "Heberto Padilla, the First Dissident," was awarded a trip to the Soviet Union for his controversial 1968 poetry anthology *Fuera del juego* (Out of the Game) and who emerged as a dissident modeled on the Soviets.

There was a visible Eastern European presence in Cuba prior to the Revolution, primarily composed of Jews escaping fascism. According to Zeta Dacosta, female Soviet immigrants who came after the Revolution were generally not as visible since they inserted themselves into their husbands' families and "were not able to settle en masse in one particular place."[2] On the other hand, the "technicians, advisors, and their wives, all from the very same countries. . . . did garner a lot of attention." They settled into the "recently built Alamar neighborhood (of Havana) and the residential zone adjacent to the Lenin Hospital in Holguín."[3] Their children attended Russian schools, which *polovinas* also "had the right to attend."[4]

Estimates of the number of *polovinas* currently living on the island vary. Dmitri Prieto Samsonov and Polina Martínez Shvietsova have estimated that around fifteen hundred children and five hundred grandchildren who are the products of marriages between Cubans and citizens of the former Soviet Union reside on the island.[5] In *Los rusos en Cuba* (Russians in Cuba), Alexander Moiseev and Olga Egorova estimate that in 2009, between three and ten thousand persons from the former Soviet Union were living on the island "permanently."[6] Most of these children have Cuban fathers and Soviet mothers. Dacosta speculates about the racial and sexual inscriptions in the coupling. "Young Cubans returned to the island with a college degree under one arm, and a beautiful *ojimar* (blue-eyed) girl on the other. . . . It is noteworthy that of those who came home with this degree and a girl on their arms the majority were blacks and mulattos. Not denying their honest feelings and love for their wives, many of these men . . . enjoyed the fact they were able to get beyond the barrier of racial prejudice."[7] Cubans like to say that few Soviet men coupled with Cuban women because Cuban men are so desirable that Cuban women would not want to go elsewhere. However, the fact that few men from the Soviet Bloc were brought back home to Cuba may also speak to gender and social factors that impeded the realization of relationships between Cuban women and foreigners.

The biculturalism of the children of these mixed marriages treads on theoretical discussions about whether the *ajiaco*, the characteristic Cuban stew introduced by Fernando Ortiz in 1939 as a metaphor for Cuban identity, is really as malleable as it is sometimes understood to be. Are the principal ingredients of the *ajiaco*—the European, the African, and the Chinese—"justly" transculturated? Whether the *ajiaco* can incorporate new elements and "dish out" the same syncretic Cuban identity is questionable. Just as the conventional and outdated US "melting" pot can be interrogated for its assimilationist ends and across-the-board unevenness, so can the *ajiaco*. While the Revolution sought to provide equal rights for all, some Cubans are more "endorsed" than others. Enduring racial prejudice is one of the main obstacles to the formation of the idealized *ajiaco*. In the first decade of the twenty-first century, some children of Cuban and (former) Soviet parents sought to carve out a space in the public sphere to speak about themselves, as well as to claim what they conceive to be their "minority" status.

Proyecto mir_xxi_cu, the group formed by adult children of former Soviets and Cubans, grew out of the Russian club that reunited young people at the home of Gabriel Calaforra, a scholar and former ambassador, primarily to speak Russian and discuss cultural and historical matters. Project Mir's founders, Polina Martínez Shvietsova (born 1976) and Dmitri Prieto Samsonov (born 1972), comment in their essay ". . . So, Borscht Doesn't Mix into the *Ajiaco*? An Essay of Self-Ethnography on the Young Post-Soviet Diaspora in Cuba" on the importance of Calaforra's club for their socialization. The name of the group, Proyecto mir_xxi_cu—the Spanish word for "project," followed by the Russian for "peace," "world," or "community," then twenty-one in Roman numerals, referring to the twenty-first century, and finally "cu," suggesting an Internet domain originating in Cuba—indicates a virtual Cuban experience, an experience that has since resulted in a powerful expression of real dissidence. The name, symbolizing a new, more nebulous world network, defies a nationalistic sense of belonging; that this group did not have any Internet presence at all is ironic, but not particularly unusual for the Cuban experience, given that Cubans have had limited and sporadic access to the web.

These young Soviet-Cuban artists and intellectuals were also affiliated with the Hermanos Saíz Association, a state-sponsored organization for young artists. In 2007, Hermanos Saíz and the Russian embassy backed the cultural event Encounter of Compatriots in Cuba, and the embassy has become increasingly supportive of the work of this generation over the years. How successful Project Mir actually was at organizing young people of dual origins across the island is arguable, but it was clearly able to raise public awareness of different affective zones of the Soviet-Cuban connection.

Since the dissolution of Project Mir in 2007, Martínez Shvietsova has headed up similar cultural events, such as a commemoration in May 2009 of St. Cyril and St. Methodius Day (the Byzantine Greek brothers credited with the creation of the first Slavonic alphabet in the ninth century). Many former members of Project Mir have left Cuba. The Ukrainian-Cuban poet, musician, and painter Igor Capote Omelchenko (born in the Ukraine in 1968), soon after helping to articulate the group's goals, emigrated to Spain; the musician, journalist, deejay, and English teacher Pavel Capote Patapov moved to Thailand; the Ukrainian-Cuban Víctor Pérez Demidenko, who at the time was studying physics, moved to Egypt; Mikhail Luna Larin, who worked as a doctor, moved to Moscow; and his brother, Fidel Luna Larin, a former student of biology, tragically committed suicide. According to an August 22, 2009, e-mail interview with Dmitri Prieto Samsonov, some of the group's members were more active than others. For example, Capote Omelchenko, Capote Patapov, and the writer Andrés Mir were simultaneously involved with activities at the Russian embassy and at the Orthodox Church. The quest for recognition of their existence has since taken on new venues. Martínez Shvietsova's projects have gained institutional endorsement, including (at least ostensibly) the endorsement of the Russian embassy.

The fact that Soviet immigration was a consequence of the revolutionary alliance between Cuba and the USSR makes it distinct from other experiences of migration to Cuba (e.g., Jews, Chinese), and Cuban views toward the Soviets have evolved over the years. The immediate distancing from the Soviet Union after its dissolution has given way to a more general memorialization. The May 2009 roundtable hosted by Rafael Hernández of *Temas* magazine— "Huellas culturales rusas y de Europa del Este en Cuba" (Russian and Eastern European Cultural Roots in Cuba)—exemplifies this shift. Speakers at the roundtable included Prieto Samsonov; Zoia Barash, a Ukrainian translator and film scholar who resides in Cuba; José Miguel Sánchez Gómez, science fiction writer; and Jorge Cid, Cuban expert on Russia and the Soviet Union. Undoubtedly, some of the impetus that contributed to this newfound interest in the topic can be attributed to these young people's self-ethnographic projects.

In March 2004, Proyecto mir_xxi_cu collaborated on the first of two events with the word "*Koniec*" (End) in their titles—a name that, written in the Latin, not in the Cyrillic, alphabet, suggests that the group understood itself from the start as a translational project. "*Koniec*" is one of the most recognizable Russian words in Cuba, predictably appearing at the end of Soviet television programs and films. "*Koniec*" is almost as familiar as "*tavarich*" (comrade) or the phrase "*niet, tavarich*" (no, comrade). But "*koniec*" marks an ending on a symbolic level and a return to an empire that, for more than half of their lives, the participants in the event called home. Martínez Shvietsova delineates the meeting's scope:

> Koniec? was the first event where they proposed to analyze and inves-
> tigate the influences of the Euro-Asian imaginary in Cuba: the traces
> that they left on various generations of Cubans, the almost totalitarian
> presence of the intelligentsia from the extinct USSR, bringing together
> for the first time several young artists and intellectuals who are *aguas-
> tibias*. . . . Koniec? is not the end as the chosen title for the event indi-
> cates. Koniec? is the beginning and the continuation of our keeping
> alive the traditions of our Russian mothers and of the best scientific and
> artistic works that the former-Socialist countries left for thirty years.[8]

This declaration shows the group's investment, from their inception, in exploring their own genealogy and having a place to do so publicly. Furthermore, like other groups who consider themselves an ethnic or racial minority, they desire to convert an epithet into a powerful signifier of union. A constant in their projects is to uphold what is "theirs," to highlight the loss of wholeness that serves as a creative force, to document the bonds of their community, and to be recognized by Russians influential in the Cuban sphere.

## A CHRONICLE OF THE SOVIET-CUBAN STRATOSPHERE

To get a better sense of the cultural and political stakes, let us examine Prieto Samsonov's poem "Jurel en pesos" (Yellow Tail in *Pesos*). "Jurel en pesos" is a rereading of Virgilio Piñera's 1943 "La isla en peso" (The Island's Weight), which expresses the poetic subject's dissatisfaction with capitalism, with his positioning in Cuba, and with his inability to reclaim his homeland, using the characteristic Cuban motif of national identity — food.

> La maldita circunstancia del dólar por todas partes
> es como si ya no pudiera respirar más acá de
> [los arrecifes
> donde quince años atras se trabara este cuerpo.[9]

The damned circumstance of the dollar everywhere
is as if I can no longer breathe any further than
   [the reefs
where fifteen years ago my body was all tangled up.

A few verses later, it becomes clearer that his dissatisfaction is related not only to the economic instability associated with the inefficacy of the national currency within an increasingly market economy, but also to the loss of sensual objects. This situation stirs up the poetic subject's recollection of his ethnic inheritance.

Pero aún, con su precio en pesos
nunca será como aquella *selyodka* con cebolla
que solía probar en casa de mi abuelo
cuando comíamos carne, y pescado,
   y otra vez carne.[10]

But still, with its price in *pesos*
it will never be like that *selyodka* with onions
that I used to try at my grandfather's house
when we ate meat, and fish,
   and meat again.

Distinct layers of nostalgia are uncovered—for the period when Cuba was supported by the Soviet Union, when consumer goods were accessible in *pesos*, and for the place that held those savory products, "back in the USSR."

El pueblo de ellos se ha tornado un lugar caro
   [y absurdo
   y otra vez absurdo
que se llama mercado negro.[11]

Their village has become an expensive
   [and absurd place
   and again absurd
that's called the black market.

The utopic island experiment can no longer satisfy the Russian fruit, but neither can the other half; the poetic subject ends up betrayed by his forefathers' dreams for solidarity and asphyxiated by the dollar. Prieto Samsonov's disparagement is crucial to identifying one aspect of his generation's zeitgeist.

The present can only be compared to the superimposed past, which, in "Jurel en pesos," was almost organic. No foundational myth, however, can relieve the pain of the subject's hybrid and unsatisfied identity. The closest the Project Mir generation gets to forging one is *Ánima fatua* (Fatuous Soul), an autobiographical novel by Anna Lidia Vega Serova published in 2007, but it resists speaking for the collective.

Prieto Samsonov's distrust for capitalism is evident not only in his poem but also in his blog, published in *Havana Times*, an online journal in English wherein the author regularly critiques United States policies and raises awareness about bureaucracy and closed-mindedness inside Cuba. With degrees in biochemistry, philosophy, law, and anthropology, Prieto Samsonov is exceptionally gifted, and it would be impossible to read his ideological and aesthetic convictions merely as exemplary of the Soviet inheritance in Cuba. In his 2009 "Military Bases in 'Our America,'" he tells an anecdote about a disagreement that he had with his Irish neighbor in London regarding the veracity of certain historical narratives. He was startled by her reaction to his comment that the Soviets were victorious against fascism, a fact that is often reiterated in official Cuban rhetoric: "The Americans won the war!" she declared. Rather than succumb to the Russian nationalism that he felt brewing in him upon hearing such a statement, he instead felt compelled to berate present-day US imperialism.[12] In another entry, "The Moon Landing and Woodstock Anniversaries," also from 2009, he conveys his surprise at having heard US astronauts speak on a news program with a "tremendous sense of reverence" that sharply contrasted with his impression of "ugly" Americans. The Americans he knows, he says, are "not so romantic, they drink a lot of beer, eat steak and popcorn, and they like to watch American football on TV, even when they're in England."[13] But then, out of this nationalistic and stereotypical distrust of the United States populace emerges a critique of what is not remembered from the same time period, as well as more recent and clearly less benign anniversaries that did not make their way to Cuban television, such as the twenty-year anniversary of the massacre in Tiananmen Square or the fall of the Berlin Wall. Prieto Samsonov repeatedly makes comparisons between the Soviet tactics of silencing and contemporary Cuban ones: for instance, the Soviets did not broadcast the US landing on the moon in 1969, and Cuban television persistently ignores global events that might cause agitation in the populace.

Whether it be in Prieto Samsonov's distaste for Michael Jackson's US brand of postmodernism, the equivalent of unfettered individualism, or in his discussion of the importance of under-disseminated books in Cuba from crucial Socialist thinkers such as Trotsky and even early Lenin, his entries resonate with the politics of binational contemporaries who attempt to read Cuba through an imagined Soviet lens and to identify with revolutionary critical politics of the global left. Such a lens is profoundly anachronistic, since the Soviets no longer exist and it has been difficult for Cubans to keep up to date with matters in the former Soviet Bloc since the fall of the Berlin Wall, although in very recent years, along with increased economic collaboration, this too is changing.

Prieto Samsonov is vocal when it comes to ideological matters. For example, at the aforementioned *Temas* roundtable, having compared the Soviets to the diverse Spanish, Yoruba, Chinese, Arab, and Jewish diasporas, all of which count on constitutionally permitted associations on the island, he affirmed the necessity of establishing such an association for citizens of the former Soviet Bloc in Cuba, an idea that has been in the making for some time. According to Prieto Samsonov,

> Civil society of the post-Soviet diaspora in Cuba is diametrically opposed to that of the Chinese communities: they count on 13 associations, all founded before 1959, many of which are very active, and on a certain amount of official institutional support; the former Soviets, with a number comparable to Chinese descendents, do not possess any organization of their own.[14]

One of the main obstacles to such an organization might be interethnic battles; that is to say, a so-called Soviet association in Cuba might be the last place that the Soviets, as an interethnic group, would have a real presence, and what such an association might mean for the future would likely exceed the cultural realm.

To understand the significance of Prieto Samsonov's cautious critiques of national and international incidents requires more contextualization. One clue is provided in his "Trotsky in Havana," a *Havana Times* post in which he speaks of the value of books published abroad by and about Trotsky entering the national sphere at the Cuban book fair and of the presence of Trotsky's followers in Cuba, some of whom form part of the group "Revolución bolchevique: Historia de la URSS y Cuba, Análisis crítico socialista desde el siglo XXI" (Bolshevik Revolution, History of the USSR and Cuba. Critical Socialist Analysis from the Twenty-First Century), founded in 2007 by the Juan Marinello Center. Two years prior, in 2005, the Unión de Escritores y Artistas de Cuba (UNEAC; Writers and Artists Union of Cuba) hosted Las Otras Herencias de Octubre (The Other Legacies of October), a symposium that sought to bring new life on the island to lesser-known Socialist thinkers, to the October Revolution of 1917, and especially to thinkers who were cast aside by the Cuban Revolution. That same year, the Haydée Santamaría collective, under the auspices of the Hermanos Saíz organization, led by Prieto Samsonov, sponsored the foundational symposium on the recuperation of Trotsky—an event that was well attended by Project Mir members.

The perspective from which Prieto Samsonov examines Cuba in his blog is often filtered through his understanding of Russian and Soviet culture and history. For instance, in "The Pravda of Reggaetón," Prieto Samsonov takes a simplistic and polarizing look at reggaeton, upholding the popular genre for the truths that it conveys, as he delves into the meaning of *"Pravda"* for contemporary Cuba. "Reggaeton has a unique quality: it has something that the Russians call 'Pravda.' That word, which was the title of the main Bolshevik, and later Soviet newspaper, means not only 'truth' or 'justice' but also something like 'testimony,' 'shared living experience,' or 'moral rectitude.'"[15]

The author's implementation of the word *"Pravda"* is not extraneous, but rather is indicative of the desire to reassert a perhaps confused version of the Soviet past in the Cuban present. Much like nineteenth-century *crónicas*, blogs specialize in seemingly spontaneous reflections upon daily life and news events of import to their authors. It is in this way that we can consider Prieto Samsonov's somewhat hasty commentary on reggaeton, in which he evokes a Russian Christian existentialist, hardly known in the Cuban sphere, by the name of Nikolai Berdyaev, "who in the mid-20th century gave a brilliant analysis of *Pravda* in Russia and its role in the subversion of czarism and the Bolshevik ascendance."[16] Prieto Samsonov neglects to mention that along with many other philosophers of his epoch, Berdyaev was sent into exile by the Bolsheviks for his embrace of creativity. Had the comparison been more explicit, the *Pravda* would have been far more explosive.

### DISFIGURED MATRIOSHKAS

The co-founder of Project Mir and the winner of the Gaceta literary prize in 2006 for the short story "17 abstractos de una agenda" (17 Abstracts of an Agenda), Polina Martínez Shvietsova has been instrumental in bringing attention to the Soviet-Cuban imaginary in the twenty-first century. That award marked not only the launch of the author's career, but also of the public coming into consciousness of the peculiar circumstances of inhabiting this dual identity. In both her photographic series and award-winning short stories, Martínez Shvietsova bears witness to the complicated dynamic of metropolis and periphery by adorning her naked body in diverse national and intimate paraphernalia and by deconstructing the grand history of the Soviets and Cubans on the most personal and corporal level. Her photographic performance is potentially transgressive in a number of ways: for its pornographic content in a nation that prohibits pornography, for its grotesque implementation of revolutionary logos, and for its placement of world flags upon the bare female body.[17] In her work, her body becomes the repository for the encounter of ex-centric and

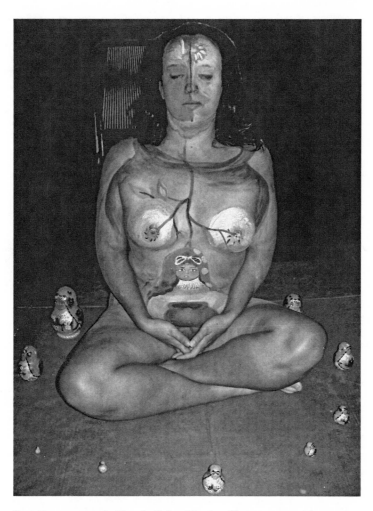

Posición 2 con matriushkas, *by Polina Martínez Shvietsova, copyright 2006.*
*Courtesy of artist.*

dominant belief systems and ideologies that include Buddhism, Judaism, and
Russian new age, along with flags from Cuba, Russia, Switzerland, the United
Nations, Lithuania, France, and Italy. In addition to the ideological decals, she
is adorned with symbols of excessive consumption, such as cigarettes, empty
alcohol bottles, coffee cans, and trinkets.

Referring to the nesting dolls that entered Russian handicrafts in the late
nineteenth century and that much later, during the Soviet period, became part
of Cuban material culture, the word "*matrioshka*" is not only included in the
titles of many of Martínez Shvietsova's photographs, but is also a play on the

*Matriushka escondida, by Polina Martínez Shvietsova, copyright 2006. Courtesy of artist.*

form that her obsessions take. In *Posición 2 con matriushkas* (Position 2 with Matrioshkas), the artist sits cross-legged with matrioshka dolls placed in a circle around her and a matrioshka painted on the core of her body, an orange painted on one breast, and a lime on the other, her face two-toned in red and orange, reflecting an uncomfortable syncretism. *Matriushka escondida* (Hidden Matrioshka) positions the matrioshka figure — smiling this time — in the same location around the stomach of the artist with two matrioshka dolls guarding the painted image. The rest of her stomach region is covered with numerous flags that do not have their own space on her corporal canvas. They overlap in a messy way that is itself contrary to the autonomous nation-state. While reminiscent of Manuel Mendive's well-known ritualistic performances of Cubanness in public spaces, which display painted bodies of all shapes, colors, and sizes, some of which are traditionally sexy and others grotesque, Martínez Shvietsova's body paintings are distinct in several ways: first, in their full embrace of the aesthetic that the artist herself refers to as "morbo," meaning taking pleasure in the morbid, and second, in their utter disrespect for the conservation of myths.

Martínez Shvietsova's short stories, like her visual work, critique authoritarian discourses. For instance, the sketch-like structure of "17 abstractos de una agenda" stylistically exhibits the fragmented nature of being both Cuban and Russian in Cuba. To the question of whether the post-Soviet Cuban experience entails a postmodern logic, this story would speak in favor of such an assessment.

The metatextuality of "17 abstractos de una agenda" is instantly perceivable. The dialogue in the fifth abstract evokes the underside of searching for institutional support and representation on the island.

> —Hola, ¿ustedes son polovinas?
> Me dirijo al grupo con timidez desafiante. Estamos en Tarará, donde
> el embajador de Ucrania ha organizado un buffet. Uno de ellos gira 180
> grados y me ataca:
> —¿Y tú quién blíat eres?
> —Yo, Pamyla Shvietsova. Me cago en tu madre. ¿Y tú?
> Pero el embajador ya retoma la palabra por el micrófono y nos insta a
> todos a rezar y a brindar.[18]

> —Hello, are you *polovinas*?
> I address the group with challenging timidity. We're in Tarará, where the
> ambassador from the Ukraine has organized a buffet. One of them does
> a 180 and attacks me:
> —And who the blíat are you?
> —Me, Pamyla Shvietsova. Fuck your mother. And you?
> But the ambassador took the microphone again and urged us to pray
> and toast.

The fact that the event takes place in Tarará is itself telling. Tarará, an area on the coast to the east of the city of Havana, once a neighborhood that housed Soviet officials, became in 1990 a refuge for approximately twenty-four thousand victims of the 1986 Chernobyl disaster, primarily from the Ukraine, but also from Russia and Belarus.[19] It is not the history of the region that particularly concerns Martínez Shvietsova, but rather the urgent present, wherein the hybrid protagonist, while taking advantage of what the Ukrainian ambassador has to offer—a buffet with "deliciosos bocadillos de importación" (delicious sandwiches with imported products) and Cuba libres (rum and Coca Cola drinks)—involves herself in a courtship of a more transgressive nature carried out with a combination of Cuban *choteo* and Slavic humor. Paul Allatson's succinct history of the term *"choteo"* is useful to keep in mind as we analyze Martínez Shvietsova's writing:

> Jorge Mañach (1940) defined *choteo* as a collective street-level anti-authoritarian sensibility that mocks and satirizes its targets, the agents of social order, decorum, and power. . . . the Cuban American José Muñoz (1999) argues that it is a transcultural signifier, encoding within it the long historical interplay between African and Spanish peoples in Cuba. . . . *Choteo* for Muñoz thus becomes a key strategy for self-assertion, identity construction, and critique of dominant cultural protocols.[20]

The first rude and simultaneously flirtatious question is addressed to the protagonist by a co-patriot named Misha in the Russian language, translated in the story's glossary for outsiders. They are insulting each other as a mode of fast intimacy, disrupting both the decorum of the occasion and conventional literary monolinguism.

The concept of hybridity that is elaborated in Martínez Shvietsova's short fiction is ripe for discussion because its relation to postcolonial renderings of the term tells us something about the ontology of being both Soviet and Cuban. Robert Young's definition of hybridization in the colonial context helps elucidate Martínez Shvietsova's narration:

> The colonial desiring machine, whereby a culture in its colonial operation becomes hybridized, alienated and potentially threatening to its European original through the production of polymorphously perverse people, who are, in Bhabha's phrase, white, but not quite: in the nineteenth century, this threatening phenomenon of being degraded from a civilized condition was discussed as the process of "decivilization."[21]

By no means can this concept be directly applied to the Soviet-Cuban experience; many felicitous and pained hybrids are manifest in Cuban cultural production. One such instance is the protagonist of "17 abstractos," Pamyla Shvietsova, who appears to be the author's alter ego, possessing the same initials and last name as the author. The inability to fully inhabit either the Soviet or Cuban nationality is painful, but unlike in Prieto Samsonov's poem, in which a loss of integrity is experienced, in this story, the subject is always fragmented and desiring from the start.

Pamyla Shvietsova perceives herself as inhabiting a monstrous version of hybridity. No identities nest neatly within the confines of her character, as they would within the matrioshka; instead, as Misha blatantly puts it: "Eres mi matriushka sicópata, eres mi matriushka sicópata; inexplicablemente me repetía el muchacho que me atacó" (You are my psychopathic matrioshka, you are my psychopathic matrioshka, the boy who attacked me repeated). Repetition and mimicry are definitive aesthetic and political strategies within the story. In abstract 2, Pamyla gets a ride in an old American van and asks herself, "¿Qué sentiré después de hacer el amor?" (What will I feel after making love?) In the next sequence, however, the description changes slightly. "Voy montada en una vieja camioneta rusa y ya no me pregunto nada" (I am riding in an old Russian van and I no longer ask myself anything). Her experience in the van is of greater interest due to the picture she paints of her surroundings—"la gran marcha patriótica del 13 de junio" (the great patriotic march of June 13) and "el dolor . . . franco y silencioso" (the pain . . . frank and silent). The sensual scenery of "plástico reciclado" (recycled plastic) speaks to the condition of the second or third world in which she resides. She has commonalities with colonized subjects and holds the United States, Cuba, and the Soviet Union responsible for the resultant disfigured and subjugated relationships.

In the first short abstract, the protagonist seduces and repels the reader with her existence. "Hibridez de la doble nacionalidad. Sobrevivientes sin contexto ni ontología. Aguas tibias entre el fuego del ser y el hielo de la nada." (Hybridity of double nationality. Survivers without context or ontology. Lukewarm waters between the fire of being and the ice of nothing.) However, it is in the final abstract that existence is called into question.

> Ebriedad de la no nacionalidad. Sobremurientes del hipervínculo
> y la ideología. Socialipsistas remando en un iceberg que parece un
> caimán. . . . 17 instantáneas fuera de foco. 17 abstractos de una agenda.
> 17 primaveras rotas de una sola pedrada y que ninguna esquirla se llame
> nunca Pamyla.[22]

> Inebriation from no nationality. Agonizers of the hyperlink and of ideology. Socialipsists rowing into an iceberg that looks like a caiman . . .
> 17 instant photos out of focus. 17 abstracts of a diary. 17 springs broken
> from just one stone throw and that no fragment is ever called Pamyla.

This conclusion urges readers to disbelieve the diary, yet at the same time, out of sympathy for the inexistent subject, they resist and inevitably feel sympathy. The simulacrum of this ensemble does not negate the affect that it produces. The neologism "*socialipsista*" (socialipsist), echoing "Socialist" and "solipsist," speaks to the sense of ideological confusion and chauvinism, captured in the resemblance of the iceberg to the caiman, the usual description of the island's geography. The poetic "*sobremurientes*," literally, those who survive death and live in that state, echoes "*sobrevivientes*," meaning survivors, the word with which Martínez Shvietsova introduces her protagonist.

This sequence of poetic episodes pays homage to Julian Semyonov's novel *Seventeen Instants of a Spring* (1968), a popular spy novel featuring the Soviet spy Stirlitz, from which Martínez Shvietsova adopts her title. The protagonist calls her lover Vlady "Whiskey," but his dislike of that name leads her to rename him "Vodka." Then she brainstorms other possible names from Russian military history that she might use, but she suspects he would not know them, since he, like her potential readers, is not as knowledgeable of Russian culture as she is. She is thus alienated within a world for which she needs to continually translate.

The perpetual in-betweenness of the character entices the postmodern sensibility. Pamyla announces that "en la portada de mi primer y único libro, Pushkin se sentará entre John Lenin y Vladimir Ilich Lennon en el parque de 15 y 6" (on the cover of my first and only book, Pushkin will sit between John Lenin and Vladimir Ilich Lennon at the park at Fifteenth and Sixth). Martínez Shvietsova molds post-Soviet to postcolonial desire by way of this exchange of names and surnames. Vladimir Lenin, the icon of Soviet history, and John Lennon, the icon of popular culture, are repositioned by the Cuban-Russian architect of her own genealogy.

One of the most outrageous moments occurs when the protagonist critiques *Ostalgie*:

> En el cine ponen *Goodbye Lenin*, un filme alemán. Desde las butacas, oímos los gritos afónicos del Osezno Misha, desgañitándose como en el Estadio Olímpico de Moscú. Está eufórico, no sabemos por qué. La acomodadora lo apunta con su linterna y amenaza con hacerlo expulsar.
>
> Misha le mienta a la madre en ruso y también en ruso amenaza con quemar aquel cine de mierda si no lo dejan en paz.
>
> —Mir, mir, mir, mir, mir, mir—le repite en voz de falsete.
>
> La acomodadora sonríe y se retira. Misha permanece en silencio, con la cabeza de Lenin volando en helicóptero desde Berlín hasta los cristales miopes de sus gafas. Hace muecas. Nadie en el grupo lo nota, pero yo sé que él se muestra eufórico para no echarse a llorar.
>
> "Goodbye Misha", escribí esa noche en mi agenda.[23]

At the cinema, they are playing *Goodbye Lenin*, a German film. From the seats, we hear the shouts of the Bear Cub Misha, screaming as if he were in the Olympic stadium of Moscow. He is euphoric; we can't figure out why. The usher points to him with her lantern and threatens to make him leave.

Misha insults her in Russian and threatens, also in Russian, to burn down that shitty theater if they don't leave him in peace.

— Mir, mir, mir, mir, mir, mir, he repeats in a falsetto voice.

The usher smiles and goes away. Misha remains in silence with Lenin's head flying in a helicopter from Berlin to the myopic lenses of his glasses. He makes faces. No one in the group takes note of him, but I know that he looks euphoric so as not to cry.

"Good-bye, Misha," I wrote that night in my diary.

Pamyla interprets what it must mean to dream about a Socialist system in a society in which it has disappeared, executing the interpretation from a position that shadows that other society, from a compromised position about which we learn more in the penultimate abstract. No longer on an American or Russian bus, Pamyla mounts a Cuban one and is immediately harassed by the driver, who says that she can ride for free if she touches his member.

No le respondo nada. Él tampoco insiste. Nos acercamos a un semáforo y lo veo tapársela con la camisa. Se inclina hacia mí. Lo dejo. Me susurra algo en la oreja y me extiende su tarjeta de presentación.

La leo al vuelo. Es de Soviexportfilm, una empresa fantasma. Definitivamente, vivimos en una película. De guerra o de amor, no sé. Igual en el semáforo de pronto me bajo sin decirle adiós.

El hijo de puta me pareció un pobre tipo al final. Si me hubiera pagado, entre la pena y el asco tal vez se la hubiera podido tocar.

I don't respond, nor does he insist. We arrive at a traffic light, and I see him cover [his penis] with his shirt. He leans toward me. I let him. He whispers something in my ear and hands me his business card.

I scan it quickly. It's from Soviexportfilm, a dummy corporation. Without a doubt, we live in a film. About war or love, I don't know. Still at the traffic light, I get out without saying good-bye.

The son of a bitch seemed like a poor guy to me in the end. If he had paid me, between the pity and the disgust, I might have touched it.

Martínez Shvietsova establishes a brilliant metaphor for the nation in this story. The bus, which represents Cuba, is, like Soviexportfilm, "una empresa fantasma" (a dummy corporation), a term that challenges the notion that Cuba and the Soviet Union were brethren in an ideological quest. Cuba, it would seem, served as a vehicle for the Soviet Union, and Soviexportfilm turns into a phantom of a previous enterprise beneficial to the empire. Cuba remains a vehicle, but now that the Soviet Union no longer exists, who benefits from its remaining in that position? This is a serious question raised by "17 abstractos de una agenda." If for Dmitri Prieto Samsonov the Soviets are implemented primarily for their Aesopian value for Cuba, for Polina Martínez Shvietsova, they are an important dimension of an authoritarian Cuba against which she rebels.


## THE BILDUNGSROMAN OF THE HALF-BREED

The Soviets as an international political entity are neither explicitly nor even allegorically the subject of Anna Lidia Vega Serova's writing, but rather, more generally, they are analyzed and critiqued as individuals in personal settings. Her 2007 novel *Ánima fatua* is not the first work in which she narrates a complicated relationship to hybrid identity. Her collection of short stories, *Limpiando ventanas y espejos*, published in 2001, contains numerous allusions to the ties that bind some of her characters to unusual invented landscapes. In "Proyecto para un mural conmemorativo (técnica mixta)" (Project for a Commemorative Mural [Mixed Media]), the narrator creates a skeleton for the poetic bonds between an Afro-Cuban seducer who engenders the narrating "creature" with an apparently extraterrestrial woman/mother, between the garbage that is her enveloping present and the distant snow that is itself extraterrestrial. Narrated in forty poetic segments, "Proyecto" challenges the conventional structure of the short story and could easily have been a source of inspiration for Martínez Shvietsova's "17 abstractos." Where and what might "CASA" (home) be is a question that preoccupies the narrator, as she is haunted by distant lullabies that do not resemble her present. The mural of the story's title commemorates the uncanniness of the narrator's autobiography as well as the Soviet-Cuban experience explored on the level of smaller units, setting the stage for *Ánima fatua*.

*Ánima fatua* maps a journey to the Soviet Union, around it, and back to Cuba in the late 1980s that is fraught with disunion and sorrow, but also joy and desire. The protagonist comes of age in the Soviet Union at the time when a supreme ideology of the twentieth century, symbolically "responsible" for giving birth to this hybrid protagonist, is seemingly falling apart. While a similar story is shared by numerous Soviet-Cubans, Vega Serova hesitates to be grouped into such identitarian projects. In an interview with María del Mar López-Cabrales, who asks her whether the Soviet-Cubans have a group conscience, Vega Serova avoids inserting herself definitively within that community. "Existen personas que intentan agruparse, hacer cosas. Se reúnen, hacen fiestas, tienen proyectos culturales, etc. . . . En diciembre se planea hacer una expo colectiva. Posiblemente yo participe" (There are people who try to group together to do things. They meet, throw parties, have cultural projects, etc. . . . In December, they're doing a collective exhibition. Perhaps I'll participate).[24]

*Ánima fatua*, characterized by a difficult-to-achieve stylized simplicity and freshness, is impossible to read without recalling emblematic road novels such as *On the Road*, by Jack Kerouac, or novels such as *When I Was Puerto Rican*, by Esmeralda Santiago, but in contrast to the protagonists of the more well known ethnic coming-of-age novels, Vega Serova's Alia neither looks for nor finds a facile solution to the problems that emerge from her binational development. Alia, a "historical casuality," is a victim of abandonment by her Afro-Cuban father and abuse by her Russian mother, a couple that once found each other compelling and exotic in the city of bridges, Leningrad. When Alia's mother can no longer cope with the failed relationship with her Cuban partner, she takes her daughter and her younger son back to her homeland, where from a very young age, Alia must seek modes of assimilating in order to combat the overwhelming prejudices around her. While the violence of being the "other" emanates primarily from her aging grandparents, she also feels herself to be the gossip of the town, empathizing with her mother's sense of guilt for having pro-duced "esa niña, gorda, fea, retardada, como una evidencia, y la cara marchita frente al espejo, como una evidencia" (that girl, fat, retarded, like evidence, and that withered face in front of the mirror, like evidence).[25] Alia imagines the murmurings of the town: "'Estuvo casada con un cubano.' '¿Un cubano?' 'Como lo oyes, un CUBANO.' '¿Negro, supongo?' '¡Negrísimo!' 'Pobrecita.'"[26] ("She was married to a Cuban." "A Cuban?" "Just as I said. A Cuban." "Black, I suppose?" "Very Black!" "Poor little thing.") This provincial sense of tragedy at having wed an Afro-Cuban is far from the narratives of greatness regarding the Soviet-Cuban solidarity that were disseminated within the sphere of inter-national relations. In this way, even if Vega Serova's autobiographical fiction resists being read as a testimony of an era, it still shows the underside of a mar-riage that in the 1970s and 1980s was viewed as exceptionally promising.

As a child, Alia forms multiple personalities to distance herself from the vio-lence of such an experience. That of Sofia appears only briefly but is significant:

> Le gustaban las canciones y los cuentos tradicionales rusos, las conver-saciones largas y las fiestas populares. Me presenté al examen el sábado siguiente y lo pasé con éxito. Canté *Katiusha*, que venía cantando desde el círculo infantil, conté la historia del pescador que se quedaba sin un solo deseo cumplido por culpa de la avaricia de su mujer, y recité el poema de Liérmontov sobre el velero solitario que tanto le gustaba a Liena.[27]

She liked traditional Russian songs and stories, long conversations and popular parties. I appeared at the exam the next Saturday and passed successfully. I sang "Katiusha," which I'd been singing since nursery school. I told the story of the fisherman who was left without a single wish fulfilled because of his wife's greed, and I recited Lermontov's poem about the solitary sailboat that Liena liked so much.

Melodies that may have haunted the narrator of "Proyecto conmemorativo" are mastered by Alia at a young age so that she can transcend the prejudices of the dominant community and become even more "white" or "Soviet" than those in power. These moments in the autobiographical fiction shed light not only on what it might have meant to be an immigrant in Soviet lands, but also on the holes within the ideology of Soviet equanimity and greatness.

The racial prejudices within the Soviet Union come to the fore in *Ánima fatua* to an extent that has not yet been fictionalized elsewhere. The reason that Alia's Soviet maternal family looks down upon her is that she is her father's daughter, a fact that explains her "barbarous" behavior. Zeta Dacosta pays special attention to these aspects in the novel as they relate to the larger community of Soviet-Cubans.

> For example, Alia, the *polovina* character in the novel *Ánima fatua* [Fatuous Soul], who in Russia can seem somewhat exotic, as the daughter of a black man who, as the character herself says, was in reality "only a fairly light-skinned mulatto, of course," is accepted as white in Cuba, just as she might have been in the time of *Cecilia Valdés*. Thus, *polovinas* are not troubled or worried about race, which may explain why they are somewhat lost or invisible. They are seen as *mestizos* but defy classification: moreover, they ignore it. At most, they admit to a minimal or quite ambiguous reference relative to their parents' origin. Because of this situation, they are satisfied and comfortable with the way in which society sees them, because being *different* always presents a challenge.[28]

Dacosta's assessment of Soviet-Cubans' relationship to race coincides with Prieto Samsonov and Martínez Shvietsova's thesis in ". . . So, Borscht Doesn't Mix into the *Ajiaco*?" wherein Cuban artists from the Soviet diaspora resist embracing their hybridity as a way of assimilating within the Cuban national realm. Having interviewed three artists — the painter and writer Ernesto González Litvinov; the editor of the online journal *Esquife* in its first incarnation, Andrés Mir; and the painter and writer Vega Serova herself, along with eleven subjects from the Soviet diaspora in Cuba — Prieto Samsonov and Martínez Shvietsova suggest a discrepancy between how the artists see their work as fitting in with the Cuban sphere and its very real binational influences and identifications. While the degree of Alia's oppression may be unique, given her familiar circumstances, many other visual and narrative testimonies of the less savory aspects of the union permeate contemporary Cuban culture.

## SEXUAL IMMIGRATION

If we are to more fully understand the repercussions of the artistic and political endeavors of ethnic minorities in Cuba, it is necessary to contextualize them in the broader picture of the Soviets in Cuba. As *Ánima fatua* indicates, marriages between women from the former Soviet Union and men from Cuba literally and symbolically remain interesting for present-day Cuba. According to Moiseev and Egorova, some thirteen hundred women from Russia and other former republics still live in Cuba.[29]

*Cuba mi amor* (Cuba My Love), the first documentary that addresses the topic, was made by the French-Togolese filmmaker Penda Houzangbe, who, born in 1979, studied at the film school in San Antonio de los Baños, graduating with this project in 2004. The twenty-three-minute film, yet to be released, focuses on the late Natasha Balashova. The Russian daughter of a Bolshevik, Balashova came to Cuba in 1969, nicknamed herself "Bolchevique," and formed a club for Russians called The Rodnikí (Springs) Ethnographic Cultural Center. Balashova remarks in the documentary that the kind of migration in which she partook was "sexual," although it was officially called "matrimonial." Balashova's story is unraveled as she regards photographs of her youth, among which is a particularly striking one taken on the day she met her darker-skinned Cuban husband at a campfire beside birch trees, a commonplace in the Soviet-Cuban imaginary. She emotionally portrays her love of Fidel, and while one of Balashova's friends complains of her devotion to the nation, another adds a passionate stanza to the patriotic song "Guantanamera," which she affectionately calls the Slavic stanza. The documentary suggests that Balashova's patriotism toward the Soviet and Cuban nations comes from the same apparently heartfelt embrace of internationalism, an internationalism that is even stronger in light of the disappearance of her homeland. "Porque nosotros sí somos soviéticos" (Because we are Soviets indeed), Natasha utters, expressing a sentiment toward a no-longer functional identity.

*Todas iban a ser reinas*, a fifty-four-minute documentary directed by Gustavo Pérez, explores the lives of seven women from the old Soviet Union who faced, for the most part, similar predicaments regarding the lack of interest their embassies showed in them, their lack of financial means to "return" home, and as was the case with Balashova, without a nation that is their own—the Soviet

Union—to which they can return. The documentary starts out with the same premise as *Cuba mi amor*—exploring the fate of women from the Soviet Union on the island—but the implications that can be drawn from it about the relationship between the Soviets and Cubans are more intense, as they are inspired by a more apparent and intimate empathy. The artists see their own youth and dreams reflected in the diverse stories of the Soviet women who reside in their own Camagüey. In a beautiful unpublished letter to her daughter, the producer, Oneyda González, details the almost year-long process that began with approximately one hundred interviews with women from the former Soviet Union and concluded with the film's premiere.

> One day, I found myself in the hospital with a Ukrainian. Let's say it was a sonorous encounter. She spoke in Spanish and her accent seemed strange with regards to the languages that we hear these days. When I was able to identify it, I asked myself, and what became of the Russians? You were very little, but surely you remember your uncle Frank's wife. When the Soviet Union disappeared, these women remained, but under different conditions: that is what we tried to discover.

This familiar yet uncanny sound led González to convince her partner, film director Gustavo Pérez, to take on the project of documenting the testimonies of these women from the former Soviet Union; the film, González noted, would be "an investigation into the social project that was expressed in a magazine that [she] read as a young girl: *The Soviet Woman*." She continues:

> In the magazine, which was regularly distributed in Cuba, those women were seen as models to be adhered to, as exotic as the immense country in which they lived. They were intellectuals, artists, doctors, and even cosmonauts, whose professional development guaranteed the happiness of their home and their own realization.

The loss and failure evident within the documentary is given even more depth through these words, which describe not only a bygone era but also a transnational feminist perspective that, having formed González as artist and mother, may be in danger of being lost in future generations. González's sentiment cuts to the explosive gender politics around transnationalism and hybridity that affect not only the children of these Soviet women, as seen in the production of the Project Mir generation, but also Cuban women at large who came of age in the 1980s with models of beauty that were imported from the Soviet Bloc.

*Todas iban a ser reinas* was shown on March 23, 2006, at a cultural institution in Camagüey. The documentary was the first of its kind to treat the topic of

Soviet-Cuban personal relationships in a historical framework, a topic that previously had been institutionally ignored. A provocative debate—one of many to follow—ensued. The film aired on Camagüey television two days later, significantly, just once, with tremendous support from viewers. Screenings of the documentary took place in venues that could accommodate only a limited public. The documentary screened at the Cine Infanta and in the Caracol Sala of the UNEAC in Havana as part of the International Film Festival, as well as at a number of other festivals. Most of this story could easily sound like that of any number of independent documentaries made elsewhere in the world, including in the United States, with the difference that in Cuba, it is largely the state apparatus, rather than the market, that works to control a film's impact. With the new Russian-Cuban friendship now in center stage, the documentary has taken on a new life within the nation and abroad with an international distributor. This is a sign of the power of the hegemony to contextualize and reinterpret, a peculiar yet also common strategy in dealing with culture. In fact, with the presence of the former Soviet "queens" at many of the screenings, the documentary has given them a space in which to speak about their experiences.

*Todas iban a ser reinas* begins with a Latvian woman singing about the "*ostrov svobody*" (island of freedom); the film then cuts to the sea and its sounds, and immediately after, to a Ukrainian speaking about having been taught to sing the "July 26th Hymn" in Russian. Another interviewee echoes, "Aquella 'Guantanamera,' aquella 'Guantanamera' . . . Me enamoré, me enamoré y yo pensé que un día yo tengo que aprender este idioma" (That "Guantamera," that "Guantanamera," I fell in love, I fell in love, and I thought that one day I had to learn that language). The document's haunting power lies in the fact that these women's out-of-placeness in Cuba and more general inability to envision themselves anywhere else is symptomatic of Cubans' disillusionment as a whole. What the filmmakers found in these female lovers was not just of intimate and singular importance, but was also a metaphor for Cuba. At least initially one might conclude that it was this kernel of identification that led to the documentary's questionable viability for Cuban television. Before turning to the revelations of disillusionment, let us first listen to the pangs of passion and love that characterize their marriages:

> Yo conocí a un estudiante cubano que después se hizo mi esposo hasta ahora y hasta que la muerte nos separa. Yo, una letona veinteañera ordinaria para mi punto de vista y un compañero exótico con espendrum con su piel bronceado porque estamos en julio . . . Con sonrisa esa espléndida de cubano que me mató, me mató, me deslumbró, me llevó acá y me mató para el resto de mi vida . . .
>
> Me pareció un muchacho muy serio, muy bonito, pero muy bonito,

muchísimo bonito que nuestros rusos . . . Me gustaba su forma de ser alegres, naturales. Un día en una fiesta nos presentaron allí y no nos separamos más.

I met a Cuban student who later became my husband until now and until death do us part. Me, a twenty-something Latvian, ordinary, from my point of view, with an exotic guy with an Afro and bronzed skin since it was July . . . With that splendid Cuban smile that killed me, it killed me, it dazzled me, it brought me here and it killed me for the rest of my life . . .

He seemed to me a very serious boy, very handsome, really handsome, much more so than our Russians . . . I liked his way of being happy, natural. One day at a party they introduced us, and we were never apart again.

These voices, sometimes in evidently broken Spanish, sound as if they formed part of an operatic chorus injected with a good dose of kitsch rooted in the 1970s and 1980s; the fictional mother of Alia in *Ánima fatua* would fit in. The history of each witness cannot escape the larger history of the nation, and in this way, the symbolic honeymoon faces setbacks. The Latvian describes how she and her family were denied lodging at the hotel beside the airport in Moscow back in 1990; in retrospect, she speculates it was either on account of her being Latvian or her husband's being Cuban. That same, still-in-love Latvian also states: "Porque yo dejé atrás una vida en un país desarrollado . . . es morir y nacer en otras circunstancias, en otro país, en otro medio, en otro mundo . . . Es como morir y nacer de nuevo en otro nivel" (Because I left behind a life in a developed country . . . it's like dying and being born in other circumstances, in another country, in another atmosphere, in another world . . . It's like dying and being reborn on another level). Her first explanation of what was happening in Moscow in the late 1980s and early 1990s can be considered a post-Perestroika reflection, emerging in a place where ethnic prejudices that had been previously buried are exposed. The characterization of the island as having been underdeveloped reflects a postrevolutionary moment in the sense that the failure of the Revolution is suggested. Nevertheless, it manifests some discrepancy in the manner of perceiving development. It is in the Soviet Union, that supposedly developed country, where she states that she had her first experience with inhumanity.

What happens to the island of freedom, the "ostrov svobody"? The documentary's "prologue" features Gabriela Mistral's poem, from which the documentary takes its title: "Todas íbamos a ser reinas de cuatro reinos sobre el mar . . . lo decíamos embriagadas y lo tuvimos por verdad" (All of us were to be queens, ruling four realms beside the sea . . . drunk with our story-telling, we truly did believe).[30] The poem suggests how intricately tied such gendered diasporic and national conditions and positions are to each other. The word "todas" ("all," in the feminine) belongs as much to diasporic subjects as it does to the film's creators and the potential spectators, for whom the film could be emasculating.

It is extremely difficult to assess the complex dynamic of the film's impact. Independent Cuban journalists reported the replacement in December 2007 of Rebeca Burón Marín, director of Televisión Camagüey, for broadcasting the documentary.[31] Víctor Fowler Calzada, in his review of the documentary, reveals the film's menacing edge and poignancy when he transforms its title from third-person plural (*iban*) to first-person plural (*íbamos*):

> *Todas íbamos a ser reinas* is the chronicle of a dream that disappeared (that is, friendship among countries or a relationship of equals between development and underdevelopment); a game of winks with present-day Cuban life (the interviewed subjects compare the country as it was when they arrived with the one that exists today); a small exploration of our identity (culture shock is illustrated through the difference in customs); and a consideration of the displacement of identity, through the work with these people who no longer play the central role they used to in national life or in the interests of their governments, who appear to have remained stranded in a void.[32]

In fact, "*Todas íbamos a ser reinas*" is what the documentary ought to be called, elucidating that play of winks at contemporary Cuban life. The documentary, which Reina María Rodríguez also calls "*Todas íbamos a ser reinas*," serves as a point of departure for "Nostalgia," in which she states:

> Among colorless matrioshka dolls, tapestries scraped by the tropical sun, textiles defeated by humidity and dust, these mature and portly women sing Russian ballads on camera. Nostalgia returns throughout their stories in displays of the oblivion marked on their faces, on their movements. Obscurity: they let it hang like an amulet among other tokens. And there it resides, like a ghost, presaging disillusionment.[33]

Some critics' interpretation of these women as stranded suggests that the film works principally as a metaphor for these critics' own situation, living in a country from which, as the novelist Wendy Guerra has said, "todas se van" (all leave). However, let us not evade less symbolic fates of Soviet women on the island. In July 2007, another Russian woman who came to the island for love, Elena

Varelevna Verselova (she had lived in the Isla de Juventud and was president of the Acción Democrática Pinera), was not permitted such nostalgia and was instead deported for "dissident activities." Her fate drew attention to these so-called Russian women on the island. Anthony Boadle of Reuters picked up this parallel in an article entitled "Russian Women Stranded in Cuba since USSR Fall,"[34] a title that does not quite accurately characterize the mixed sentiments of the women interviewed in the documentary.

In *Todas iban a ser reinas*, the forgotten, once heroic warriors of love and country are resurrected to reflect upon the casualties of both the Soviets and the Cubans. While their gender roles are largely left unquestioned—the Latvian, for instance, declares in an almost conventional fashion that it is her role to follow her man—almost every other concern is put into question. The women hardly converge on any issue, and in this way, the film debates education, home, economy, and children on the island. To a large extent, they hold down a broken fort in Cuba whether they want to or not.

> Yo amo esta tierra y amo el pueblo cubano. Esto sí es verdad: yo tengo dos patrias, eso sí voy a repetir muchas veces, yo tengo dos patrias, la patria donde yo nací y la patria donde yo vivo. El pueblo cubano miro como un pueblo mío . . . [El] calor y las mentiras no los soporto . . . Entonces desde aquel momento, suspendieron el idioma ruso en toda la enseñanza . . . Esa palabra sentí con mucho dolor, la palabra "desmerengamiento" . . . No hay manera ni de pagar la visa. No hablando del pasaje.
>
> I love this land and I love the Cuban people. This is the truth: I have two homelands, I am going to repeat this many times, I have two homelands, the homeland where I was born and the one where I live. The Cuban people I look at as if they were my own . . . Heat and lies, I can't put up with them . . . Then, from that moment on, they stopped teaching the Russian language . . . This word I felt with much pain, the word *desmerengamiento*.[35] There's no way to pay for the visa, not to mention the airfare.

The pain that the Ukrainian who lived in Cuba for over thirty years feels about the breakup of the Socialist Bloc is existential. Although the authenticity of the documentary genre leads spectators to believe in its verisimilitude, it is essential to keep in mind that, like fiction, *Todas iban a ser reinas* is a negotiation between interlocutor and witness, manifesting the relationship between host and guest. This is a sore topic, especially for a Revolution whose principal goal has been that of national sovereignty. In this way, the documentary considers the themes of hospitality and the treatment of the other, even when this other was, at a different point in history—a very recent point in history—representative of a hegemonic entity.

The documentarians' own sense of identification with these women's diverse stories of romance, belief, passion, and disillusionment also emerges in Lissette Solórzano's *Érase una vez . . . una matrioshka* (Once upon a time . . . there was a matrioshka), a photographic exhibit that formed part of the 2009 Havana Biennale and that in February 2010 was tied to *Todas iban a ser reinas* when the two projects were displayed together, along with the work of Russian-born Canadian photographer Olga Chagaoutdinova at the Pabellón Cuba as part of the International Book Fair of Cuba. The use of the imperfect tense in both titles is most suitable for expressing nostalgia. However, Solórzano's project, more so than the documentary, illustrates the presence of designated foreign spaces within the domestic sphere by foregrounding her subjects' ties to the Russian Orthodox religion, whose significance within Cuba greatly increased with the consecration of a magnificently ornate church in Old Havana in 2008 that stands out among the decaying buildings around it with its impressive height, gold cupolas, and crosses. It is not the exterior that captivates Solórzano, but rather the parishioners and the practices inside.

Through what Argel Calcines calls Solórzano's "anthropological sensibility," she documents her subjects' religious practices, their domestic space, and their family ties. While her interest in them likely stems from nostalgia for the Soviet period in Cuba, she refrains from incorporating her subjects in a narrative of defeat and instead casts them in one of revelation and discovery.[36] The promotional materials for the 2009 Havana Biennale, written by the curator Hilda Barrio, stress just that: "More than 40 years have passed so that these Matrioshkas, already 'burnt by the sun' accept kindly the call of the artist Lissette Solórzano to revive their personal stories, to be registered in this singular photographic essay." Calcines, who himself took an active part in the Soviet-Cuban experience, having studied at the Energy Institute in Moscow in 1987, describes Solórzano's process in the following manner: "Black and white portraits, but with enough shades of gray to show the authors' moderation in penetrating into that 'underground' community of those who 'endured History.'"[37] The Russian Orthodox Church, so visually distinct from conventional Cuban landscapes, provides a remarkable backdrop for photographing Soviet women on the island and for showing their responsibility in the continuation of traditions far from home, their complacence in their surroundings, and even their transcendence.

While *Todas iban a ser reinas* primarily documents a sensibility of disquiet wherein women are seated alone in their homes, Solórzano's photographs show them with their heads covered, before religious altars, along with their mixed-race and multiethnic families. Solórzano's visual narrative retains a sense

*From* Érase una vez . . . una matrioshka, *by Lissette Solórzano, 2009.*
*Courtesy of artist.*

of wholeness that is frequently missing from representations of a nation that is typically pictured as splintered by political and economic migrations. This sense of wholeness is portrayed through images of family unity; adornment, in the form of matrioshka dolls, samovar, Russian hand-painted wooden spoons, collections of ceramic figurines of *muzhiks*, horses, flowers, and tapestries; and a set of diasporic images of the family's life in both countries that could be compared to the Cuban-American experience.

These auto-ethnographic, documentary, and literary projects by and about the diaspora of Russians in Cuba and Russian-Cubans begin to reveal a complex narrative of Cubans' ideological and geopolitical orphanage from the Soviet Bloc and reconnections with different parts of the world, including Russia. The generation of Proyecto mir_xxi_cu has proven to be exceptionally important for drawing attention to the presence not only of Soviet phantasms but also of real former Soviet women on the island who inhabit a multilayered ethnic history. For some of these women, replacing the word "Soviet" with another ethnic category can be difficult. The literature emerging from the children of Soviets and Cubans explores what it means to inhabit a historical accident in ways that history is unable to convey. Gustavo Pérez and Oneyda González's film and Lissette Solórzano's photography, if read as Cubans' own attempts to render this unusual Cuban syncretism, are inspired by a similar quest to know more deeply these foreigners living among them who were once part of the nation's triumph. For the filmmakers, the Soviet women are not only reminiscent of a transnational past with elements of which to be proud, but are also analogous to the abandoned Cuban present. For Solórzano, Soviet women become a source of pride and the basis for envisioning the unique multicultural fabric of Cuba.

# CHAPTER TWO

# Crossed Destinies

*I*n the short fiction and performances that I examine in this chapter, the destinies of the Soviet Union and Cuba are crossed within
the lives of the characters. The resonances of relationships between Soviets and
ordinary Cubans, who in some cases have no biological ties or even intimate
or prolonged interactions with each other, are evidenced within the analyzed
texts.

The most dramatic example is Pedro Manuel González Reinoso's kitschy
drag character, a "Russian" woman Lawrence La Fountain-Stokes would call
a *"transloca"* on account of the character's eccentric negotiation of space and
sexuality.[1] By placing his unique performance in dialogue with other creative
renderings of the Soviets by Cubans, I highlight the overall queerness of the
Soviet-Cuban union. With lightning speed, González Reinoso recollects and
molds together different time periods and contact zones, reminding us why a
purely historical approach to the topic at hand is not adequate.

In other works, the more violent sides of cultural contact are also explored.
Voyeurism, one of the main themes of Cuban writing in the Special Period,
takes on new significance as Soviet/Russian and Cuban neighbors merge with
one another. For example, in "Clemencia bajo el sol" (Clemency under the
Sun), by Adelaida Fernández de Juan, a Cuban man's infidelity and the collapse of the Soviet Union become the impetus for a Soviet woman's return to
her "homeland" and for her Cuban neighbor's realization of the Soviet woman's
destiny. In Jorge Miralles's "Fotos de boda" (Wedding Photos), Cubans'
struggle to detach from the Soviet narrative can be truthfully illustrated only
within a surrealistic and blurry portrait. Similarly, in the play *Sputnik*, by Ulises
Rodríguez Febles, the Cuban and Soviet landscapes merge in the imaginary,
showing the difficulty of extricating memories, especially when those memo-

ries have familiar roots. The sexualization of the ideological union between the Cubans and the Soviets as an allegory for the geopolitical dissolution and the new chaotic world order takes on a far more humorous tone in Ernesto Pérez Castillo's "Bajo la bandera rosa" (Beneath the Pink Flag) and the novel *Haciendo las cosas mal* (Doing Things Wrong). The two nations overlap upon the lives of the protagonists.

### RED DRAG

Pedro Manuel González Reinoso (born in 1959) narrates repeatedly the invention of his character "La Rusa Roxana Rojo" (The Russian Roxana the Red), whom he started performing at El Mejunje Club in Santa Clara, Cuba, the mecca of drag on the island, in the early 1990s. Roxana Rojo's fictional voyage to the island from the USSR is central to González Reinoso's queer aesthetics, which implodes the Cuban narrative of brotherhood and solidarity of the 1960s through the 1980s.

For this Cuban drag performer and writer, the Soviet territory persists within the Cuban imaginary to elucidate several unsettling and enchanting aspects of Cuba's past, present, and future. González Reinoso's multigeneric and exceptionally fragmented creations reflect the zeitgeist of post-post-Soviet times. As the Soviet empire vanishes from the world stage, it continues to re-anchor itself in Cuba, in what the protagonist of Polina Martínez Shvietsova's short story "17 abstractos de una agenda" (17 abstracts of an agenda) calls a phantom, or shell, corporation. In fact, in Adelaida Fernández de Juan's prologue to the 2010 edition of *Vidas de Roxy ó el aplatanamiento de una rusa en Cuba* (Lives of Roxy or the Bananification of a Russian in Cuba), she uses the word *"fantasma"* (phantom) to describe the doubling that entraps its author, González Reinoso. In her words, "Pedrito allows himself to be entrapped by his other half, by the other phantom that inhabits him, and that is sometimes one, and at others, his counterpart."[2] This notion of being entrapped by the Russian woman serves as an appropriate allegory for distinct aspects of the political machinery in Cuba as well.

Having been an economist and an accountant for about twenty years, González Reinoso describes some of the rationale behind his curious career change in Judith Grey's 2003 documentary *Sin Embargo*: "When the Special Period intensified, I gave up, and became a hairdresser. This gave me more freedom. I invented a character. She was created in 1994, at a time when tolerance for the gay movement began to develop. We're all made of bits and pieces, like all Cubans, I'm no exception." Like many of his compatriots, González Reinoso identifies scarcity as the impetus for invention. The snippets from Soviet Bloc history and culture that González Reinoso implements to create his character are especially exacting.

In the following passage, González Reinoso takes a parodic spin on the material leftovers from the Soviet bloc:

> Yo creía que el pugilato por el refrigerador *Dosvidania* tras la Zafra de los millones en el 70 me abriría al respeto y a la exoneración. Ni siquiera la olla *Ruskii* que gané antes, junto al odio palpitante de mis excompañeros de trabajo por el despojo masivo del *Poljov* (despertador pareciera, de bajas pasiones), o la (o)diosa lavadora *Aurika* destroza-trapos, ni la radio *Órbita* (controlada y meridiana, en su paseo celeste), o la bicimoto *Berjuvina* escánda(hum)osa que me auxilió dando botella, en la pesca del divino respaldo huesimuscular que el diseño original no le incluyera. Ninguna de esas hipotéticas inmunidades para después, me servirían.[3]

> I thought that all the clawing for a *Dosvidania* refrigerator after the how-many-million ton harvest of 1970 would win me the respect and protection a vanguard worker should have coming to her. But no. And neither did the *Ruskii* pressure cooker I had already won, nor the *Poljov* watch (with its low-passion alarm), the *Aurika* washing machine (clobberer of clothing), the *Orbit* radio (controlled and with limited hours) nor the *Berjuvina* motorcycle (with its enormous racket) on which I could cruise around in search of the divine backrest missing from its design. All these brought me the palpable animosity of my ex-workmates, but not the hypothetical immunity I had supposed.[4]

All of these products are immediately recognizable both to Cubans who may still be using some of them and to anyone who grew up during the Soviet years. The consumer goods from the Soviet Union were notorious because, reliant upon "heavy industry to produce" them, their aesthetic was immediately recognizable as distinct from that of the West, and, in addition, they possessed a debatable functionality.[5]

Soviet appliances are an enduring topic of interest for Cubans. The controversial Yoani Sánchez blogged about Cubans accruing debt unknowingly through the acquisition of appliances such as the Chinese Panda television on the nation's merit system — a system with roots in the Soviet period whose merits, according to Sánchez, have come under doubt. "Being on duty for the Committee for the Defense of the Revolution (CDR) or going to the criticism meetings have lost their attraction because it doesn't appear that the reward will be the allocation of a washing machine, a telephone line or a portable radio."[6] La Rusa's humorous assessment of the function of these goods is that she read the situation incorrectly: what she thought would bring her moral superiority only made others envious of her. In this way, La Rusa Roxy Rojo mocks the workings of sociability within the Socialist system in Cuba.

Who is this Roxy we come to know in her distinct manifestations? About his principal character—whose full name is Roxana Petrovna Krashnoi y Vladivostova—the authorial personage states:

> A veces, por razones de coacción, le toma meses a la triunfal resurrección. Y es precisamente ahora, allí, entre antiguas reminiscencias y actuales bastidores que reincorpora el carácter de la soviética ausente como una invocación o como una venganza. Han sido años de vivir la vida cubana de una rusa importada e impostada. Nacida en la extinta Unión Soviética, en tiempos cercanos a la posguerra, había sido concebida en campos de mucha concentración (a saberse si de Stalin o de Hitler), pudo escapar (de alguno de ellos) gracias a las maniobras tenebrosas de su madre quien montada *nadiesabecomo* en barco danés hacia *Ellis Island*, hubo de perderla otra vez en el trayecto. La muy locuela, mientras su madre dormitaba, pasó la noche atormentando con tacones hurtados, al Capitán de la nave que la llevaría a *"tierras de libertad judeo-cristiana."* Era enorme la alegría desbordada de la niña y no compartida por la tripulación, que enojada y somnolienta, la lanzó al mar.[7]

> Sometimes, due to circumstantial causes, the triumphal resurrection may be delayed for months. Yet it's in that dressing room, surrounded by old backstage business and modern memories, that I take on my character, a stranded Russian woman long ago imported into Cuba like a vengeance or a prayer. Born in the former Soviet Union, perhaps (or perhaps not) around the end of the Second World War, she was conceived in a camp of utmost concentration—whether Stalin's or Hitler's, who knows? She escaped thanks to certain dark maneuvers of her mother, who managed—*no-one-can-say-how*—to board a Danish ship bound for Ellis Island but then lost her daughter en route. On that voyage to *"the shores of Judeo-Christian freedom,"* the impetuous Roxy spent one night tormenting the ship captain by stamping her heels above his head while her mother slept. The girl's brimming joy was not shared by the crew, who threw her into the sea.[8]

These statements concerning Roxy's accidental immigration to Cuba, this "phantom company," also have the effect of pushing the Soviet period into the past by simultaneously enacting revenge upon it and memorializing it, not through statues and official commemorations but by pointing out the absurdities of the Soviet-Cuban narrative of solidarity. As González Reinoso communicated to Yamil Díaz Gómez,

> I see doing this spectacle in Cuba as a revenge against the Russian grayness, against the years that we shared with that omnipresence in our cultural and economic life. Russian that was propagated in an official form through schools and on the radio. My brother studied Civil Aeronautics in Kiev; my father went to Armenia. All that amalgam of Russification I incorporated into this crazy character, into my Roxana, this out-dated, incongruent fiction.[9]

González Reinoso's project both mocks and pays homage to what the Cuban people have inherited from the Soviet Union, a nation that, while it did not colonize Cuba in the same ways that the "West" colonized the "Orient" or the "North" the "South," imposed itself in a way that makes it valid to compare post-Soviet culture in Cuba not only with post-Soviet culture elsewhere, but also with postcolonial art in other parts of the world.

Numerous literary works by Latin American and Caribbean writers have incorporated transvestism and a drag performance both as a theme and as a style within their writing. José Donoso's *El lugar sin límites* (1966; The Place without Limits) is both carnivalesque and tragic; Pedro Lemebel's *Tengo miedo torero* (2001; Bullfighter, I'm Afraid) is a thriller set during Augusto Pinochet's dictatorship, and Mayra Santos Febres's *Sirena Selena vestida de pena* (2000) explores a Caribbeanness that continually exceeds neoliberal boundaries. In these and other works, transvestism and drag challenge heteronormativity and its implications for political and social issues. Transvestism is central to Severo Sarduy's theorization of the neobaroque: "Play, loss, waste, and pleasure, that is, eroticism in so far as it is an activity that is always purely ludic, that is no more than a parody of the reproductive function, a transgression of the useful, of the 'natural' dialogue of bodies."[10] González Reinoso is an heir to both Sarduy and Reinaldo Arenas, and proof of that affiliation is in the *choteo* to which he subjects them. With respect to Sarduy's "Los travestis," González Reinoso replies, "No hizo falta llamarse *Kallima* ni paja-mariposear por París para batirse en retirada; tan sólo, chorreantes alas" (It was not necessary to be called *Kallima* nor to behave like a butterfly throughout Paris to back out; just dripping wings).[11] Of the fourth book in Arenas's *pentagonía*, *El color del verano* (The Color of Summer), Reinoso comments, "Como el rojo *color* de Las Arenas (en su verano)" (Like the red *color* of The Arenas [in his summer]).[12] In Arenian fashion, González Reinoso immediately warns the reader about the unclassifiable nature of his work. Rejecting the notion of "writer," he affirms his joy in "mis(x)tificar las vidas, disfrazarlas de alegorías, a-*tributos* y engañifas que las tomen medianamente soportables" (mys[x]tifying lives, dressing them up with allegories, wheeling and dealing so that they pretty much put up with them).[13] In *Vidas de Roxy*, González Reinoso neither completely allegorizes drag nor documents the performer's trials and tribulations; rather, he brings to the written page the performance of the protagonist of his spectacle.

*Vidas de Roxy* is divided into three parts. The first, "(Pre)visiones de 'artista' que se construye mientras (re-a)visa 'sus argumentos'" ([Pre]visions of 'Artist' That Is Constructed While He [Re]vises His Arguments), alternates between the textual creator and his creation. The second part, "Sucesión segunda: 'Sus argumentos'; "La Académica se (dis)pone a vacilar" (Second Succession: His Arguments; The Academic Is Ready to Have Some Fun), is comprised of texts, according to the narrator, "extraídos de su *cahiers* de bitácora" (extracted from his diary notebooks). The third part, "Terminal Tercera: Mis argumentos" (Third Terminal: My Arguments), is the creator's attempt at a critical explanation through a mockery of the genealogical tree.[14] At the same time that *Vidas de Roxy* ridicules filial ties through lengthy explanations of the character's conception and subsequent abandonment, González Reinoso is overflowing with gratitude toward those who encouraged his writing—Laidi Fernández de Juan and Reina María Rodríguez figure at the top of the list.

Each section of *Vidas de Roxy* contains an epigraph from Charles Baudelaire's "In Praise of Cosmetics" from *The Painter of Modern Life*, which Reina María Rodríguez says functions as a "prolepsis."[15] Like Sarduy's *Cobra*, which begins with the transformation of Cobra into the star of her midnight drag show, the establishing shot of *Vidas de Roxy* is the artist's making-up of Roxy through the application of cosmetics.

> Comienza por una base tubular de *pancake* que esparce por la frente y los pómulos usando los dedos—un tono *deep-olive* de *MacFactor*—con equilibrio de alquimista entrenado en no resaltar al esconderse bajo emplaste, el cutis modificado.[16]

> [He begins] with a *pancake* base, a *deep olive Max Factor* shade, using two fingers to spread it over his forehead and cheeks with the balance of a skilled alchemist so the doctored skin reveals no bulges or bumps.[17]

The hypercosmetic aesthetic of González Reinoso rejoices in the associations of meanings, especially between the artificial nuances and the worldly nuances of the same word, "cosmos." The drag libretto's indulgence in this cosmetic aspect complicatedly relies on both the neobaroque and Soviet kitsch.

González Reinoso's performance and libretto elucidate multiple and simultaneous temporalities in global Cuba, while exposing the difficult way that transnational contexts became embedded within the performer's own biography. In this light, González Reinoso's project may be understood as a supreme instance of vernacular cosmopolitanism vis-à-vis the hegemony's internationalism. While drag performances often participate, albeit on the periphery, in the star system by imitating and parodying international divas, La Rusa Roxana Rojo is engaged with another paradigm, that of exploiting transnational folklore. She is the epitome of the matrioshka in Cuba, destitute and "stranded," and part of communities of women, some of whom are celebrated within Penda Houzangbe's *Cuba mi amor*, Gustavo Pérez and Oneyda González's *Todas iban a ser reinas*, and Lissette Solórzano's *Érase una vez ... una Matrioshka*, discussed in Chapter 1 — even obtaining their fifteen minutes of fame in the wake of the new Russian-Cuban friendship. González Reinoso's own biography and the performance of La Rusa Roxana Rojo, as well as the presentation of *Vidas de Roxy* at the 2010 International Book Fair of Cuba, dedicated to Russia, are best understood as part of this spectrum.

Having studied Russian at the military academy and acquired familiarity with the Soviet/Russian mentality from his neighbors in Caibarién, González Reinoso integrates Russian along with English into La Rusa's chaotic and imperfect performance. Although González Reinoso did not travel outside of the island until 2011, his performance of La Rusa Roxana Rojo is fueled by references to Russian and Soviet literature and film, exemplary of the *transloca*. For La Fountain-Stokes, who coined the term, *transloca* is not about the

> unstable, or in between, or in the middle of things, but rather ... the core of transformation — change, the power or ability to mold, reorganize, reconstruct, construct — and of longitude: the transcontinental, transatlantic, but also transversal. The word *transloca* itself consists of the polysemic prefix "trans-" (from the Latin for "across" or "over") and the Spanish word *loca*, meaning "madwoman" and widely used in slang as a synonym for "effeminate homosexual." To be a transloca is to disidentify with dominant social mores in the sense advanced by José Esteban Muñoz (1999) ... *Transloca* (or the transloca state) is a (queer) extension of the historically important (and culturally and geographically specific) concept of *transculturación* (transculturation).[18]

In this sense, González Reinoso disidentifies not only with Soviet hegemony but also with the hegemony of the conventional star system adopted by many, but not all, drag queens. La Rusa Roxana Rojo's persona is exceptional on account of its Soviet inheritance in Cuba, yet it is not detached from the rest of the community of drag performers at El Mejunje either. Not only are some of the songs within the repertoire of La Rusa rendered by her co-workers, but also, La Rusa narrates important occurrences related to the Mejunje, its founder (Ramón Silverio), its artists, and its public. Like La Rusa, many of the characters performed at El Mejunje are not part of the conventional star system. Humberto Toscano Cardoso (born in 1960), the creator of the well-liked and well-known character Samantha Fox, a woman who "tries to be refined but is popular at the same time," writes about how his drag performance helps him to cope with the fact that he is HIV positive, and about how, due to some of his physical features and age, his makeup and wardrobe require more attention than the rest of the performers (more makeup and wardrobe than he sometimes possesses, since his Miami contingency cannot always support his cause). Cristal, a character created by Lázaro Martínez Mendoza (born in 1969), is by contrast "an elegant, very fine but burning and aggressive, theatrical woman" whose repertoire includes songs by the Argentine stars Valeria Lynch (born in 1952) and Nacha Guevara (born in 1940). Mario Félix Herrera Martín (born in 1968), whose name is reminiscent of the Mexican star of the Golden Age María Félix, adores the songs of the grand dames of 1960s and 1970s Cuban music. Then there is Lilli, realized by Mardiel Hernández Morales (born in 1977), whose performance was transformed upon the death of the Chicana singer Selena in 1995. Javier Lorenzo Olivera (born in 1974) is the creator of Sintia, "a bitter, crude woman, who interprets songs about repressed feelings and nightmares, shows her disdain and does not try to be agreeable with the public gratuitously." She does not "try to be beautiful or attractive" and frequently sings hits by the Spanish singer Malú (born in 1982).[19]

As José Estebán Muñoz remarks on Vaginal Davis's "terrorist drag":

> Her dark brown skin does not permit her to pass as white, the beard is obviously fake, and the fatigues look inauthentic. Realness is neither achieved nor is it the actual goal of such a project. Instead, her performance as Clarence functions as an intervention in the history of cross-race desire that saturates the phenomenon of passing. Passing is parodied, and this parody becomes a site where interracial desire is interrogated.[20]

This problematic is hardly the same as La Rusa Roxana Rojo's, but the character is similarly "homey," even organic, as Muñoz has said about Vaginal Davis.

Some of the attributes—such as self-conscious imperfection and awareness of sociopolitical and economic context within the performance—that describe regular actors at El Mejunje also characterize La Rusa Roxana Rojo. While one signature song of her performances is the 1977 hit "Rosanna" by the US rock group Toto, other performers from that same era are also celebrated. For example, at a December 2005 show that she introduced as "the worst, the most kitsch, the most raspberry," she lip-synched "Vsë mogut koroli" (Kings Can Do Anything), a 1977 hit sung by the Soviet and Russian musical performer Alla Pugacheva, whom La Rusa Roxana Rojo personified, wearing an over-the-top red cape similar to the one that had dazzled Pugacheva's audiences twenty-five years before.

The diverse repertoire of La Rusa Roxana Rojo includes Argentine Liliana Felipe's "Las histéricas" (The Hysterics); the Swedish pop group Abba; the Mexican ranchera singer Paquita la del Barrio; the Argentine Nacha Guevara, known for "Vals del minuto" (Minute Waltz) in addition to many other hits; the Europop duo from Germany called Modern Talking; the US jazz singer Ella Fitzgerald; the US queen of pop, Cher; the great Cuban pianist, singer, and songwriter known as Bola de Nieve (Snowball), a homosexual and fervent supporter of the Castro regime in its first decade, before he died in 1971; and even the current Colombian superstar Shakira, among many others that lend themselves to kitsch. Often the costumes of La Rusa—for example, a pink and green outfit with a bizarre hat—do not at all "match" the songs being performed, as is the case when she lip-synchs "Rabo de nube" (Tail of Cloud) by the Cuban hero of the *nueva trova* movement (a kind of revolutionary folk music) Silvio Rodríguez. Before the audience knows it, La Rusa reappears as Madonna with a cross covering his privates and then strips down to the actor Pedro González Reinoso singing "Puro teatro" (Pure Theater) by the Cuban American "queen of Latin soul," La Lupe. This final gesture anchors the performance momentarily and playfully in essentialism. While the Soviet and Russian inheritance surfaces at different points in the show, the point of departure for La Rusa's renditions of diverse pop music, mostly from the 1970s and 1980s, is principally an umbrella persona.

González Reinoso's analysis of his performance's relationship to geopolitics emerges in a conversation with the journalist Yamil Díaz Gómez.

> Cuando termino de maquillarme y me empiezo a poner el cuerpo —
> a base de espumitas de goma, de toallitas—, ya me siento la estrella.
> Anoche decía que ya ni siquiera soy una estrella sino un *sputnik*, porque
> había perdido el geoestacionamiento y me dedicaba a vagar. Soy como
> la basura sideral que flota y ve con calma lo que ocurre debajo, en la
> Tierra.[21]

> When I finish making myself up and I begin to put on the body—made
> out of foam rubber, little towels—, I already feel like a star. Last night I

said that I'm not even a star anymore, but rather a *sputnik*, because I had lost the geo-parking and I was dedicated to wandering. I am like sidereal trash that floats and calmly sees what happens below, on Earth.

Both González Reinoso and La Rusa Roxana Rojo bombard readers and spectators with a broad knowledge of international and national political affairs, cultural (both elite and popular) affairs, and material culture.

> Vuelve Roxana a colocarse los tacones desgastados y el vestidito Rojo punzó que ha escogido de su ropero habitual para la *performance* de hoy: trenzas rubias y pañuelo kazajo en la cabeza a lo *Alla Pugachova* (eso, *Allá*, cuando hacía sus fotos publicitadas en *Izvestia Rossía* de i-*lustre* trabajo voluntario en el *Sovjós*), quien fuera una vedette soviética como ella, que se presentó varias veces en Cuba allá por la década vigorosa de los 80 (¡seguimos apabullados con los ocho y huele *a muerto* todavía!). Aquí pegaba escasamente la música popular de los rusos por sus ruidos guturales, y esa cantante, que tenía cierta onda *pop* sirvió un po(p)co para dar *imagen* de modernidad a una cultura que siempre se asoció a cosas más zafias y sombrías.[22]

> Roxana once again tightens the straps of her worn-out high heels and the bright red dress she's chosen for today's *performance*. She's wearing blond braids and a Kazakh kerchief on her head, just like *Alla Pugachova* (when, over there, she was doing publicity shots in *Izvestia Rossía* doing illustrious voluntary farm work in the *Sovjos*). You remember her, a Soviet vedette who toured Cuba sometime in the *8os* (we remain overwhelmed with the eight and it smells *like death* still). Russian popular music was never much of a hit here because of all those guttural sounds, but that particular singer with a certain *pop* flair managed to lend a little modern *glow* to a culture we always associated with heavy and somber things.[23]

While US culture is known to seduce Cubans more than the culture of the Socialist Bloc, despite government efforts to the contrary, González Reinoso ensures that the most popular and the most esoteric of Soviet culture that was disseminated on the island is resuscitated. For example, he retells the tale of the Soviet/Russian cellist Mstislav Rostropovich (1927–2007) and his wife, the soprano Galina Vishnevskaya:

> El *Chupa-destupe-chochas* como instrumento, se acopló con cuerda aprisionada al trabuco del violonchelista *Mstislav* cuando su esposa *Galina*

regresó al bloque en los **90** por la cédula despilfarrada. Una música cre-cida en **Baikonur*** bajo los arpegios fogosos de *La Soy-u(n)z-Protón,* desde Bakú en su *antro-morfismo.*[24]

The *Pussy-sucker* as instrument coupled with the imprisoned cord on the blunderbuss of the cellist *Mstislav* when his wife *Galina* returned from the Bloc in the *90s* for their squandered identity card. A music born in **Baikonur,** under the fiery arpeggios of The *Soy-u(n)z- Proton* from Bakú in his *anthropomorphism.*

This somewhat nonsensical speech, filled with insider references and word play, is hardly intelligible, let alone translatable. "Antro-morfismo" might refer to *"antro,"* or dive, while *"morfismo"* corresponds to transformation. The density of the prose matches the strangeness of re-creating the Soviet world in Cuba through the allegory of Mstislav and Galina. Once Soviet heroes, they were de-prived of their Soviet identity for their support of dissidents.

A principal goal of the movement for imperfect cinema in the 1960s was that of challenging the star system. Julio García Espinosa's perspective on Holly-wood's fabrication of stars is well known: "Imperfect cinema rejects exhibi-tionism in both (literal) senses of the word, the narcissistic and the commercial (getting shown in established theaters and circuits). It should be remembered that the death of the star-system turned out to be a positive thing for art."[25] González Reinoso's insistence upon the resemblance of his character to the *sputnik* speaks to his own theory of geopolitical and cultural framing in the post-Soviet world; he is the imperfect star that corresponds to another econ-omy wherein cosmonauts and sputniks are the order. That is to say, it is as if La Rusa were telling the story of the Cuban Revolution through the camp perspec-tive of a tethered loser, the eighth queen of *Todas iban a ser reinas,* the faulty bildungsroman. The performance manifests a pride in the struggle to exhibit repeatedly the queerness of the Soviet-Cuban solidarity.

### "RUSAS" AND "RUSSIFIED CUBANS" OF THE SPECIAL PERIOD

While conveyed in a principally somber tone, unlike that which char-acterizes La Rusa's performance, transformations in material and cultural con-sumption post-1989 are also central within Adelaida Fernández de Juan's short story "Clemencia bajo el sol," which places gender above nationality and his-tory in its capacity to forge unquestionable loyalties. While the Cuban narrator, Cuqui, has never traveled beyond the city's tunnel, she imaginatively leaves Old

Havana through the anecdotes of her Russian neighbor, Ekaterina, and even comes to implement Russian literature as a mode of transforming tragedy into a unique solidarity between herself and this "exotic" woman.

Ekaterina's husband, Reyes, returned to Cuba with his Russian bride to re-create a Russian home, having brought all the décor from her homeland, "para hacerse la idea de que seguirían viviendo allá"[26] (to make themselves believe that they were still living over there). While the Cuban narrator envisions that man and wife have both embraced Russianness within their home, when she gets to know Ekaterina, she advises her to exchange Russianness for Cubanness as the language of the bedroom, as a means of preventing the Cuban macho from straying and seeking out another "home" in a Cuban lover.

The intimacy between the women begins, somewhat cliché-like, by way of cuisine. "El caso fue que nos acostumbramos a estar juntas. Yo comí por primera vez en su casa sopa de remolacha, col y yogur, ella me explicó que se llamaba borsch."[27] (The thing was that we got accustomed to being together. I ate beet soup, cabbage and yogurt for the first time at her house, and she explained to me that it was called borscht). This exchange is the start of their interpenetration. When Ekatarina is about to give birth to her *polovina*, the narrator performs the duty of accompanying her to the hospital. Later on, her responsibilities increase.

> Volodia nació flaco y transparente como su madre, y si usted la hubiera visto, llorando y diciéndome: spasiva Cuqui, spasiva.
>
> Me encargué de hablarle en español a Volodia; Ekaterina y Reyes solo hablaban en ruso.[28]

> Volodia was born skinny and transparent like his mother, and if you had seen her, crying and telling me: *spasiva*, Cuqui, *spasiva*.
>
> I took it upon myself to speak to Volodia in Spanish; Ekatarina and Reyes only spoke in Russian.

While transferring a mother tongue is a weighty task, the story's focus is really on the cross-fertilization of women.

Cuqui is particularly curious about the Russian's creolization process. "¿Quién ha visto a una rusa haciendo dulces criollos?"[29] (Who has seen a Russian making Creole sweets?). Having seen the effect of her efforts to nationalize Ekaterina, Cuqui becomes particularly protective of her friend, especially when she observes an allergist frequenting Ekaterina's home, supposedly to care for Volodia, but in fact she is having an affair with Reyes. She warns Ekaterina, "No es buena, no la dejes estar aquí en el cuarto"[30] (She's not good. Don't let her be here in the room). Cuqui acts as a go-between who seeks to empower the Russian guest on Cuban soil. Ekaterina, the Russian guest, like many other Soviet women in Cuba, makes a living as a translator. Survival is at stake for all the characters, and as such, Ekaterina returns with her son to Russia upon learning of her husband's affair. When Reyes's Cuban lover installs herself some months later in Ekaterina's former home, Cuqui takes revenge by physically attacking her and (supposedly accidentally) murdering her. "Clemencia bajo el sol" is her confession.

The intensity of her response to the change of loyalties comes about as a logical denouement to the bond of the two women. Cuqui's own son, just a year younger than Ekaterina's, is the result of another infidelity, her own with a married man. She copes with her own tenuous financial situation through the help of a family member and Ekaterina:

> ¿De qué yo vivo? . . . De lo que gana mi tío de las visitas de Osvaldo, y de vender arroz con leche . . . Ekaterina me ayudó mucho, muchísimo. También vivo de la ilusión de lo que he leído, a mí no me apena decir que he leído a los rusos.[31]

> What do I live on? . . . From what my uncle earns from Osvaldo's visits and from selling rice pudding . . . Ekaterina helped me a lot, very much. I also live on the illusion of what I have read. I'm not embarrassed to say that I have read the Russians.

The potential for embarrassment in sustaining oneself through Russian literature in the aftermath of Ekaterina's departure from the island, and with her, the departure of her culture, is, by far, the most significant aspect of this passage. The transition from "things Russian" occupying the realm of the exotic and unsavory to their becoming almost her own realm speaks to the adjustments made within the Cuban popular *ajiaco* to accommodate new Russian ingredients.

> Todo empezó cuando ella consiguió libros traducidos para ayudarse en su trabajo, y me animó a leerlos . . . Oígame, yo creía que los hombres rusos eran toscos y brutos como los osos, con los dedos cuadrados y los muslos fofos de no usarlos como es debido, hasta que leí *Ana Karenina*.[32]

> It all started when she obtained translated books to help her at her job, and she encouraged me to read them . . . Listen, I thought that Russian men were rough and brute like bears, with square fingers and flabby thighs from not using them as they ought to be, until I read *Anna Karenina*.

Ekaterina opens Cuqui's world to the sumptuous panorama of the nineteenth-century masterpiece—which did not resemble the picture she had of the Soviets. The disturbance arises when the stage begins to collapse.

> Los relojes en forma de llave del Kremlin que se detenían, cansados para siempre, oxidados por el salitre, y sobre todo cuando se despegó la foto inmensa de la catedral de San Basilio, que los niños usaron para papalotes.[33]

> The key-shaped clocks like the Kremlin's that stopped, forever tired, oxidized with saltpeter, and above all, when the immense photo of the San Basilio cathedral fell off and children used it to make kites.

Even the significance of décor is transformed. Prior to the literary aperture, Cuqui only knew Soviet products of the sort La Rusa Roxana Rojo ridicules, so she was not particularly surprised by the evolving function.

> Siempre le dije que las cosas rusas eran una mierda . . . Estábamos tan acostumbrados a los relojes de pulsera que pesaban una tonelada y a los zapatones que parecían de ladrillo que, cuando de pronto desaparecieron, no sabíamos que hacer. ¿Y qué me dice de la carne enlatada? No, no voy a bajar la voz, yo no tengo pelos en la lengua . . . Mucha hambre que matamos con la carne rusa y con las manzanas de pomo. Es verdad que sabían a rayo encendido, pero ¿ahora qué?[34]

> I always told her that Russian things were shitty . . . We were so accustomed to wristwatches that weighed a ton and shoes that seemed like they were made of brick that when suddenly they disappeared, we didn't know what to do. And what about canned meat? No, I'm not going to lower my voice. I don't mince words . . . We fought off much hunger with Russian meat and apples in jars. It's true that they tasted like shit, but now what?

The inability to speculate about and predict what will happen next is characteristic of much Special Period fiction, but this story highlights the process through which "things Russian"—once a shoddy stage set—are almost naturalized.

Esther Whitfield's *Cuban Currency: The Dollar and "Special Period" Fiction*, regarding the dramatic impact of Cuba's dollarized economy on Special Period fiction, is central to understanding Fernández de Juan's short story. When Cuqui observes Reyes and his lover Mireya "vendiéndolo todo, y por dólares" (selling it all, and for dollars), her passion for conserving an old world that belongs to her and her neighbor heightens.[35] Her expression of this withering away is especially symbolic. "Hasta las matrioshkas estaban allí en hilera . . . Y yo allí, viendo cómo se evaporaban los recuerdos"[36] (Even the matrioshkas were there lined up . . . And there I was, watching the memories evaporate). The sensation of being an intimate witness to shifting hegemonies pervades the cultural memory of the Soviet Bloc. In this case, as a "popular" Cuban woman, Cuqui refuses to be embarrassed, to lower her voice, and so rapidly assimilate to a new world order. She does not regret her previous solidarity, and only laments having sullied "los libros de Tolstói y de Chejov"[37] (the books of Tolstoy and Chekhov) with the blood of her violent revenge.

Similarly, a Cuban woman realizing the destiny of her "Russian" neighbor is the theme of Jorge Miralles's short story "Fotos de boda," whose fantastic and nebulous setting is explained, in part, through the characters' reliance upon old photographs taken with East German Orwo film to understand their reality.

> Aunque ahora están enrojecidas por el tiempo—o tal vez fue culpa del rollo *Orwo* que se vendió por aquella época en la La Habana—, cargarían siempre con la culpa. Todos seríamos borrados por no sé qué alquimia socialista, con la que también se fabricaron estos productos.[38]

> Although they are now tinted in red whether because of time or because they were taken with that East German *Orwo* film that they used to sell back then in Havana, the photos will always be to blame. We would all be erased by who knows what socialist alchemy; the same that was used to build these products.[39]

"Fotos de boda" manifests a lack of conformity with the present world, in which the standard way of coping with Special Period dearth is by migrating to the United States. Now living in Miami, the Cuban protagonist Yurislady recalls how the process that eventually brought her to the United States began—with the staging, years earlier, of her marriage to a Cuban who had won the special lottery to go the United States. At the same time, she remembers listening to her upstairs neighbor, an older Russian woman who arrived in Cuba as a refugee from World War II (like La Rusa Roxana Rojo), recount the story of her would-be wedding day in the Soviet Union.

Unlike "Clemencia bajo el sol," in which the Soviet-Cuban union is the impulse for Ekaterina's arrival on the island, in "Fotos de boda," the Soviet-Cuban connection is not as neatly allegorical. However, Soviet Bloc material culture and landscapes are unmistakable—the East German film and the Soviet Zenit camera, as well as landscapes of snow and *dachas* that Cubans got closer to through their country's alliance with the Soviets. The tale of the Russian refugee, who found out that her fiancé died in the war on the day that they were to wed, is deeply interwoven in the protagonist's life. Yurislady feels as if she has become hostage to the Russian's past when years later, through the mail, she receives notice of her Russian neighbor's death. "Tan perturbada estaba que necesitó apretar fuerte los ojos para comprobar que no era un sueño cuando se acercó al espejo y rozó el velo de nieve"[40] (So perturbed was she that she needed to squeeze her eyes tightly to prove that it wasn't a dream when she approached the mirror and rubbed the veil of snow),[41] expressing her sense that "otra mujer se cruzaba para cumplir su destino"[42] (her destiny was crossed with that of another woman[43]). In short, Miralles's story portrays the Soviet imaginary taking hold of a now-diasporic subject, evoking the power of such solidarities to penetrate individuals. Both his story and Fernández de Juan's are representations of a violent and impassioned merging, and a subsequent melancholic separation, of cultures.

OUTING THE ISLAND OF FREEDOM

*There were all the manuals of Marxism that you can imagine there and the complete production of Soviet publishing houses Raduga and Mir. Since the majority of the books had a red cover, those shelves looked like a brick wall. That is what I read: all the Soviet literature (not Russian, Soviet) from Volokolamsk Highway, The Old Fortress, How the Steel Was Tempered, The First Teacher, the poetry of Mayakovsky (above all, his poem "Lenin," and also "The Soviet Passport").*

PÉREZ CASTILLO, "ESCRIBIR NO ES UNA CARRERA"

If La Rusa Roxana Rojo is the eighth queen, the protagonist of Ernesto Pérez Castillo's story "Bajo la bandera rosa" (Beneath the pink flag) is her fraught son. In contrast to the melancholic tone of Pérez and González's *Todas iban a ser reinas* and the somewhat somber, even noble rendering of hybridity in Solórzanos's *Érase una vez . . . una matrioshka*, numerous contemporary short stories ridicule the marriage between the Soviets and Cubans, on racial, social, and sexual levels. "Bajo la bandera rosa," reminiscent of Reinaldo Arenas's "Viaje a La Habana" (Journey to Havana)—which itself is a carnivalesque rewriting of José Martí's 1882 book of poems *Ismaelillo* and of La Condesa de Merlín's 1844 *La Havana*—possesses an urgency regarding the desire for paternal discovery and a fear of sexual transgression. Born in 1968, Pérez Castillo and his contemporaries grew up with Soviet-Cuban solidarity and came of age around the time of Soviet Perestroika and Cuban Rectification, a commonality he shares with the renowned Novísimos's promotion of writers led by Salvador Redonet. Nevertheless, in the above-cited interview, Pérez Castillo affirms his "distance" from them; he explains that he was from a small town with an unpronounceable name in the province of Havana, did not belong to any generation per se, and spent his time in the library reading Soviet books.

As the story's title suggests, "rosa" (pink) takes the place of "roja" (red) and "rusa" (Russian), alluding to the watering down of ideology and the difficult topic of homosexuality within Communism. The story interweaves an actual past event—Cuban subjects who were sent on a mission to Siberia in the 1980s (when it still formed part of the Soviet Union) to cut down the omnipresent birch trees—and the present story of Vladimir, a Russian son in search of his father in Cuba. At the center of Vladimir's quest for identity lie two questions: Is his father black or white? Is he hetero- or homosexual? These questions are as controversial for the old Soviets as they are for the present Cuban characters. Through Pérez Castillo's invention of this post-Soviet/Russian gaze on Cuba, Cuban realities can be elucidated.

> Vladimir pensó que aquello de conseguir alojamiento gratis era algo que solo podía ocurrir en Cuba, la *Ostrov Svaboda*,[44] donde el socialismo todavía no era un cadáver, y probablemente la gente conservaba intacto el sentido de la hospitalidad.[45]
>
> Vladimir thought that getting lodging for free was something that could only occur in Cuba, the Ostrov Svaboda, where Socialism was not yet a cadaver, and where people probably conserved intact a sense of hospitality.

Whether the Cuban Revolution is itself a cadaver is the question here. *La ostrov svobody* (the island of freedom) is only nominally free because it entails other forms of exchange: sexual comforting and socialization wherein the Russian provides the alcohol. The Russian protagonist's expectation that the Cubans' hospitality toward Russians would outlast the demise of the Soviet empire is not so far from the feelings that Nadya Bakuradze ascribes to her compatriots in "The Post-Pioneer Inferiority Complex":

> Cuba unintentionally reveals psychological constructs, that "reality tunnel" necessary for a better understanding of actual processes in new Russia, in its new culture.
>
> The Cuban vector was not chosen by chance. All those years Cuba appeared as a bugaboo for democrats, as a sacred image of a Revolution-

ary Blessed Virgin, as the last socialism bastion for Communists; and as a mystical glory in intellectual circles. One's attitude toward Cuba sharply defined one's sociopolitical position. Everyone agrees: in this attitude there are a lot more emotions than rational judgments. Everyone is sure that in spite of existing and fabricated weak points "Cuba is my love" (this is the line from the popular Soviet lyrics).

Cuba turned out to be of no geopolitical interest to Russia, the ostrov svobody had been forced out of public consciousness, as part of an infantile inferiority complex.[46]

The Russians, according to Bakuradze, uphold Cuba not simply as lost brethren but as a status symbol gone astray. In November 2005, Bakuradze, as the founder and principal organizer of the first nongovernmental cultural event between Russia and Cuba, entitled the FREE DOM, led approximately twenty artists, journalists, and moviemakers from the Russian Federation to Cuba in order to establish new communication with Cuban artists and cultural institutions. Their "small" endeavor entailed screenings of alternative films and video art, along with graphic design exhibitions. One has only to take a look at *Los rusos en Cuba* by Alexander Moiseev, the last Soviet correspondent from *Pravda* in Cuba, and his wife, Olga Egorova, to discern the validity of Bakuradze's argument. More centrist Russians of an older generation, who captured the pulse of the 2010 book fair in Havana, attempt to cut the losses, uphold a history longer than the Soviets, and relive their own love affair with the island. They tell us that commercial relations go back to the colonial period; that José Martí admired Pushkin; that the intellectual Fiodor Korchavin documented the flora and fauna of the island, along with his distaste for slavery; and that there existed three Russians who fought for Cuban independence, to boot. In very little time, the sentiment expressed in the popular Soviet song "Cuba, My Love," written by Aleksandra Pakhmutova and S. Grebennikov, has been wed to renewed economic, and potentially ideological, interests.

Cubans' fictionalized projections of Russian characters then and now run the gamut. When the mother of Pérez Castillo's protagonist informs him that his real father is Cuban, Vladimir Stepánovich Ustimenko goes out in search not only of his father, but also of his Cubanness. Várvara helps her son achieve his goal by showing him a box of rifles that she suggests he sell to the Chechens in order to pay for his passage to the island of freedom. This contextualization alludes to the Russian situation that explodes in Pérez Castillo's *Haciendo las cosas mal*. Vladimir behaves as would a young apparatchik who arrives late, both to the function of an apparatchik of the Komsomol (Communist Youth) and to Havana—that is, after the Soviets have lost their privileges in this city. The signifier and signified do not align, precisely because geopolitics, as Bakuradze attests, have shifted.

The current crisis of timing is the product of a personal and collective historical discrepancy. Descending the airplane, Vladimir meets young North American Communists who are greeted by a poster—"Viva la amistad entre los pueblos de Lincoln y Martí" (Long live the friendship between the peoples of Lincoln and Martí)—rather than the inscription he saw in a photo of his father's generation: "Long live the friendship of the peoples of Lenin and Martí."[47] (Vladimir's appearance in Havana gets all sorts of mixed reactions—passport control doesn't know what to do with his passport, while the macho agents of the G-2 building, which houses Cuba's intelligence agency, are moved to tears upon his entrance.)

Várvara had picked Vladimir's father out of a crowd of new arrivals some twenty-four years before, but blames her inability to recognize him on the age of the photograph, taken with East German Orwo film, a brand whose apparent shoddiness is relived in Cuban fiction. The Soviet-Cuban relationship that is described by the women in *Todas iban a ser reinas* as romantic is here merely a fast and vulgar outpouring of desire—Vladimir's Cuban father hardly corresponds to the prototype of masculinity and exoticism outlined in, among many other places, the documentary.

> Aquí fue que la siberiana se le acercó al negrón, y con voz muy dulce, al oído, le dijo:
> —*Ti ochen interiesnik chelaviek . . .*
> Él la miró con los ojos muy abiertos, como si hubiera entendido algo, pero en verdad no había entendido ni papa . . .
> Fue su día de gloria. Nunca había besado a ninguna mujer.
> La siberiana le quitó la camisa mientras lo besaba y, como al intentar bajarle los pantalones, él le opuso alguna resistencia, pensó que se había topado con un amante diestro que prefería ir paso a paso, y creyó entonces que aquello sería mejor de lo que había imaginado.[48]

> This is when the Siberian went up to the big black guy and said sweetly in his ear:
> *Ti ochen interiesnik chelaviek . . .*
> He looked at her wide-eyed, as if he had understood, but in truth he hadn't understood a damn thing.
> It was his day of glory. He had never kissed a woman.
> The Siberian undid his shirt while kissing him, and since he put up some resistance when she tried to undo his pants, she thought she had

happened upon a skillful lover who preferred to go slowly. This would be better than she had imagined.

Vladimir finally discovers that his father was returned to Cuba not simply because a birch tree fell on him, as he had been told, but because he was a "*maricón*" (faggot). By presenting us with a character like Vladimir's father, a mediocre Russian-Cuban hybrid with pathetic dreams of becoming a great Soviet, Pérez Castillo points out the racism and the homophobia within Cuban and Soviet society. The story ends with the queening of the New Man, a theme that is repeated in many other stories.

If "Bajo la bandera rosa" transforms the concept of the "new man" into a homosexual entity who, too weak to perform manual labor in Siberia, accidentally fathered a son who arrived too late to the "island of freedom," Pérez Castillo's novel *Haciendo las cosas mal* inserts that occurrence into a whole other context in which the so-called Axis of Evil has replaced the Cold War as the decisive metaphor to describe geopolitics. The allusion to the crisis in Chechnya and to the economic burdens and ideological mismatching that Vladimir confronts in "Bajo la bandera rosa" is but one of many strands within *Haciendo las cosas mal* that weaves together numerous plots and media, evoking postmodernity in its fragmentation and lack of chronology, as well as scenes from Russian *skaza* (folktales) and Pushkin in its *costumbrista* (focus on local color) and often cynical portraits of the post-Soviet world.

The Internet is key not only in bringing together disparate peoples around the world—some of whom were intricately linked in the not-so-distant past—but also in taking them out of their niches and turning them into migrants or refugees. *Haciendo las cosas mal*, however, does not mourn a different order. Its acceptance of things, as bad as they are, contrasts with the tone Pérez Castillo uses to describe ideological and economic disasters in his blog by the same name (www.haciendolascosasmal.blogspot.com), which regularly attacks the most famous of Cuban bloggers, Yoani Sánchez. To understand the memorialization of the Soviets in Cuba, it is impossible to ignore the extent to which mechanisms of control and secrecy continue to operate. The complacency toward the Cuban government evident within Pérez Castillo's blog appears to be far from the more sarcastic positions in his fiction.

In the novel, Svetlana, the archetypical post-Soviet woman who must fight for a better life, is center stage. The world into which she was born and for which she was formed no longer exists, and therefore she must "*aterrizar*," or land, and adapt to the new circumstances utilizing a different vocabulary.

The novel begins with a brief e-mail Svetlana writes in broken Spanish to a native speaker in Spain. Vladimir arrives at José Martí airport, as did the protagonist in the short story, and then Svetlana is introduced.

Svetlana es rubia. Es castaña. Es trigueña. Es pelirrojo. Tiene el cabello rizado, corto, largo, muy largo, lacio, rapado. Sus ojos son azules. Verdes. Negrísimos. Marrones. Grises. Tiene un ojo verde y otro azul. Su piel es muy blanca. Morena. Canela. Rosada. Muy tostada por el sol. Svetlana mide 1.75, 1.72, 1.67, 1.91, 1.60. Pesa 60 kilos. 54, 65, 59, 63 . . .

Esa es Svetlana, según sus datos de inscripción en sitios tales como www.chicasdeleste.com, www.rusaslindas.com, www.mujeresrusas.com, www.turusa.com, www.mujeresrusas.net, www.eslavas.com, www .brideinrussia.com, www.rusiamia.com, www.mujeresrusasbellas.com. Sólo algo permanece invariable en cada perfil: Svetlana siempre se llama Svetlana.[49]

Svetlana is blond. She has chestnut hair. She has dark brown hair. A red-head. She has curly hair, short, long, very long, straight, shaved. Her eyes are blue. Green. Very black. Brown. Gray. She has a green eye and a blue eye. Her skin is very white. Brown. Cinnamon. Pink. Very toasted by the sun. Svetlana is 1.75, 1.72, 1.67, 1.91, 1.60. Weighs 60 kilos. 54, 65, 59, 63 . . .

This is Svetlana, according to the registration statistics in sites like www.chicasdeleste.com, www.rusaslindas.com, www.mujeresrusascom, www.turusa.com, www.mujeresrusas.net, www.eslavas.com, www .brideinrussia.com, www.rusiamia.com, www.mujeresrusasbellas.com. Only one thing remains constant in each profile: Svetlana is always named Svetlana.

This initial passage would lead readers to believe that Svetlana is a woman who is seeking a way out of Russia through marriage to a Western man. This vision of a newly capitalistic East as a desperate and seemingly losing venture haunts the Cuba of *Haciendo las cosas mal*, but characters in the novel who reside in Cuba are not protected by their state from the new global ramifications of the post–Cold War world.

In Pérez Castillo's fiction, the Soviet world cannot be utilized entirely for its Aesopian value, as Dmitri Prieto reckoned it could, since the beginnings of the aftermath of Socialism are already experienced on the island even though Venezuela replaces the Soviet Union, at least for the purposes of slogans. "Chávez: Nadie detendrá el avance victorioso de Cuba y Venezuela"[50] (Chávez: No one will stop the victorious advance of Cuba and Venezuela).

Furthermore, the "Svetlana" plot in *Haciendo las cosas mal* is complicated by the fact that she reappears in Cuba as the daughter of Cuban diplomats who named her "Svetlana" when they were on a mission in Moscow. Her parents "llevaban una larga carrera, de embajada en embajada por el mundo, aunque al principio el 'mundo' se limitó al mundo socialista"[51] (had a long career, from embassy to embassy throughout the world, although in the beginning the "world" was limited to the Socialist world). Tired of being surrounded by Cuban functionaries and their children in foreign lands, Svetlana returns to Cuba and comes to have a sketchily defined ménage à trois with the narrator and a Cuban by the name of Rubén. One day Svetlana, who believes she speaks Spanish perfectly, but does so only roughly at best, states: "Nosotros, que disfrutamos el un alma cultivada en lo bello y un criterio entrenado en la percepción de lo hermoso, solo tenemos un camino para expresar nuestra la genialidad: hacer algo mal, genuinamente mala"[52] (We, who enjoy a soul cultivated in the beautiful and a viewpoint trained in the perception of the splendid, we have only one path to express our, the genius: to do something badly, genuinely bad). With this strangely worded proposal in mind, she conceives of plans to enter into the "submundo de nuestro interés"[53] (the subworld of our interest). Svetlana's investigation into how the other half lives leads her to scout out a French boyfriend and to leave behind her Rubén, who, devastated by her abandonment, overdoses.

Another "Svetlana" studied Slavic Philology at the University of Kazan and possesses a postgraduate degree in Metatextual Analysis as well as a master's in Comparative Culturalogy. But, once again, such a formal education — and these degrees are just a few of her many qualifications — prepares her for nothing. Svetlana's great-grandfather José was actually a Cuban who fought alongside the Republicans in Spain before joining Franco's troops to fight Hitler. When his Communist past is discovered, José ends up in a concentration camp. Once he's liberated and his connection to Hitler is discovered, the Soviets send him to Siberia, where he weds Svetlana's great-grandmother, also named Svetlana, and they remain together until the day he leaves to search for a little cow that he baptizes Katiusha. Unfortunately, while he's away, Svetlana kills herself trying to imitate the Italian neo-realist film she watched on her Krim television set without subtitles and only sporadically dubbed by the well-known Alexander Popov from Moskfilm.

One day the young great-granddaughter Svetlana, unsuccessful in her attempts to leave Russia "for love," discovers a message in her junk e-mail recruiting for the Israeli Mossad. A short time later she goes to Cuba, "residuo de la guerra fría, refugio habitual de terroristas, y uno de los más importantes pilares del terrible eje del mal"[54] (residue of the Cold War, habitual refuge of terrorists, and one of the most important pillars of the terrible axis of evil). The George W. Bush rhetoric regarding "the Axis of Evil," which condemned Cuba along with other nations that did not share his view of the world, is ridiculed in this passage. Interestingly enough, the so-called terrorist is none other than the character of Vladimir from "Bajo la bandera rosa," who is now called by his nickname, Volodia, in the novel, and it is with him that Svetlana departs to France, where the Mossad insists he be brought.

*Haciendo las cosas mal* is especially fascinating because it positions Cuba within the new global order, in full recognition of the fact that the "island of freedom" of the era that defined *Todas iban a ser reinas* no longer exists. Whereas in "Bajo la bandera rosa" the dream of the Socialist world is represented as immensely flawed and even hypocritical, in *Haciendo las cosas mal* capitalism is looked upon with equally stern and critical eyes. To play or "fight" in the new world does not require being the best, as is often believed, but being the most mediocre. Pérez Castillo's stories, like La Rusa Roxana Rojo's performance, illustrate a Cuba extraordinarily bound to discrepant temporalities. Many expect Cuba to follow the course of the rest of the Soviet Bloc, especially as it remains tied to the structures set forth by the Soviet Union. Yet Cuba is already living that destiny and transcending it within a new Leftist order.

Ulises Rodríguez Febles's play *Sputnik*, which premiered on April 27, 2007, at Cuba's National Theater, has in common with *Haciendo las cosas mal* the general structure of interrelated stories of former Soviet and Cuban characters whose lives are tied together through the historical union between the two countries. Both works also take place in an almost virtual imaginary space where the two countries overlap and where the characters have a difficult time figuring out where they are and where they want to be, both geographically and ideologically.

The first scene consists of a woman selling magazines from the Socialist Camp, shouting out the titles of all those publications that would soon vanish from the Cuban stage:

> Vendo *Novedades de Moscú* . . . *Sputnik*. Cómpreloooo. Lo mejor de lo que se escribe en el uni . . . verso . . . oooo (**Se le traba la lengua**) Se lo dice Juana Estanquillo . . . Las noticias verídicas, sensacionales, emotivas de la URSSSSSS y todo el campo soci . . . (**Se le traba la lengua**) soci . . . Aquí . . . Si quiere conocer . . . ¡Vaya . . . ! No se pierda leer ninguna de sus páginas. Escuche . . . (**Los personajes de la obra entran y compran Sputnik**)[55]

> I've got *News from Moscow* . . . *Sputnik*. Get your copy nooooow. The best of what is written in the uni . . . versssse. (**She stammers**) You heard it from Juana Estanquillo . . . True, sensational, exciting news from the USSRRRRRR and the entire Soci . . . (**She stammers**) Soci . . . Here . . . If you want to know . . . Come on . . . ! Don't miss any of its pages. Listen . . . (**The characters of the work enter and buy Sputnik**)

The collapse of the Soviet Bloc is conveyed through the linguistic breakdown in the peddler's speech. The concepts cannot be uttered because the news within the pages invalidates the message she is accustomed to conveying. To utter "universe" would be to admit the precariousness of its dissolution and the impact it could have on the publication's readers by leading them to reinterpret the significance of former monumental figures. The characters evaluate headlines, such as "Stalin personalmente tiene la culpa de todos nuestros males— dijo un orador en el mitin de la Plaza Puskín"[56] (Stalin is personally to blame for all of our evils—a speaker said at the Pushkin Plaza meeting), and react differently depending on their proximity to the news. One Cuban assesses the circumstance vis-à-vis the efficacy of nearby buildings, while another immediately waxes nostalgic about his five marvelous years in the USSR. The "Russian" woman, on the other hand, is more worried about her Cuban husband's infidelities than the faraway events. Other headlines, such as "Ayer en mi fábrica eligieron un director. El que nosotros quisimos, no el que nos impusieron"[57] (Yesterday at my factory, they elected a director. The one we wanted, not the one they imposed upon us), speak to the violent insistence upon a new civil space in the Soviet Union that could not be imitated on the island, as the prohibition of these journals in Cuba, soon after this scene, makes evident. This incapacity to adopt aspects of the transforming Soviet political sphere conditions the narrative toward the surrealistic overlapping of Cuban and Soviet landscapes wherein the tropical sun gives way to the Moscow winter, and the realities of the depicted pages come alive. With the arrival of Glasnost and Perestroika in the Soviet Union, Cuba stopped receiving Soviet newspapers as a means of sustaining the ideological rhetoric of its revolutionary nationalism. Many were left stranded without the Soviet publications—*Novedades de Moscú*, *Tiempos nuevos*, and *Sputnik*—that had begun to serve them as guides in navigating their own difficulties and hopefully emerging on the other side, not necessarily on a path toward democracy or capitalism, but to a reformed Socialism.

In the play *Sputnik*, Raúl, an Afro-Cuban character, is the first to speak about the necessity of prohibiting the circulation of *Sputnik* magazine because he spots his son, Pablo, a student in the USSR, in a photograph displayed in the pages of the periodical. His son has been arrested at a protest, and Raúl fears the consequences of Pablo's transgressive behavior when he returns to the University of Havana. Raúl insists that even if all his son wanted to do was to observe or to report on the problem there, he was mistaken, because "eso es problema de los rusos"[58] (that is the Russians' problem).

This moment in the Soviet media was intense, as described by George Black in an article that appeared in *The Nation* in 1988: "[Cuban bookstores have] the sad look of dumping grounds for Progreso Publishers' remainders, with yellow-

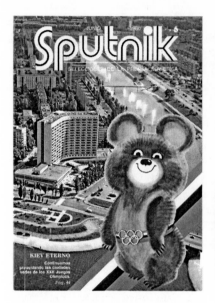

Cover of Sputnik, June 1980.     Cover of Sputnik, March 1980.

ing piles of old Bulgarian party statutes and textbooks on bovine tuberculosis, Gorbachev's book, *Perestroika*, also arrived in huge quantities and sold out in no time. The inability of the newsstands to keep *Novedades de Moscú* (Moscow News) in stock has become legendary."[59] It is difficult to envision these leftovers of Sovietization and the frenzied crisis without recalling the very first representations of the shifting literary terrain within Tomás Gutiérrez Alea's 1968 classic film, *Memorias del subdesarrollo*, in which there is a close-up of the newly revised bookshelves, on which are displayed *Somos hombres soviéticos* (We Are Soviet People; a hammer and sickle on the cover) and *Gagarin* (with his portrait on the cover).

The covers and tables of contents of *Sputnik* are a testament to the distinct degrees of Sovietization. Take, for example, the June issue in 1980, the year of the XXII Olympic games in the Soviet Union, and the excitement that *Sputnik* transmits to its readers in Cuba through images of the mascot Misha with the city of Kiev in the background, or the folkloric Soviet beauty on the cover of the March 1980 issue, whose image dwarfs the Soviet monuments shown in the background. The end of the decade was ripe with crisis, as the following cover headlines from 1988 make clear: "Rusia cristianizada" (Christianized Russia), "La Perestroika y nuestra responsibilidad" (Perestroika and Our Responsibility), and "Acusación contra Stalin" (Accusation against Stalin).

In 2009, I happened upon four copies of *Sputnik* on a bookshelf at a café at the bus station in Havana, placed there as if they were copies of current newspapers for customers to peruse while they ate or drank. The May 1989 cover below read "Stalin y Trotski" and "Ese fantástico mundo de Rusia" (That Fantastic World of Russia); a section of its index was dedicated to Perestroika and another to Glasnost and democracy. Those sections of the magazine had been torn out—perhaps in 1989, or perhaps twenty years later, perhaps as an act of censorship, perhaps as an act of memorialization. Perestroika is still taboo, just as the depoliticized Misha and Cheburashka are still missed.

Rodríguez Febles's play foregrounds some of the issues most tangible for Cubans regarding Soviet nationalism and identity construction. The nostalgia that is perceptible within *Todas iban a ser reinas* is equally so in the Soviet character in the play, Tatiana, who yearns to return to typical Soviet foods and landscapes after she, like Ekaterina in "Clemencia bajo el sol," discovers that her husband is having an affair. Her inability to dominate her surroundings causes her to practice bilocation and to become obsessed about her own identity. She confounds her interlocutors, who are used to different signifiers. For example, she utters, "Extraño la comida lituana" (I miss Lithuanian food), to which her husband responds, "Pero si eres rusa, Tatiana" (But you're Russian, Tatiana). "Pero mi abuelo era lituano" (But my grandfather was Lithuanian).[60] She claims that her son, Igor, is Russian, and that his Cuban father's influence is negligible, even though Igor's pigmentation immediately marks him as a *jabado*, or as the characters say, "Jaba'o," "[a] light-skinned, kinky haired [*mulatto*]."[61] Tatiana proves her son's Russianness through his predilection for speaking and eating like a Russian, listening to Russian cartoons and Russian music, and knowing

*Cover of* Sputnik, *May 1989.*

his mother's customs. Tatiana's chauvinism prevents her from remembering that her mother had banished her years before for marrying an Afro-Cuban. Her husband, on the other hand, is not interested in the specifics of nationalities, but rather in how they are disseminated and imposed upon him. "Pues mis jefes cubanos me trataron de imponer las tuyas. ¿O no? Las creencias soviéticas"[62] (Well, my Cuban bosses tried to impose your beliefs on me. Didn't they? Soviet beliefs).

When Manuel, a Cuban who studied in the Soviet Union for years, is expelled for having fought with a Russian, he seeks out Tatiana—"la rusa," as he calls her—when he returns to Cuba. He hopes she can help him in his search for clues about the whereabouts of his wife and son, both "lost in the Soviet Union." Tatiana similarly corrects his denomination of her. Manuel's "Russian" family never makes it to the island, but he is far from the only one who feels abandoned. The "Soviet" characters confront their own ignorance toward their new homeland and to their professional conditions on the island. Would they be able to continue making a living teaching Russian? "No sabemos lo que somos. Hasta el PCUS va a desaparecer."[63] (We don't know what we are. Even the Communist Party of the Soviet Union is going to disappear.) One "Soviet" who is particularly mournful even proposes killing Gorbachev in honor of his grandfather, who fought the Nazis.

The upside-downness of the present penetrates even the world of the deceased. Had the peddler's late husband not considered the Soviets as "los mejores del mundo" (the world's best), her son, Carlos, would not have gone off to "congelarse cortando madera" (freeze himself cutting wood).[64] The peddler expects that her late husband would turn over in his grave if he were to find out how distant the Cubans and the Soviets had become, as she remarks that she always told her son, "No debías haber dejado a la venezolana" (You shouldn't have left the Venezuelan).[65] The choice of a Venezuelan girl as a mother's ideal partner for her son is undoubtedly informed by the extratextual twenty-first century alliance between Cuba and Venezuela.

The hybrid biological and historical identities of Rodríguez Febles's characters are also reflected in the accompanying music, which at times is a mix of Russian and Cuban and at other times reminiscent of the sound tracks of Soviet Bloc cartoons. As Tatiana prepares to return to her no-longer-existent homeland with Carlos Igor, the son she has with Carlos, a debate over her son's race and nationality ensues. Carlos Igor says, "Dice que soy negro" (He says I'm black). His mother responds, "No eres negro. Eres . . . ruso." (You're not black. You're . . . Russian.) To which Carlos Igor replies, "No soy ruso. Soy jaba'o." (I'm not Russian. I'm jaba'o. I've got white skin with black-people's hair.) Such a response in Cuban argot does not satisfy Tatiana. "Eres jaba'o. Y ruso. Naciste en el Dnieper." (You are jaba'o and Russian. You were born in Dnieper.)[66]

The economics of Tatiana's plan of escape are equally problematic. Between her staying and leaving comes a Minsk motorcycle that Carlos claims as his property because he earned it in Siberia, where he went "para mejorar a cortar madera en la Siberia"[67] (to better himself, to cut wood in Siberia), a phrase reminiscent of a popular Cuban racist way of thinking: "Hay que casarse con una blanca para mejorar la raza" (You have to marry a white to improve the race). His revelations continue: "Irme a la Siberia fue el mejor camino que encontré para sentirme alguien. Para ser diferente a los demás negros."[68] (Going to Siberia was the best path I found to feel like I was somebody. To feel different from the other blacks.) The character's perspective on his initial motivation to travel to Siberia remains steadfast and shows how the evolutionary nation was incapable of abolishing completely enduring racial paradigms. Carlos is not the only one who is plagued by the turmoil of the transition from a Communist Soviet Union to a newly capitalist Russia. The precariousness of Cubans' struggle to grasp the profanation of sacred categories is especially evident in Raúl's revelations about the role of the Soviet Union in his own family. His wife drugs herself just to cope with her son's imprisonment and blames everything on Raúl for sending their son to what was once "el mejor país del mundo"[69] (the best country on earth) but that in post-Soviet times is a place where it is impossible to distinguish a party head from a mafia head and where violence can strike at any time.

The inferiority complex that motivated some Cubans to travel to the Soviet Union is mirrored in Tatiana's overwhelming sense of alienation once she knows Carlos is having an affair. "Sin país, sin familia, sin un lugar donde asentarme. No soy nadie, ni nada. Por favor . . . Déjame ir tranquila."[70] (Without a country, without a family, without a place to settle down. I'm no one, I'm nothing. Please . . . Let me go in peace.) Tatiana's impending departure, however, is by no means gentle, even though singing bullfinches are witnesses to the scene. Victim to uncertainty about whether she will be recognized once in Smolensk, whether "[le] abran la puerta de la isba" (they open the door to the log hut for her), Tatiana hears "palabras ininteligibles en ruso y español" (unintelligible words in Russian and Spanish).[71]

A more overarching meaning of the play, suggested by all of the cross-fertilized subjects analyzed in this chapter, is that of an extraordinary disorientation that takes hold of Cubans and former Soviets alike. They represent the mirage in which they once lived and whose remnants they continue to inhabit and perform repetitively, as they struggle to put together the pieces to compose a new world whose contours they have yet to define.

# CHAPTER THREE

# Cuban Intermediaries

*Until a few years ago, a trip from Havana to Moscow was a prize awarded only to "national heroes of work," to "national vanguards," to those who "excelled," or as in my case, to student leaders who "deserved" a "good vacation" in the grand Hotel Rosilla in the very center of Moscow, beside the Kremlin where a gentleman named Lenin showed himself to be asleep and old. In those years of prosperity everyone aspired to board one of Aeroflot's IL-62s and sample caviar while the 9,550 kilometers went by.*

GUILLERMO MORALES CATÁ, 2002

N o Hollywood director has yet to "discover" a "barbarian's" account of the Soviet Bloc and of members of the former Soviet Bloc, of which many exist—some even ripe for cinematographic adaptation. As Jorge Ferrer states, "Less is known about Cuban attempts to capture the USSR on film . . . In fact, the younger brother also wanted to show the face of the Other."[1] With Cuban travelogues from the 1960s in the background, this chapter focuses on Cuban artists' rendering of travels to the Soviet Union (and the impact of these travels) from the mid-1980s to the present. It addresses the extent to which Cubans' visions of the so-called West are altered when they travel to the so-called East, as well as, in the Aesopian vein of Prieto Samsonov, the extent to which their assessments of the East influence their predictions about the future of Cuba.

Morales Catá's characterization of the abrupt transformation in the significance of travel to Moscow during Soviet times compared to post-Soviet times is just one of many testimonies by Cubans about the Soviet Bloc and Russia. Two of the earliest and most complete accounts of the Soviet Union are found in the writing of Samuel Feijóo and in the cinema of Roberto Fandiño. The histories of Feijóo's and Fandiño's travels to the Soviet Union stand out among more recent "travelogues." Feijóo, an autodidact, primarily known as a poet, but also as a novelist, painter, magazine editor, and folklorist, traveled to, among other destinations, the Soviet Bloc throughout the 1960s and 1970s. He published his observations in, among other places, *Islas*, the journal that he founded in 1958 and edited from the Universidad Central de Las Villas. He also collaborated with the translator Nina Bulgakova on *Poetas rusos y soviéticos*, a 1966 anthology that was responsible for the earliest canonization of Russian and Soviet poetry on the island.

Antonio Bermejo Santos claims that in the 1960s *Islas* neither spoke about the increasing penetration of Soviet Marxism on the island nor focused on "those affiliated with *Pensamiento Crítico* and the Department of Philosophy at the University of Havana, or those first graduates of the Soviet Union, who played an appreciable role in the conception of the programs of study of the Schools of Revolutionary Instruction."[2] However, according to Bermejo Santos, in the 1970s, *Islas* did include many articles written by Soviet collaborators: "The influence of the massive expansion of Soviet Marxism in the publishing houses and centers of teaching in the country throughout the decade made it into *Islas*."[3] Feijóo's travelogue of his 1964 journey to the Soviet Union as a cultural diplomat, published in the 1967 issue of *Islas*, which was dedicated to the October Revolution, reflects a subject who is personally and politically at home in the Soviet world. In a discussion with the popular wartime poet Alexei Surkov, recalled in the travelogue, Feijóo states: "Here, I find a marvelous union of the spirit of the nineteenth century along with the scientific spirit of the twentieth. The people talk as if in ballads and the sputnik flies through the skies."[4]

Feijóo's solidarity with the Soviets leads him to declare to his hosts a few days into his trip, "Until now there has not been nostalgia for my country friends, etc. I remain in my land."[5] These seemingly benign words convey a pronounced sense of belonging, but they are not as harmless when one takes into account other convictions of Feijóo's about the Soviet Union that had serious consequences on the island. Emilio Bejel reminds us: "The leftist writer Samuel Feijóo led a campaign against homosexuals from the pages of the newspaper *El Mundo* and, after an extended trip to the Soviet Union, proclaimed that homosexuals no longer existed there."[6] His infamous and oft-cited statement from a 1965 interview in *El Mundo*—"No homosexual represents the Revolution, which is a matter for men, of fists and not of feathers, of courage and not of trembling"[7]—was instrumental in the ensuing years of repression in Cuba.

Around that same time, Roberto Fandiño represented a less idealized Soviet world in *Gente de Moscú* (People of Moscow), a sixteen-minute documentary released in 1963. As Ferrer affirms in "Around the Sun: The Adventures of a

Wayward Satellite" (the only article to date to analyze the documentary in any depth), Fandiño was part of a team from ICAIC, the Instituto Cubano de Arte e Industria Cinematográficos (Cuban Institute of Cinematographic Art and Industry), that traveled to Helsinki for the World Festival of Youth and Students. Having wished, even before the Cuban Revolution, to make a documentary about Moscow, Fandiño asked Alfredo Guevara, the president of the newly founded ICAIC, for permission to do so. This detail is important since, unlike some of the other creators discussed in this chapter, Fandiño did not form part of the masses of scholarship students and workers awarded with travel abroad. Unforgettable, precisely for its lack of monumentalism, lack of "ballads" and "sputniks," Fandiño's *Gente de Moscú*, for Ferrer, "a stolen portrait of Moscow," was not the vision that the Soviet Union wished to portray of itself. The documentary is filled with incongruent and mundane images. Rain soaks people's feet; the Kremlin is first seen inverted and then right side up. The buildings' immensity contrasts with the smallness of the people; haunting music contrasts with the bark of a dog. The film cuts to an amusement park, to people playing dominoes, a hammer and sickle, a rocket blasting off. Through shots of minimal urbanscapes, the bells of the Kremlin are heard. And finally, children are seen dancing and singing in the countryside. Ferrer details the process by which the seemingly innocuous documentary was cast into oblivion.

> Alfredo Guevara, president of the ICAIC, shows it to the Soviet Ambassador in Havana. He complains: *Gente de Moscú*, the ambassador would have said, showed a city peopled by vagrants and the morally decadent, a Moscow without workers. Guevara, who had liked the documentary, stated that in Cuba they weren't governed by the aesthetics of social realism and that they considered it a valid documentary. So much so that ICAIC submitted it to compete in the 1963 Leipzig All German Festival for Cultural and Documentary Film, in which it won the Friendship Among Peoples award. Naturally, Fandiño's short film was never shown in the Soviet Union. It didn't have any luck on Cuba screens, either.[8]

Fandiño compares his own film's destiny to that of Sabá Cabrera Infante's *P.M.* in the sense that neither portrait was driven by a commitment to a particular future. Guevara's support of Fandiño's documentary in the midst of Moscow's rejection indicates that Soviet and Cuban ideologies had not yet become as interchangeable as they would some years later. Having gone into exile in the late 1960s, Fandiño is reported by Ferrer to have continued to remember his time in Moscow fondly, even though his documentary does not convey triumph. Feijóo's upbeat travelogue and Fandiño's mundane portrait of the Soviet

Union capture the anecdotal and personal qualities that correspond to the emerging Soviet-Cuban friendship, far more monumentally staged in Mikhail Kalatazov's 1964 film, *Soy Cuba*.

As noted by the Brazilian director Vicente Ferraz and the Cuban scholar Carlos Espinosa Domínguez, had Hollywood directors Martin Scorsese and Francis Ford Coppola not championed the joint Soviet-Cuban production *Soy Cuba*, the film would not have been rediscovered in the early 1990s and would have only been seen as a misinterpretation of the Cuban people.[9] That misinterpretation nevertheless holds interest. What were Cubans in the early 1960s to the Soviets? Cubans were hot-blooded, sexy, impoverished, and in need of being civilized—not particularly distinct from how they were seen by the US. When speaking about his own people in the 1960s and 1970s, Fidel Castro also frequently addressed their want of civilization. In a speech he delivered in 1972 to a group of Cuban scholarship students and to the Cuban embassy in the Soviet Union about the technical impoverishment of his nation, he stated: "We cannot consider ourselves even semi-civilized. Within a few years, we will be semi-civilized. We still will not be civilized. And I think one of the goals that we must propose for ourselves is civilization."[10] Informed by historical materialism, Castro's concept of civilization is far from the better-known colonial antinomy of "civilization" and "barbarism" that still harbors within Cubans' writings about their experiences in the Soviet Union. For Cubans and Soviets alike, detaching the West, viewed as an exclusive, capitalist entity, from the connotation of "civilized" was a difficult task.

Interviews with Cubans involved in *Soy Cuba*, conducted by Vicente Ferraz in his 2005 documentary *I Am Cuba, the Siberian Mammoth*, indicate the extent to which Cubans traditionally, socially, and culturally identified with the West, as well as their uneasiness with having been perceived by filmmakers from the East as a sinful Caribbean island and a tropical Socialist paradise that was, at the same time, a Wild West. Future policies would try to eliminate any trace of a prerevolutionary time.

Bárbaro, the protagonist of Jesús Díaz's novel *Siberiana* (2000), is a twenty-five-year-old black Cuban journalist who is sent by the journal *Bohemia* to Siberia; the time frame is left unclear. Bárbaro's personal goal in traveling to the Soviet Union is to lose his virginity. Having grown up in a marginal environment, the teenage Bárbaro escapes the home of his seemingly lascivious and dark parents and searches for refuge in the home of the General, the lover of his young aunt, Lucinda, who is a mere six years older than he and whom he sexualizes. Thinking that he would find solace in the General's home, he is instead sexually abused by him and, as a result, becomes confused about his own sexuality later in life. The bisexual Afro-Cuban deity Changó serves Bárbaro as a motif that helps him regularly reflect upon his own racial and sexual identity.

Once in Siberia, Bárbaro falls in love with his interpreter, Nadiezdha Shalámov González, who is proud to be Siberian and the daughter and wife of political prisoners. "Para ella ser siberiana significaba pertenecer al pueblo elegido, al escalón más alto de la trágica superioridad que a sus ojos le otorgaba el mero hecho de haber nacido rusa"[11] (For her being Siberian meant belonging to the chosen people, the highest rung of the tragic superiority that, in her eyes, the mere fact of having been born Russian bestowed upon her). Her husband, Alexander Petrovich Kirilov, never recovered from his time in the Gulag. Her mother, Angustias González, was a refugee from the Spanish Civil War. Throughout the novel, Nadiezdha recounts to Bárbaro the grueling conditions of life in Siberia; she and her male companions also taunt Bárbaro about the differences between the way of life in the East and in the West. Once Bárbaro finally conquers Nadiezdha, it is almost time for him to return to Cuba. The ending, however, is much more unfortunate than the separation of two lovers. Bárbaro suffers a fatal illness, the result of having subjected his body to extreme degrees of heat and cold in honor of his love.

*Siberiana*'s author himself traveled to Siberia, where he, along with many other Cubans, co-directed *La sexta parte del mundo* (The Sixth Part of the World), a 1977 Soviet-Cuban documentary that pays homage to the October Revolution. Given the multinational character of the Soviet Union portrayed in this documentary, Díaz's description of the rough Siberian landscape, climate, and way of life in *Siberiana* is no surprise and, as Mario L. Guillot Carvajal states, is "one of the virtues of the book."[12] The epic rhetoric characteristic of *La sexta parte del mundo* contrasts sharply with Díaz's *Siberiana*, published nine years after the disintegration of the Soviet Union. One review of *La sexta parte del mundo* compares the "frames that show the unity in diversity" to a "bouquet of very well chosen and combined flowers": "above the languages, dialects, dances, and customs, modes of completely new conduct are imposed."[13] To some extent, *Siberiana* plays the ethnic and national differences of its characters off how Cubans feel about their own racial identities. The novel's lack of attention to character development makes it read more like a folktale than a novel, but insofar as it drives home generalized, almost cliché-like differences between Cubans and Soviets, it is fascinating.

Tuvo una arqueada al respirar abiertamente aquella peste insoportable como la de una letrina, hecha de la hediondez del grajo, los pedos y los

eructos de col agria de Tolia y de Chachai, el chófer, un buriato peque-
ñito y sumamente ingenioso, de largos bigotes lacios, que ya dormía
como un tronco y que aun en este estado mantenía aquella semisonrisa
irónica que lo acompañaba siempre, distanciándolo de los rusos . . . En
la súbita oscuridad Bárbaro se olió los sobacos, comprobó que apesta-
ban a azufre y se sintió tan mal como les hubiese faltado a su madre y
a Lucinda, para quienes un negro apestado era un ser absolutamente
detestable. Pero él no lo era, les susurró evocándolas, apestaba porque no le quedaba otro remedio, no era su culpa que no hubiese baños,
inodoros ni siquiera urinarios en aquel lugar salvaje. Tolia y Chachai,
por ejemplo, sí eran verdaderos cerdos, ni siquiera echaban de menos la
carencia de duchas e incluso se daban el lujo de burlarse de él por su ob-
sesiva necesidad de higiene. Por los menos Chachai era buriato, bajito y
amarillo, pero Tolia era ruso, blanco como la leche, aun así se compor-
taba como un puerco y encima se reía de él y lo retaba a sostener las más
estúpidas competencias, como un reno siberiano.[14]

He felt like gagging upon breathing in that unbearable smell similar to
a latrine's, composed of the stench of body odor, the farts and burps of
Tolia's sour cabbage, and of Chachai, the chauffeur. He was a small and
immensely ingenious Buryat, with a long smooth mustache, who already
slept like a log and even in this state maintained that kind of ironic
semi-smile that distanced him from the Russians . . . In the sudden dark-
ness Bárbaro smelled his own armpits, proved that they smelled like sul-
pher, and felt as bad as if he had lost his mother and Lucinda, for whom
a smelly black man was an absolutely detestable being. But he wasn't
detestable, he murmured, evoking them. He smelled because there
wasn't anything he could do. It was not his fault that there were no bathrooms, toilets, or even urinals in that savage place. Tolia and Chachai,
for example, were really pigs — they didn't even miss having showers and
went so far as to laugh at him for his obsessive need for hygiene. At least
Chachai was Buryat, short and yellow, but Tolia was Russian, as white as
milk, and even so, he behaved like a pig and on top of it, laughed at him
and challenged him to participate in the most stupid competitions, like
a Siberian reindeer.

A popularly held Cuban sentiment (with its own racial implications) is that the
Soviets smell bad because they do not bathe regularly. Bárbaro's sense of both
inferiority and superiority is apparent. For Cubans live in the tropics and per-
spire a lot, and in order to prevent the *catinga* (body odor) from getting out of
hand, they bathe religiously.

Inscriptions of race and odor pervade Caribbean culture. In Tomás Gutiérrez Alea's *Memorias del subdesarrollo*, for instance, Sergio asks one of his lovers whimsically, "And what do you like better, the smell of Russians or the smell of Americans?" She responds with a lack of interest in politics, suggesting that "smells" in general are richly nuanced in Cuban Spanish.[15] Many writings by Cubans referencing the Soviet odor speak to their own racial panic. At the same time, extreme pallor is not thought of as especially attractive, as suggested by Bárbaro's favoring the Buryat, who is, at least, "yellow." And in that way, Bárbaro ventures that he is aesthetically better off—a sensation that is pervasive among Cubans.

Another story in which Cubans' aesthetic superiority is represented is Antonio Armenteros's "La fracasada inmortalidad doméstica" (The Failed Domestic Immortality), published in the 2005 short story collection *País que no era* (Country That Was Not).[16] Born in 1963 in Havana, Armenteros is the author of five books of poetry, including his 2000 collection *Nastraienie*, a Russian word that does not have a precise English translation. It means something along the lines of "melancholic atmosphere"—the mood that also characterizes *País que no era*. In 1985, Armenteros went to study the automatization of nuclear and conventional plants in the Soviet Union, where he lived on and off until 1991, in Moscow, Leningrad, and a small city by the name of Novovoronets.

In "La fracasada inmortalidad doméstica," a Cuban is drinking at a tavern accompanied by two other foreigners when a nose-less Crimean by the name of Serguéi—Gogol-style—introduces himself and joins their party. The Cuban narrator decides that accompanying him back to his house would be a good way of figuring out "cómo era que vivían en realidad los soviéticos"[17] (how the Soviets really lived). Serguéi's wife, Ania, feeds them as he leads a conversation about Cuban boxers until passing out from inebriation. The "sujeto blanco como la leche" (subject as white as milk) is then put to bed by Ania and the Cuban, who finds Serguéi's body to be as grotesque as *Siberiana's* Bárbaro finds the Russian's. Many Cuban characters reveal abjection upon encountering Soviets. The feeling of *morbo* that Polina Martínez Shvietsova, for example, makes explicit in her auto-representation of a disfigured matrioshka could be viewed as her looking at her own "Russian" body from the outside, as would a Cuban, and the abjection that such an encounter elicits.

Like a good guest, the Cuban of "La fracasada imortalidad doméstica" settles down to sleep, but before he knows it, Ania reappears naked, offering herself. When the guest's reaction is not exactly what she had wished for, she protests, "¡Así es la hospitalidad rusa!"[18] (This is Russian hospitality!)—a hilarious and also daunting statement, given the events to come. The protagonist conveniently buys into this logic and imagines Pushkin and balalaikas as the sound track to their lovemaking, along with "El alacrán" (The Scorpion) by Afro-Peruvian Nicomedes Santa Cruz. Both Soviet and African American (in Martí's sense of "Our America") cultural and folk traditions echo in his head—the strange tension between them characteristic of the entire volume. Amazingly, Ania's husband seems unbothered by the new lover and even encourages the Cuban's return. His nonchalant reaction to his wife imploring the Cuban protagonist to drop by more frequently alienates the Cuban even more. The story ends tragically: Ania cuts her veins in front of her one-time guest because he did not prolong his visits. The tale ends with his classification of the husband as "mucha *realia* rusa" (much Russian *realia*). That is to say, "otro día absurdo del Este"[19] (another absurd day in the East), a pithy summary of one of the seemingly most frivolous yet "poisonous" or scorpion-like of tales in Armenteros's collection. What happens to a Cuban when bitten by the Soviet scorpion? In this case, he walks away unscathed, but confused.

While Bárbaro's experience as a black foreigner in the Soviet Union also has its picturesque absurdities, it is much more complex—he hardly conquers, nor does he get out alive, able to be amused by the absurdity in the difference in cultures. One of the many key words in Díaz's novel is "*salvaje*" (savage). It signals that in Siberia, Bárbaro (barbarian), in foreign territory where he is called "*chorni*," meaning "black" in Russian, has the potential to dominate the epistemological field, because he is, in a sense, the privileged traveler who, although looked down upon for his blackness, knows other places and ways of being. Those who host Bárbaro in Siberia try to convince him of his incapacity to camp in the rugged and unforgiving territory.

> En el auto donde regresaban al hotel [Nadiezdha] intentó otra vez convencerlo de que permaneciera en Irkust, argumentado que un negro sufriría demasiado en los campamentos del Baikal-Amur. Bárbaro calificó aquel argumento de racista.[20]

> In the car when they were returning to the hotel [Nadiezdha] tried once again to convince him to remain in Irkust, arguing that a black man would suffer a great deal in the campgrounds of the Baikal-Amur. Bárbaro considered that argument racist.

Soon thereafter, Bárbaro bursts out that "ella no era más que una racista de mierda y que ni los cubanos ni los negros eran tontos"[21] (she was no more than a fucking racist and that neither Cubans nor blacks were foolish).

*Siberiana* also portrays in fiction the decisive attraction that's remarked upon in both Pérez's and González's film, as well as Solórzano's photographs. "Por un lado, su condición de negro lo definía como un *nierus* absoluto; por otro, justamente el color de su piel y las características de su pelo lo hacían extraordinariamente atractivo para los siberianos"[22] (On the one hand, being black defined him as an absolute *nierus*; on the other, it was precisely the color of his skin and the characteristics of his hair that made him extraordinarily attractive to Siberians). As a definitive *nierus*, or non-Russian, the protagonist of *Siberiana* expresses his dismay at this new environment, which contrasts so sharply with that of his homeland: "Cuando empezó a bajar la escalerilla batida por el viento, cuya base estaba semihundida en la blancura de la nieve, se dijo que había arribado a otro mundo"[23] (When he began to descend the little steps shaken by the wind, whose base was semi-buried in the whiteness of the snow, he said to himself that he had arrived in another world). His words echo the Latvian's in *Todas iban a ser reinas*, who speaks of "dying and being reborn in other circumstances, in another country, in another atmosphere, in another world."

Bárbaro retreats into a maternal matrix that, although ultimately conditioned by white Europeans, places him in a position of superiority at least in his imagination: "*Chorni, chorni, chorni*. Aquello no podia ser verdad . . . no soportaba que aquellos salvajes lo escudriñaran con la vista como si el salvaje fuera él."[24] (*Chorni, chorni, chorni*. That could not be true . . . he could not put up with those savages scrutinizing him with their looks as if he were the savage.) Bárbaro refuses to be encapsulated by his name, "the barbarian," or by the word "*nierus*," a derogatory term used by the Soviets to refer to non-Russians or foreigners. Curiously, only in rare circumstances do Bárbaro's professional credentials exempt him from the ignorance of the Soviets.

What it means to be foreign in the Soviet Union and in Russia is also one of the most important themes of José Manuel Prieto's work, especially in his 1997 *Enciclopedia de una vida en Rusia* (Encyclopedia of a Life in Russia) and in *Livadia* (1999, published in English in 2000 under the title *Nocturnal Butterflies of the Russian Empire*), the first and second parts of Prieto's Russian trilogy, whose final installment is the 2007 *Rex* (published in English in 2009). Having been sent to Novosibirsk, Siberia, at the age of nineteen to study electronic engineering, Prieto (born in Havana in 1962) spent twelve years in the Soviet Union, significantly more than other Cuban exchange students, and married a Siberian woman. Both *Enciclopedia de una vida en Rusia* and *Livadia* describe a moment soon after the collapse of the Soviet Union. Prieto's characters cope with the abruptly transforming limits of geography, ideology, and comportment having been informed by an empire that, in the words of *Enciclopedia*, was composed of prisoners who

> tenían la sensación de galopar en plena libertad: hombres y mujeres en su habitat natural sin alambradas ni dispositivos de alarma a la vista. El IMPERIO era un mundo paralelo, un universo autosuficiente en el

que se podía hallar a "trotamundos" que, sin embargo, nunca lo habían abandonado.[25]

had the sensation of galloping in full liberty: men and women in their natural habitat without wire fences or alarm devices in sight. The EMPIRE was a parallel world, a self-sufficient universe in which one could find globetrotters who, nevertheless, had never abandoned it.

The writer/protagonist of *Enciclopedia* entered into this empire from Cuba. He is a foreigner who knows something about the "beyond" of the empire, but it remains uncertain whether his conception of the "beyond" can easily be envisioned as the West, which the inhabitants of the empire so coveted and with which they had a specular relationship: "OCCIDENTE: Es el espejo donde Rusia se mira todas las mañanas para reajustar su propia imagen"[26] (OCCIDENT: It is the mirror in which Russia looks at itself every morning to readjust its own image). As is the case with *Siberiana*'s Bárbaro and Martínez Shvietsova's shell corporation, Cuban subjectivity is not aligned to either the East or West.

A definition of the term *"nierus"* is provided in *Enciclopedia* from the position of an outsider with a deep understanding of the hierarchies within Soviet and Russian society:

> Otra vez platicaba con un amigo en un lugar público, y una mujer, tomándonos quizá por NIERUS (no rusos representantes de alguna minoría nacional del IMPERIO) se volvió indignada: "¿Pero por qué no hablan *en ruso*? Llevan media hora hablando en esa lengua de pájaros y me tienen la cabeza hecha un verdadero rollo. ¿Cómo no les da vergüenza?" Después nos estudió mejor y ESCUPIÓ al suelo . . . Con los años y el acontecer de *La caída de la casa Usher* fui testigo de un cambio mental traumático, la inversion de polos de los *rus* ávidos de una vida plena, OCCIDENTAL, sin patatas hervidas ni pepinillos en salmuera.[27]

> Another time, I was talking to a friend in a public place, and a woman, taking us perhaps for NIERUS (non-Russian representatives of some national minority of the EMPIRE) became indignant: "But why don't they speak *in Russian*? They have spent the last half hour talking in this bird language and they've turned my head upside down. Aren't they embarrassed?" Then she took a closer look at us and SPIT on the ground. Over the years and with the occurrence of *The Fall of the House of Usher* I was witness to a traumatic psychological change, the inversion of poles of the *Rus*, eager for a full OCCIDENTAL life, without boiled potatoes or gherkins in brine.

The sarcastic and distanced tone that is achieved through, among other techniques, a literary allusion to another crumbling house hardly shields the narrator from the violence signaled in capital letters. This narrator makes several distinctions that are not apparent in *Siberiana*; Bárbaro does not understand Soviet culture in the ways that Prieto's narrators do. The connotations of the term "*nierus*" in Prieto's work are even more provincial than in Díaz's. According to *Enciclopedia*, the Russian characters who cannot even imagine an "other" from beyond Soviet borders transform soon after into subjects desperately hoping to *become* the other, that is, denizens of the West.

*Siberiana* is less politically controversial than the work of Jesús Díaz that many know from the journal *Encuentro* (which he founded in 1996) or from his novels, such as *Las cuatro fugas de Manuel* (2002, Manuel's Four Escapes), which also takes place in the East. Emilia Yulzari points to significant linguistic decisions Díaz made that possess political connotations. For instance, Nadiezdha's last name, Shalámov, "also could be characterized as a homage to the dissident writer Varlam Shalamov, prisoner of the Gulag and author of *The Kolyma Tales*, published in times of Perestroika."[28] The speeches by distinct Soviet authorities to which Bárbaro is subjected reveal flaws in the rhetoric regarding Soviet-Cuban intimacy, while Bárbaro's observations shed a different light on the "greatness" of the Soviet Union. Cuba is imagined by those Bárbaro encounters in Siberia as both "una isla muy pobre" (a very poor island) and "un país moderno, ya que estaba situado en pleno Occidente, un universo absolutamente mitificado en Siberia, objeto, a la vez, de la más profunda idolatría y del mayor desprecio"[29] (a modern country, since it was situated right in the Occident, an absolutely mythologized universe in Siberia, object, at once, of the most profound idolatry and of the greatest scorn). As the Cuban government advocated and even sculpted a way of life that was meant to lead Cubans to a Marxist-Leninist material reality, the Siberians understood themselves to be the authentic denizens of the Eastern margins who were only then going through modernization. For instance, the words of welcome from the chief engineer, Igor, come as somewhat of a surprise, as Bárbaro has been treated as such a "barbarian" in his daily transactions.

> Constituía un inmenso honor recibir al que iniciaba la lista, que además tenía las virtudes de ser occidental y periodista, por lo cual, con sus escritos, haría famosa en todo el mundo a Siberia, el continente más grande del planeta, la tierra con mayores reservas de agua, petróleo, oro y minerales estratégicos en todo el universo. ¿Qué le faltaba a Siberia? . . . transporte . . . y eso era justamente lo que estaban haciendo ellos, los heroicos constructores del ferrocarril.[30]

It constituted an immense honor to receive the first on the list, who in addition had the virtues of being from the West and a journalist, and as such, with his writings, would make Siberia famous around the world — the greatest continent on the planet, the land with the greatest reserves of water, petroleum, gold, and strategic minerals in all the universe. What did Siberia lack? . . . transportation . . . and that is just what the heroic constructors of the railway were doing.

Such hyperbolic language was disseminated in Cuba through various media. While the Cubans back home were consuming the narratives about the magnitude of Soviet steel and technology, Bárbaro was dealing with the lack of a decent toilet. "¡Qué mundo de locos aquel donde los baños tenían vapor y látigos en vez de agua y jabón!"[31] (What a crazy world that one, where bathrooms had steam and whips instead of soap and water!) In this way, the novel challenges what it means to be developed.

The response of Bárbaro's interpreter to his complaint cuts to the core of the more foolish of Cold War rhetoric — rhetoric of a nation that sought to model its technological development on that of the Soviet Union.

> Las famosas letrinas de los campamentos volantes de Siberia . . . disponían de tres comodidades que las hacían superiores por definición al más exquisito de los inodoros occidentales.[32]

> The famous latrines of the mobile encampments of Siberia . . . had three comforts that made them superior by definition to the most exquisite of Occidental toilets.

Nadiezdha's tone is facetious, as the last of those "comforts" — frozen, and therefore inodorous, excrement — makes clear.

*Siberiana* delves into issues of race that could not be buried successfully by Marxist-Leninism. On the one hand, as a member of the Eastern Bloc, Bárbaro is supposed to be "equal." Yet, the "Easterners" see him as both more modern and, undoubtedly, as more southern (as an African). In that way, the narrative of progress is far from neat. These Cuban characters' memories of their experiences with the Soviets contrast sharply with Feijóo's affection for them. Cubans' experiences abroad in the Soviet Bloc were, in fact, multiple and varied.

As *Rex* shows, the encounter between a post-1991 Russian and a Cuban continues to be determined by racial signifiers, yet the consequences are distinct. While *Rex* is not a travelogue, its protagonist, who desires to be called Psellus, like Michael Psellus, the eleventh-century stammering Byzantine historian and philosopher, is a Cuban who, having lived in the Soviet Union and Russia, knows the intricacies of the post-Soviet Russian mentality. In Prieto's post-Soviet world, divested of international solidarity, a "bárbaro" could not possibly be construed as modern. Psellus scams his way into being hired as a tutor for Petya, an eleven-year-old child of a Russian family who escaped to Marbella, Spain, from the Russian mafiosi, whom they, in turn, had scammed into buying counterfeit diamonds. The story unfolds in the form of Psellus's narration about instructing Petya in all realms of knowledge through the "Book," which is not of singular origin, and about his concocting a hoax to civilize this family (in the most banal way of educating their son and the more baroque way of "restoring" their connection to royalty). While Proust's *Remembrance of Things Past* is the source of numerous citations, the "Book" represents the amalgamation that is literature, into which Psellus and Prieto struggle to insert these menial characters — and to insert themselves not as mere commentators (like ourselves, readers), but as the Writer of the Book. Psellus is a trickster who outdoes the colonizers at their own game. A mere impostor of a tutor, hired to restore gravitas to this money-hungry pair of Russians, he falls in love with Nelly, the lady of the household, and comes to be responsible for her husband's and her own conversion into czar and czarina.

Some of Psellus's descriptions of his relationship to the masters of literature and his perception of his surroundings could be interpreted as colonial mimicry, characterized by Homi K. Bhabha as "the desire for a reformed, recognizable Other, as a subject of a difference that is almost the same, but not quite,"[33] or even analyzed through Henry Louis Gates's theory of the "signifying monkey," wherein citation entails greater flexibility and play vis-à-vis the hegemonic sphere, or the "original."[34] The novel, though, does not seem to hold the Soviets responsible for colonization. Instead, the Soviets are only mentioned once, and are not specifically linked to the journey of the protagonist — a cannibalizer, a one-time citizen of the Second World, on the threshold of "money." Territory is no longer the principal determinant of hierarchies. As Psellus falls for Nelly, he is reminded of the relationship between Humbert, the "europeo estragado o desencantado y Viejo"[35] (ravaged or disenchanted old European[36]), and Lolita, "la vulgar y joven Americana"[37] ("the vulgar young American girl"[38]), but he sees himself in the reverse role. Your mother, Psellus tells Petya, con su apellido compuesto, los lunares negros en su pecho, representaba los encantos de una antigua civilización, pero todavía gozable, llena de jugo. Y que yo, un torpe y joven americano, representaba la vulgaridad y la torpeza, aunque lleno de ímpetu y demás.[39]

with her hyphenated family name and the black moles on her breast, represented the enchantment of a civilization that was antique but was still ripe for enjoyment and full of juice. And I, an inept young American, represented vulgarity and ineptitude, though full of drive and all of that.[40]

In this passage, Psellus momentarily positions himself as the barbarian who seeks to be close to the legacy that he attaches to Nelly. However, just as Nelly is not a csarina from a European Russia—she is a post-Soviet wife of a mafioso whose house is strewn with "manuales sobre la vida en Occidente"[41] (instruction manuals for life in the West[42])—so Psellus is not a pauper from the New World (he is an educated Cuban struggling to survive in a post-Soviet world). In this way, Prieto unfastens entirely geopolitical signifiers from the hinges upon which they rest in the works of other Cuban writers.

Regarding the current relationship between the Russians and the Cubans and its being informed by a past legacy, no other scene captures the complexity as well as when Psellus spies a "Sasha." A "Sasha" is this man in front of a reception desk with "cabellos rubios y [un] porte difícil, la pesadez de un nuevo rico que todo el tiempo quiere dar a entender . . . su nuevo estatus"[43] (blond hair and awkward bearing, the ponderousness of a nouveau riche who must constantly give to understand . . . his new status"[44]). He is spotted in Spain in Psellus's search for possible guests to invite to the party that will convert the Russian mafia living in Marbella into royalty and will restore the monarchy. The stakes of recollecting the Soviet-Cuban alliance in contemporary times are revealed in the following passage:

Y me sentí atraído por aquella cara desconocida, aunque muy familiar ¿en su generalidad?, enternecido y sonriente por la luz fluorescente de un gusto tan vulgar y predecible. Atravesé el hall para conversar un poco, amistoso. Siempre les extraña, déjame decirte, ser interpelados por mí. Son mis amigos pero no lo saben, reniegan de mí, de mi amistad. Juntos, les decía, en las trincheras del socialismo. ¿Qué tal? En las trincheras ¡y del socialismo! Pero ya casi junto a él cambié de idea iluminado claramente por el grueso reloj de oro macizo que se le adelantó en la muñeca al levantar el teléfono minúsculo, la pantallita azul a la oreja rosada . . . Pasé por su lado y me limité a llamarlo: ¡Sasha!, un nombre

inventado, uno cualquiera. Se volteó sorprendido. Y sin apartarse el teléfono de la oreja me estudió de pies a cabeza y me espetó: "*Nu, I kak banani v etom godu v tvoem Gondurace?*" *¿Qué tal están las bananas este año
en (tu) Honduras?* (O de dondequiera que seas, quiso decir.)

El habla ultrajante, el tono. Al punto que me hizo lamentar haberme
dirigido a él. Urgido él mismo a abandonar las profundidades asiáticas,
poco dado a fraternizar con un ex aliado, todo eso. Vastas zonas de su
pasado totalmente claras para mí: desayunos con salchichón barato no
hacía ni tres años, huevos duros en el cupé de un tren para el viaje de
dos días, una madre ahora mismo y un padre en Rusia.[45]

And I felt attracted by that unknown face, unknown though familiar—in its general aspect? Touched by a vulgar and predictable taste,
smiling through the fluorescent light. I crossed the lobby for a chat,
friendly. They always find it odd, let me tell you, to be addressed by me.
They are my friends but don't know it; they deny me and my friendship. Together, I would say to them, in the trenches of socialism! How's
that? In the trenches! The trenches of socialism! But now, almost next
to him, I changed my mind, his face clearly illuminated by the massive
gold watch that slipped forward on his wrist as he raised the tiny telephone, little blue screen to pink earlobe . . . I walked past him and limited myself to calling: Sasha!—a name invented on the spot, any name.
He turned in surprise . . . And without taking the phone from his ear he
studied me from head to toe and spat back: "Nu, I kak banani v etom
godu v tvoem Gondurase?" Well, how are the bananas this year in your
Honduras? (Or, wherever it is you're from, he meant.)

The cutting phrase, the tone. To the point that I regretted having addressed him. He himself in a rush to abandon the Asiatic depths, little
taste for fraternizing with a former ally, all that. Vast zones of his past
totally clear to me: breakfasts of cheap sausage not three years ago,
hard-boiled eggs in the train's café car for the two-day trip, a mother
and a father back in Russia.[46]

This scene manifests the Russian's impulse to pass for a denizen of the West.
"Sasha" detects "Psellus" to be a southern "barbarian," the effect of a more discernible colonial experience—that of the banana republic, such as Honduras,
as opposed, perhaps, to the "dummy," or "shell corporation," that Martínez
Shvietsova equates with Cuba. His southern characteristics, presumably, are
racial, but Psellus himself, even before, preempted "Sasha" with his own racial
X-ray—Sasha's coloring is different from that of this distant member of the
previous Soviet empire. When Psellus begins to work for the Russian mafia

family in Spain, he tells them he is Spanish, and when he reveals to them that he is Cuban, they do not react. The slippage is supposed to go unnoticed and does not provoke a loss of confidence in the mentor or our narrator. To recall the "trenches of socialism" in the post-Soviet moment, as Psellus does, is contrary to the motivations of his previous "brethren's" passage toward the West.

In Prieto's 2001 *Treinta días en Moscú* (Thirty Days in Moscow), the proto-fictional narrator's awareness of his foreignness is molded into his understanding of Russians' visions of themselves as innately foreign—a phenomenon that is not easily comprehensible at least within *Enciclopedia*'s definition of "nierus." Forming part of a series of seven books by different authors, published by Mondadori in the Año Cero (Year Zero) collection, that were envisioned as a historic document of the most important cities at the new millennium, *Treinta días en Moscú* takes its readers through a tour of the newly capitalistic Moscow, illustrating how its inhabitants negotiate the remains of their recent Soviet totalitarian past by reconstructing a dynastic past to buttress their personal identities. A compilation of individual biographical sketches, *Treinta días* comes together through the narrator's commitment to showing how dramatically the city's denizens have changed since the last time he was there as a resident in the city. Referencing his engagement with Russian society of the early 1990s, the eyewitness ties himself to the fictional protagonist—J.—of his renowned novel, *Livadia*.

In all of his writing Prieto portrays his engagement with Russia almost as if it were an accident, detached from the international compromise that resulted in so many Cubans residing in the Soviet Union. Ascribing this phenomenon to both *Enciclopedia de una vida en Rusia* and *Livadia*, Rafael Rojas remarks: "The few times, in these two novels, the narrator admits that he is Cuban, he does it as if he were to confess an originary defect, a ridiculous randomness, an embarrassing condition."[47] While I would not agree with Rojas's account of the shame, Prieto's writing does emphasize the randomness of origins. For instance, while *Livadia*'s J. claims that he arrived in Russia "para estudiar óptica, aunque sin terminar la *carrera*"[48] (to study optics, but I didn't graduate[49]), his assertion is never linked to the masses of other students whose trajectories of study in Russia (note the use of Russia, here, and not the Soviet Union) paralleled his own.

The narrator of *Treinta días en Moscú* is fascinated by the extremes to which Russians go to envision themselves through their relationship to that which is from the West. In describing an artisans' market, a place that usually features local production, the narrator comments on Russians' fascination with the West:

> Y como el país está fascinado por Occidente, venden, por ejemplo, cerámica importada de producción masiva, plata mexicana, incensarios

indios, gnomos de plástico. Vender piezas laqueadas rusas sería de poco prestigio y provecho. Pregunto a la vendedora: "¿Tiene alguna jarra con algún lema en ruso?" Y la sola pregunta ya delata en mí a un extranjero. Tampoco lo hubiera hecho cuando vivía aquí, es cierto.[50]

And since the country is fascinated by the Occident, they sell, for example, mass-produced imported ceramics, Mexican silver, Indian incense burners, plastic gnomes. To sell Russian lacquered products would be of little prestige and benefit. I ask the vendor, "Do you have a pitcher with a Russian motto on it?" And the question itself reveals me to be a foreigner. I wouldn't have done it either when I lived here, that's for sure.

This West is not the West that was the Other to the East of *Siberiana*, nor is it an array of characteristic staples from the United States and Western Europe. Rather, it corresponds to Russians' preferences in taste and the globalized circuits of goods. It looks more like the Russia that La Rusa Roxana Rojo observes from her place in Cuba, to which she desires to adapt in order to become part of the New World order.

The experienced traveler is not startled by his own otherness, nor is he preoccupied with his own or his nation's positioning in a global order, in part because the divisions that were once celebrated have "melted into air."

Prieto explains former Soviets' ability to navigate foreignness and assess hybridity as being the result of the immense migrations that occurred within the former empire. The narrator is ethnically inquisitioned and reduced to his foreignness as he practices the same art of observation. "Paso junto a un miliciano a quien le basta verme de espalda para determinar que soy extranjero"[51] (I pass a military man who only needs to see me from behind to determine that I am a foreigner).

Es muy fuerte en Moscú el contraste con ciudades con una migración de más lejos. La gradación racial es aquí más ligera, más tenue, pero una vez que se ha aprendido puedes sorprender gratamente a cualquier mujer, estableciendo finamente, con ojos de conocedor, de qué nación del imperio proviene. Toma años, pero no hay nada que pasme más a una persona-mujer que el cálculo exacto, el despeje exacto de su sangre. Más ahora que antes, porque han recordado que alguna vez también fueron nobles, hurgan en sus pasados y se sacan príncipes yakutos o buriatos, dinastías calmucas. Y afloran, en efecto. ¿No son principescos los rasgos de las mujeres que entran a la disco, delgadas, sus rostros como cubiertos por máscaras de fino oro? Cuidados por los mismos cosméticos occidentales sus pómolos étnicos.

Y sentado allí con la cerveza en la mano, con solo hacer resbalar la vista por las mujeres que entran, elaboro mentalmente una lista de pueblos tan extensa como en la Ilíada o en Herodoto: chechenas, georgianas, abjazianas, bashkirias, daguestanas, yakutas (y todos los mestizajes con los rusos que a su vez son mestizos, preciosamente mestizas, las rusas, aun las que tienen los ojos azules y el pelo claro. En otra combinación de colores, sí [como en otro cuadrante de Warhol], pero que exploradas al tacto no se diferenciarían un ápice de un rostro chino. Sólo el cuenco de los ojos, quizá, pero el óvalo, los pómulos, la caída del cabello. Tártaras, ucranianas, komies. No del blanco al negro y al asiático marcado, sino en una velada, sfumata transición. Y algunas que das por sentado que son de madre tártara o Georgiana o Armenia, resultan rusas de madre y padre, pero que, miméticamente, en un lugar donde no se es verdaderamente bello sin un poco de sangre ajena, imitan la coloración, un perfil mestizo).[52]

There is a strong contrast between Moscow and cities where migration took place longer ago. The racial gradation is lighter here, more tenuous, but as soon as you've learned how, you can pleasantly surprise any woman, finely determining, with the eye of a connoisseur, which nation in the empire she comes from. It takes years, but there is nothing that shocks a person—a woman—more than the exact calculation, the exact sorting out of her blood. More now than before, because they have remembered that at one time they were also nobles, they poke around in their pasts and they take out the Yakut or Buryat princesses, Kalmuck dynasties. And they flourish, in effect. Aren't the features of the women who enter the disco—thin, their faces covered as if by masks of fine gold—princesslike? Their ethnic cheekbones cared for by the same Occidental cosmetics.

And sitting there with a beer in hand, with just glancing at the women who enter, I draw up a mental list of villages as extensive as in the *Iliad* or in Herod: Chechens, Georgians, Abkhazians, Baskirians, Dagestanians, Yakuts (and all the mixtures with the Russians, who are themselves mixed, beautifully mixed, Russian women, even those who have blue eyes and light-colored hair. In another combination of colors, yes [as in another quadrant of a Warhol painting], but when explored by touch cannot be distinguished in the least from a Chinese face. Only the hollow of the eyes, perhaps, but the oval, the cheekbones, the fall of the hair. Tartars, Ukranians, komies. Not a marked shift from white to black and to Asian, but rather a hidden, *sfumata* transition. And some who you took for granted had a Tartar or Georgian or Armenian mother turn out to have parents who are both Russian, but who, in a place where no one is truly beautiful without a little foreign blood, mimetically imitate the coloration, a mestizo profile).

While this expression of racial polyphony contrasts with the racial landscape of Cuba, one would be hard-pressed to say that the framework used by the narrator to describe hybridity and to interpret race is entirely unique; rather, as for Bárbaro in *Siberiana*, it is already highly tuned and measured against a Cuban lens. As a knowledgable witness, he has assimilated the Russian way of confronting racial difference to such an extent that he identifies himself within their categorization.

The Assyrian nation, in particular, is the one that captures the narrator's attention when a doorman informs him that the Assyrians are the shoeshines in Moscow. The notion of Assyrians in Moscow in the new millennium, when their nation was destroyed between 612 and 609, creates dissonance in the narrator. He cannot quite get his head around the fact that this doorman is Assyrian, as opposed to Armenian or Azerian (whom we are told Russian housekeepers refer to as blacks); Azerians are the "mal caucasiano"[53] (bad Caucasian). It is as if a remnant of a faraway time permeated the streets of Moscow. He confirms the veracity of the doorman's genealogy years later upon reading a book about the Gulag (likely Jacques Rossi's *The Gulag Handbook*, which was published in Russian in 1987 and in English in 1989), in which Stalin is said to be called "Gutalin," or shoe polish, since he was said to look Assyrian, the ethnicity of many shoeshines in Moscow.

The one in charge of this game of recognition in *Treinta días en Moscú* is the narrator, and while he is frequently interrogated for his "papers," his actual Cuban identity is kept undercover. The exception is in the book's concluding chapter, "En el aire otra vez" (In the Air Again), when the Assyrian shoeshine marks him as a Cuban, after which he marks her as Assyrian. In the book's final words, "¿Y en el pasaporte tiene escrito así: 'asirios?' Claro (se ríe), ¿y en el tuyo, cómo está escrito, 'cubano'?"[54] (And in the passport is it written like this: "Assyrians?" Of course [she laughs], and in yours, what is written, "Cuban?") It is the only moment in which the narrator is mirrored in another, as if the female shoeshine beats him at his own game by attaching him to his passport. At the same time, the story of the Assyrians is so seemingly far removed that he almost fictionalizes himself in this very exchange. The fact that his Cuban identity is revealed almost if by accident suggests a degree of identification with these denizens of Moscow who are at once particularly grounded — fixing the soles of people's shoes — and in the air, not only because they had to escape carnage on various occasions, but also because they are then viewed as almost outside of time. The location of the shoeshine's little shack in front of a Mexican restaurant points to the destination of the narrator's travels: he is returning to Mexico.

The other moment in which the national identity of the narrator surfaces is when he remarks upon Moscow's musical landscape of insipid pop being disrupted by a Cuban septet. Just a few years before, it would have been inconceivable to have heard this music anywhere outside of "Bayamo, Sancti Spíritus, Ciego de Avila, en lo más profundo de Cuba"[55] (in the deepest of Cuba). He comes upon the music in a café while overhearing some women speak about another locale called Scandinavia's Summer Café. This juncture speaks to his experiences of consumerism and to the appearance of globalization in the post-Soviet landscape. In the 1990s, especially in the post–Buena Vista Social Club 1990s, Cuban music experienced a boom, and the most local of rhythms reached unforeseen popularity. Likewise, Russians are fascinated by the tastes of the West—Swedish chefs cook Swedish specialties, serve margaritas, and even advertise in English, the language of the Soviet Union's former enemy, "in the heart of Moscow."[56] A certain brand of cosmopolitan consumption corresponds to the previously evoked aesthetic appreciation of diversity.

One of the many ways to read Prieto's explosive and postmodern Russian trilogy is as a treatise on taste, in general, and on fashion, in particular; that is, as a commentary on the nouveau riche's relationship to consumer products from the West, or those that are valued by the West though produced elsewhere.[57] In *Livadia*, the protagonist, J., a smuggler of contraband (remnants from the "now completely bankrupt" Red army), a hunter of Yazikus (rare butterflies that supposedly are extinct in the West), and an epistolarian par excellence of letters to his lost butterfly (a prostitute who desires to return to her Russian homeland), continually reflects upon his own foreign status, obliged to do so by the Russians, who refuse to consider him as a subject.[58] However, he notes early on, "Yo no era un extranjero, propiamente hablando. Había vivido demasiados años en Rusia para que se me pudiera considerar como tal."[59] (I was not exactly a foreigner. I had lived in Russia too long.[60]) In a review of *Livadia*, Gerardo Fernández Fé, a poet and translator born in Cuba in 1971, comments:

> Like the Russians, we too have been looking at the Occident for a long time. And Prieto's been doing this as well. Born in an equally feudal and constrained place, the Cuban case cannot hide its explosion, its trivialness and insignificance, its exodus, its haggling, its economic spirit, despite the disagreement with our Founding Fathers and our governing heads.[61]

Fernández Fé's observation about looking at the West is particularly interesting given how distinct the Cubans of the early Revolution felt from *Soy Cuba's* representation of them. Fernández Fé suggests that what constitutes "us" and "them" is not so very clear.

The unique positioning of the Cuban protagonist is most evident in *Enciclopedia de una vida en Rusia*, wherein the multiply named protagonist resides along a liminal access, between observing and possessing, witnessing and encompassing. This tension is most evident when he says, "En ruso, para impostor tienen (tenemos) *samozbaniets* o 'el que se nombra a sí mismo', algo muy conceptualista diríamos hoy"[62] (In Russian, for *impostor* they have [we have] *samozbaniets* or "he who names himself," something that today we would say is very conceptualist). Beyond the incertitude surrounding the speaker's position, there is the question of whether those who have and those who name are indeed the same group. The characters—José, Josef/Thelonius Monk, Anastasia Katz/Linda Evangelista—inhabit the crossroads between reality and fiction, the world lived and world ideal, as well as between the East and the West. Josef looks in the mirror and sees Thelonius, the character he is constructing in his novel within a novel, *Pan de la boca de mi alma* (Bread for the Mouth of my Soul). This idealized self-reflection is achieved through the realm of the artificial, in honor of which Prieto, like Pedro González Reinoso, implements Baudelaire's "In Praise of Cosmetics" in his epigraph.

The notion of "passing" runs throughout Prieto's oeuvre, and in *Rex*, the sense of "looking like" not only is relevant to fashion but also serves as a *modus operandi* for every aspect of reality and its representation in literature:

> Todos felices en el coche, vestidos expresamente para la occasión: tú como el niñito del grabado, con tirantes y escarpines, tu madre en su vestido rojo, el Armani de tres piezas de tu padre.
>
> Solo desentonaba el atuendo del buriato, a quien no pude convencer de que cambiara su jubón a franjas, de un paño listado de pésimo gusto, para *cockneys* o para lacayos despreciables.[63]

> Everyone in the car happy and dressed up for the occasion, you like a little boy in an engraving, wearing suspenders and ankle boots, your mother in her red dress, your father's three-piece Armani.
>
> Only the Buryat's attire was out of sync, for he could never be convinced to change his fringed doublet, made of a striped cloth that was in very poor taste, suitable only for Cockneys or contemptible lackeys.[64]

When Prieto, in his note to Esther Allen's brilliant English translation of *Rex*, reveals that his characters are "survivors of the totalitarian catastrophe,"[65] he is essentially telling us that they greedily make their entrance onto the Western stage by playing "dress up" in order to take what they feel is owed them.

Prieto's oeuvre suggests that commensurability with others is possible — a notion that is only partially discernible in works written by other Cuban travelers about their experiences abroad in the Soviet Union. Dori Laub's characterization of the isolation experienced as a Holocaust survivor is relevant to the situation of others who have been traumatized: "Her own children she experiences with deep disappointment as unempathic strangers because of the 'otherness' she senses in them, because of their refusal to substitute for, and completely fit into, the world of parents, brothers, and children that was so abruptly destroyed." Furthermore, "there could not be an audience (even in her family) that was generous, sensitive, and self-effacing enough to obliterate its own existence and be nothing but the substitutive actors of her unexplicated memory."[66] Laub's discussion of the imperative "to tell and to be heard" and of the frustration brought about by telling given that the receiver is necessarily removed from the traumatic situation has consequences for how we read the narratives of many international travelers in the Soviet Union or even Soviet survivors of trauma or ethnic discrimination. The traps within universalism and the barriers toward empathy are apparent in Jesús Díaz's *Las cuatro fugas de Manuel*. Living through a moment of immense historical transformations, each character is marked by the particular traumas and debts associated with his or her affiliations, and expects his or her interlocutor to be remiss when it comes to comprehending their significance.

The protagonist's recollection of the reaction of his Chilean friend Sonia, an exile from the Pinochet regime, to his superior's ordering his return to Cuba from the USSR is illustrative of how exceptionalism limits individuals' ability to transcend their circumstances. Neither Sonia nor the protagonist, Manuel, is able to know each other's sentiments about what the other is experiencing:

> Sabía muy bien lo que estaba diciendo, exclamó, no en balde provenía de una familia comunista, y sobre todo lleva cinco años en la Unión Soviética y tenía un montón de camaradas que habían pasado por Cuba después del golpe de Pinochet.
>
> Cuba no era ni la Unión Soviética ni Chile, razonó Manuel, dispuesto a ver hasta dónde llegaba la convicción de Natalia en aquel punto. ¡Ah, no, claro, Cuba era Cuba! Exclamó ella, ¡pero no le fuera a salir ahora con nacionalismos! . . . ¡los rusos, los ucranianos y los chilenos la tenían hasta aquí de nacionalismos![67]

> She knew very well what she was saying, she exclaimed. Not in vain did she come from a Communist family and, above all, spend five years

in the Soviet Union and have a bunch of comrades who had passed through Cuba after Pinochet's coup.

Cuba was neither the Soviet Union nor Chile, Manuel reasoned, determined to see just how strong Natalia's convictions were on that point. Ah, no, of course, Cuba was Cuba, she exclaimed. But he was not going to start now with nationalisms! . . . The Russians, the Ukrainians, and the Chileans had her up to here with nationalisms!

When Manuel is subjected to his first punishment for trying to escape from the Soviet Union—that of getting his possessions stolen and the walls of his old quarters sullied with the word *"apátrida"* (unpatriotic or stateless person)—it becomes apparent that Sonia's belief that her worldliness allows her to understand things about Cuba that Manuel cannot is a valid one.

Another situation similarly suggests the impossibility of going beyond the particularity of national roots, inheritance, and experiences. Manuel is witness to a heated discussion between Sonia and Sacha, a Ukrainian, wherein at the end, the inability to speak for the "other" is reaffirmed. "'¡No hables de Ucrania!' conminó Sacha. '¡Qué sabes tú de Ucrania!'"[68] ("Don't talk about the Ukraine!" Sacha warned. "What do you know about the Ukraine!"). Note that the last phrase is a rhetorical question that assumes the answer is "nothing." If the degree of ignorance about his homeland that Manuel encounters throughout his peripatetic sufferings is any indication, the logic behind such rhetoric of exceptionalism is at least to some extent defended within the novel.

Nevertheless, on one occasion Manuel incorporates analogies as a strategy of survival, and in that instance, the exceptionalism of Cuba is momentarily broken down. Having been sent by his friends Sonia and Sacha to a farm outside of Kiev both to hide from authorities and, at the same time, help an old couple work their land, he fantasizes:

> Los pinos de Ucrania eran caobos de Cuba; los manzanos, plátanos; el trigo, caña de azúcar; las rosas, rosas. Pero tarde o temprano despertaba de aquellas ensoñaciones porque ni su madre ni su abuelo aparecían nunca por sitio alguno y la finca de Holguín era sencillamente inconcebible sin ellos.[69]

> The pine trees of the Ukraine were the mahogany trees of Cuba; the apple trees, banana trees; the wheat, sugar cane; the roses, roses. But sooner or later he would awake from his daydreams because neither his mother nor grandfather ever appeared anywhere, and the farm in Holguín was simply inconceivable without them.

This daydream, characteristic of exiles—something Manuel hardly realizes that he has turned into—only works for a short period, and he soon awakens to the fact that he is in a largely inhospitable environment.


## THE CUBAN WANDERYEARS

One poet who was ahead of his time in identifying what the journey to the Soviet Union meant for him as an individual, more than as a patriot, is Emilio García Montiel (born in 1962 in Havana) because he narrates a place and calls it by a name that does not correspond to Cuba's collective history. Like Prieto, García Montiel has this propensity to speak about the category of "Russia" in a manner that, according to Rafael Rojas, initiates a precocious subjectivity:

> *Cartas desde Rusia* (1988), Emilio García Montiel's early poetry collection, perhaps was the first indicator of this subjectivity in Cuban literature. There no one ever speaks of the Soviet Union, always of Russia and of a Russia that is arrived at by sea, from Istanbul, crossing the Mediterranean and the Black Sea. In those poems, Moscow was a city of grand boulevards and of cafes on the corners, like a grey replica of Paris, where the family letters are read and written and where excursions to the outskirts, to dachas of great writers, like the house of Leo Tolstoy and Yasnaea Poliana, are more important than the visit to Lenin's mausoleum. The trip to Russia was presented, by García Montiel, not as a student duty, but rather as an adventure and a betrayal.[70]

In *Cartas desde Rusia* (Letters from Russia) (1986–1988)—and especially in García Montiel's poem by the same title, recently republished in his collected works, *Presentación del olvido* (Introduction to Oblivion)—he portrays the Soviet Union as, most of all, a way to travel outside of the island, to have access to other parts of the world. As Rojas asserts, the very title captures the personal mood of García Montiel's experience. Unlike the Ukrainian from *Todas iban a ser reinas*, who asserts her belonging to the Soviet world, or even Samuel Feijóo, who was convinced of the spirit of solidarity with the great Soviet nation, García Montiel focuses on the Russia where he actually studied and not on the entire Soviet Union, to which his homeland envisioned it was sending him. The emphasis on worldliness, rather than prescribed internationalism, in García Montiel's poetry is also evidenced in its traversing different countries without any special political attachment. In the poem "Cartas desde Rusia,"

García Montiel narrates the sense of adventure and desire that compelled him to lie to his country and his mother:

> Como un buscador de oro me escapé a esta tierra.
> Mentí a mi país y a mi madre que me creyeron un hombre de bien ...
> Yo deseaba un viaje, un largo y limpio viaje para no pudrirme
> Como veía pudrirse los versos ajenos en la noria falaz de las palabras.
> Yo deseaba cosas flexibles y silvestres, calladas y útiles
> Con su filo asentado en la vieja nobleza del hombre
> Y cosas que no eran más que otro país y otras ciudades
> Las ciudades de graves monumentos y de mujeres altas
> Las que nos traen el deseo por lo desconocido[71]

> Like a searcher for gold I escaped to this land.
> I lied to my country and to my mother who believed me to be a good
> man ...
> I desired a trip, a long and clean trip so as not to rot
> The way I saw the verses of others rotting on the fallacious Ferris wheel
> of words.
> I longed for flexible and wild things, silent and useful
> With their edge sharpened upon the old nobility of man
> And things that were nothing more than another country and other
> cities
> The cities of solemn monuments and tall women
> Those that bring us a desire for the unknown

Wanderlust takes over the poetic subject, who endeavors to rest his eyes on other peoples and contemplate, rather than Soviet chauvinism, the infinity of the sea through which he is led on his voyage to the Soviet Union: "No mintieron las cartas ni los libros de viaje. En el mar se descubre el infinito ... De Algeciras a Trípoli, de Brindis a Estambul." (Neither the letters nor the travel books lied. In the sea, the infinite is discovered ... From Algeciras to Tripoli, from Brindis to Istanbul.) García Montiel's later poetry, *El encanto perdido de la fidelidad,* can be characterized by disillusionment, but the trip to Russia that he narrates in the mid- to late 1980s signifies an opening to the world.

The biography of Antonio Álvarez Gil (born in 1947 in Melena del Sur, in the province of Havana) has several points in common with that of other Cuban travelers to the Soviet Bloc, but he arrived in the Soviet Union at an earlier point in the Soviet-Cuban affair than most. Sent to the Soviet Union at nineteen years of age to study chemical engineering in 1966, he spent one year in Kiev and five years in Moscow, only to return to the country some years later, employed by COMECON as an expert in international relations. Having lived in the USSR for a total of eleven years, Álvarez Gil married a Russian woman and eventually moved to Stockholm, Sweden. The stories in *Unos y otros*, published in Cuba in 1990, focus primarily on young Cubans' struggles with their manhood as played out in romances and friendships. They reveal conceptualizations of individual and collective success, and often, characters' experiences in the Soviet Union are a measure of their personal development. His Soviet Union is perceived, for the most part, in positive terms by the young adults who study abroad there, though some of the texts do raise questions about the Soviet-Cuban friendship. "Tres cerditos" (Three Little Pigs) tells the story of three young men who studied together in Havana and then in Moscow for six years, and who, upon their return to their homeland, are given the task of constructing a chemical plant in a remote village. The three friends are torn apart when two must return briefly to the Soviet Union to direct a workshop — a mission that will also permit them to return to their Russian wives. The narrator, Pepe, wed to a Russian who is already on the island with him, remains, performing each of his assigned tasks with excitement. He endlessly imagines the reactions of his companions to the transformations he is helping carry out.

> ¿Y qué dirían Armando y Pablo cuando vieran todo esto y lo compararan con las barracas roñosas que dejaron al partir para la URSS? Por otro lado . . . un omnibus destartalado y sin puertas cubría la ruta y para de vez en cuando junto a nuestro comedor.[72]

> And what would Armando and Pablo say when they saw all this and compared it to the grubby barracks that they left upon leaving for the USSR? On the other hand . . . the route was covered by a beat-up and doorless bus that stops every now and then by our dining hall.

Pepe is faced with something else entirely upon reuniting with his former buddies. Their blindness to what labor means is revealed by their reaction to Pepe's appearance: "¡Coño, Pepe! ¿Cómo tú andas? Te veo bien."[73] (Damn it, Pepe! How're you doing? You look good.) His friends' reaction perplexes Pepe.

> Pero yo no sabía en qué se me podía ver a mi que estuviera bien. Yo había adelgazado, estaba muy quemado por el sol, y ni mis rústicos pantalones de mezclilla, ni la camisa de trabajo, ni mucho menos aquellas botas polvorientas y tiesas podían evidenciar que yo me encontraba "bien."[74]

> But I didn't know what they could see in me that made it seem that I was well. I had lost weight, I was very burnt by the sun. Not my rustic

jeans, or my work shirt, or even my dusty and stiff boots could suggest that I was doing "well."

When Pepe realizes that Pablo and Armando, "que estaban rosados y aún llevaban ropas extranjeras"[75] (who were rosy and still wore foreign clothes), are no longer impacted by his mundane expressions of loyalty, he decides to stay with his other friends, who though not university educated like his old buddies, do share his experiences and belong to the same social stratum. Read among other fictionalized *testimonios* of Cubans in the Soviet Union, "Tres cerditos" stands out because it presents the Soviet Union as capable of producing a recognizable and privileged sheen, comparable to the transformation that is experienced upon traveling to the West.

The horizon of expectations for young Cubans of the 1970s is portrayed in Álvarez Gil's "Una casa en medio del mar" (A House in the Middle of the Sea), a generic romance about a young man named Ricardo who falls in love on the Rossía, "uno de los transatlánticos soviéticos más lujosos"[76] (one of the most luxurious Soviet transatlantics), with Sonia, a fellow passenger. They are both en route to the Soviet Union, where they are going to study chemical engineering. Ricardo reflects on that moment sixteen years after their passionate love affair came to an abrupt halt. Sonia, he remembers, commented on the "Russian smell" about which many Cubans complain. "'¡Qué olor!'—comentó Sonia cerca de mi oído. Realmente yo no había sentido nada que no fuera normal. Eran muy cortas las vacaciones para olvidar el olor de la comida rusa."[77] ("What a smell!" Sonia commented in my ear. I had not really noticed anything out of the ordinary. My vacation had been too short to forget the smell of Russian food.) Ricardo appreciates difference and responds, "Cada cocina y cada pueblo tienen su olor . . . los cubanos también tenemos el nuestro."[78] (All cuisine and all people have their smell . . . We Cubans also have ours.) However, he does not convince Sonia of the value of trying new cuisine. Upon listening to a popular Soviet song, Sonia confessed that "nunca comprendía cuando hablaban los soviéticos, y mucho menos si cantaban."[79] (I never understood when the Soviets spoke, and much less if they sang.) That said, en route to the Soviet Union, not only did she not feel nostalgia for her family in Cuba, but she "añoraba llegar y descubrir el país soviético. Quería conocer a su gente, hablar con ellos, escuchar su historia. Estaba segura que le gustaría. A pesar del clima y de la diferencia en las costumbres, sabía que iba a sentirse bien."[80] (She yearned to arrive and discover the Soviet country. She wanted to know its people, speak with them, listen to their story. She was sure she would like it. Despite the climate and the difference in customs, she knew she would feel well.) As in García Montiel's "Cartas desde Rusia," the Atlantic Ocean, and not the Soviet Union, per se, is the focus of this story about an awakening that is facilitated by the international union. If Feijóo captured a unique pilgrimage to the home away from home, the Álvarez Gil of these short stories engages a shared experience among many Cubans for whom the Soviet Union formed part of their expectations of novelty.[81]

The world encountered by readers of Álvarez Gil's *Del tiempo y las cosas* (Of Time and Things), published in Cuba in 1993, is even broader. The nationality of the protagonists is not always Cuban, and an unusual mystery and religiosity pervades the stories, which are set in small towns in the Socialist Bloc.[82] "Variaciones sobre un tema de Bulgakov" (Variations on a Theme in Bulgakov) and "Fatiga de Primavera" (Fatigue of Spring) have in common a Moscow setting and the exoticization of the Soviet sphere. The narrator of "Variaciones sobre un tema de Bulgakov" spends a strange afternoon looking for his friends' house, which, although he has visited on several occasions, he cannot locate on this one occasion. Instead a woman asks him directions to the Kremlin, an especially odd inquiry considering it is in plain sight. This bizarre sequence leads his friend to wonder if, in fact, he was bewitched that afternoon by Bulgakov's characters in *The Master and Margarita*, a novel that we are told in the revised version of "Variaciones," published in Álvarez Gil's *Nunca es tarde* (It's Never Late) (winner of the 2004 First International Prize for Short Narrative, Generation of 1927), consumed the narrator and his non-Russian-speaking Latin American friends, for whom he spent many nights translating the masterpiece. Bulgakov, as we shall see, is central to Álvarez Gil's *Callejones de Arbat* (2012) about Cubans' experiences of Perestroika in Moscow. Álvarez Gil's stories, like García Montiel's poetry, reflect the youthful mystery that the voyage abroad signified to Cuban characters, wherein their individual growth is more important than their historical subjectivity.

## PERESTROIKA AND GLASNOST UP CLOSE

In 1988, Michael G. Wilson of the right-wing Heritage Foundation reported that some students from Latin America who have been "educated in the Soviet bloc almost surely will return home committed to Marxism-Leninism, suspicious of the U.S. and indebted to the USSR,"[83] a detail that was meant to urge the United States to do more recruiting. However, Cubans' travel to the Soviet Bloc was hardly as uniform as Wilson "admonished" and, in fact, travel abroad provoked diverse reactions. What Wilson misses is that with Perestroika and Glasnost under way, many Cubans who came into direct contact with the Soviet Union from the mid-1980s to the early 1990s became highly suspicious of the "empire" to which they were supposed to loosely belong. As many of the aforementioned narratives suggest, Cubans were frequently surprised by the underdevelopment with which they were confronted. They were, after all, expecting a completed revolutionary project. The discrepancy between the exported image and the "real thing" corroborates with not only numerous informal oral testimonies of Cuban travelers to the Soviet Union in the mid- to late 1980s, but also with many fictional accounts.

Antonio Armenteros's *País que no era* (Country That Was Not) conveys travelers' experiences in the heart of the so-called International Revolution. Like the apparatchik in Ernesto Pérez Castillo's "Bajo la bandera rosa," the protagonist of Armenteros's "Misceláneas: Historias que rotan, trotan" (Miscellaneous: Stories That Rotate, Trot) arrives too late to the historical narrative of magnitude to be an actor. This sense of tardiness, however, was already inscribed within the origins of the project—hence the title of the collection of mostly interconnected short stories, "the country that was not." In the imperfect tense, the phrase does not evoke the act of falling apart, which is so frequently claimed in discussions of the Soviet Union and the Socialist Bloc in 1991, but rather its continuous nonreality. The one point at which the narrator reveals a clue to the source of longing is at the end of the snapshot-like "Misceláneas," in which he attempts to narrate to his father "algunas anécdotas, las experiencias percibidas en el país de las esperanzas del mundo, viejo, desgraciadamente el país que no era"[84] (some anecdotes, perceived experiences in the country of the hope of the world, old man, unfortunately, the country that was not). This phrase could serve as one of the many catchphrases of Armenteros's generation.

What Marta Hernández Salván has said about writers like Antonio José Ponte and Reina María Rodríguez also applies to Armenteros's collection. Hernández Salván's discussion of "Un arte de hacer ruinas" (A Knack for Making Ruins) describes perfectly this sense of disenchantment with an object that never was: "Their blind and intense belief in the Revolution made them all desire the restitution of an object that they thought was lost, yet never existed, as the narrator discovers at the end of the story."[85] The simulacrum is also pervasive within "Misceláneas." Once in Moscow, the Cuban students discuss their desperation regarding the lack of images from their homeland on television. "Cuba para los bolos no existe, tal vez sea verdad lo que nos dijo el viejo medio borracho en la panadería: ¡Ooh, Cuba, sí, Cuba, es la república No. 16 de la Unión . . . ! Y millones de epítetos escatológicos más, clásico de la cultura rusa, la inteligencia del simulacro."[86] (Cuba for the *bolos* does not exist. Maybe what the old half-drunk guy in the bakery said was true: "Oh, Cuba, yes, Cuba, it's republic no. 16 of the Union . . . ! And millions of scatological epithets more, classic in Russian culture, the intelligence of the simulacrum.) If Cuba does not exist for the *bolos* (literarily meaning "bowling pins," a derogatory term Cubans use for Soviets), then the narrative likening the Soviets and the Cubans to brethren would have to be a strategic invention.

Sometimes, in Armenteros's collection, foreign words are italicized and then defined, and at others, they are footnoted, as they are in Martínez Shvietsova's short stories. These techniques, traditionally utilized within bicultural stories, highlight for the reader what it is like to discover a foreign land. While the Cubans are attempting to penetrate the mysteries of the Slavic world, the narrator prematurely concludes that his hosts are hardly interested in his home nation. Hence, there is a lack of equity signaled by the baker's scatological epithets and his reference to Cuba as an extension of the Soviet Union, a statement that is not so distant from Rafael Rojas's description of Cuba as almost "a small tropical republic of the Soviet Union."[87]

The simulacrum about which the students in "Misceláneas" speak has many components, not least of which is culinary. The Cubans' introduction to the Soviet Union begins with a professor's explanations of Slavic food, including

> huevos a la *russe*, patatas compuestas a la rusa, con avena y miel nos surge el *Kisel*, la *Kulebiaka* o pastel de carne, arrollados de patatas con mejillones y el famoso borsch a la crema — la sopa de remolacha más apetitosa del cosmos —, la *casha*, el *Kvas* — bebida fermentada sin alcohol auténticamente rusa . . .[88]

> eggs a la *russe*, potatoes Russian-style, with oats and honey it becomes *Kisel*, *Kulebiaka* or meat pie, crushed potatoes with mussels and the famous borscht with cream — the most appetizing beet soup in the cosmos, *Kasha*, *Kvas* — authentically Russian nonalcoholic fermented drinks . . .

Let it be known that in no other part of Armenteros's collection do these dishes actually enter into the stories. Rather, they form part of the simulacrum of envisioning Cuba as a peripheral extension of the Soviet Union, about which the largely chauvinistic and provincial denizens of Armenteros's Soviet Union do not need to know. Unlike Álvarez Gil's characters, whose naïve worlds are expanded through exposure to a different culture, Armenteros's are hardly enlightened.

"Misceláneas" shows that Cubans are not the only ones who suffer at the hands of Soviet chauvinism. A drunk old woman spits on a portrait of Gorbachev, telling the Cubans, "¡Agggh, por qué y para qué hablas con nosotros en el jodido idioma de los invasores!"[89] (Agggh, why and for what do you speak to us in the fucked language of the invaders!) Then she sings "La Kamarínskaya," the national song of the Russian people, signaling the simultaneity of Russian domination and cultural hegemony.

Though adorned in a "chal de gitana" (a gypsy shawl), the old lady's origins are not immediately clear.

> ¡Esta era tierra polaca—la *terra* incognita de la *psique* humana—, vino el *tavarish* ruso u oso y se la anexó! *Panis*, les cuento de mucho tiempo atrás, de cuando *La Gran Guerra Patria*, o como les enseñan ahora a ustedes en la escuela: de cuando *La Segunda Guerra Mundial*.
>
> Sentías entre sus palabras filtrarse algo que jamás habías podido imaginar en aquellas tardes en que se ponían a jugar imitando a los héroes de *La joven guardia*. Era la conciencia mutilada, el corazón desollado, el espíritu deformado. Allí nadie pudo cumplir su destino de hombre libre . . . Rusia constituía un armonioso espejismo, lo intuiste entonces del aire: Un mundo sin escapatoria.[90]

> This was Polish land—the *terra incognita* of the human psyche—, the Russian *tavarish* or bear came and annexed it. *Panis*, I am telling you about a long time ago, about the time of *The Great Patriotic War*, or how they teach you in school nowadays, *The Second World War*.
>
> You sensed something sneak in among her words, something that you had never been able to imagine those afternoons in which you played at imitating the heroes of *The Young Guard*. It was the mutilated conscience, the flayed heart, the deformed spirit. There no one could fulfill his destiny to be free . . . Russia constituted a harmonious mirage, you sensed it then in the air: A world without escape.

Through such snapshots, which capture the differences among nations that were often grouped together as the East, the Cuban narrator perceives another side of a history about which he had been indoctrinated back in Cuba through, among other texts, Alexander Fadeyev's antifascist and Stalin-prize-winning 1945 novel, *The Young Guard*.[91] Such heroic narratives, after which the Cuban admits to having modeled himself, lose their sheen in the face of such stories of oppression—an act of awakening that can be compared to Dmitri Prieto Samsonov learning about other stories about the Second World War, once outside of Cuba.

The political-ethical system of the Cuban protagonist in "Misceláneas," like that of other young Cuban revolutionaries, was, as he elucidates, formed through great Soviet literature and film, including Chingiz Aitmatov and Andrei Konchalovsky's film *El primer maestro* (1965; The First Teacher); Nikolai Ostrovsky's *Así se templó el acero* (1932; How Steel Was Tempered); Boris Polevoi's *Un hombre de verdad* (A Story about a Real Man), for which its author was awarded the Stalin Prize in 1951, and *Somos hombres soviéticos* (1948; We Are Soviet People); numerous works by Mikhail Aleksandrovich Sholokhov, such as *Cuentos del Don* (1925; Tales from the Don); and Aleksander Bek's *La carretera de Volokolamsk* (1944; Volokolamsk Highway); among numerous other "great books."[92] However, the protagonist does not find the land of plentiful heroes.

> Todo resultó inverso, un reflejo equivocado: para Rusia en lo público solo importa la apariencia, la mentira como negación de la verdad. Aquellos seres que yo veía parecían emerger de otros relatos, otra literatura, por ejemplo: *El maestro y Margarita, Los hermanos Karamazov, El sello egipcio, La arquería de Stepanchikovo, Un día en la vida de Iván Denísovich* o *El eterno baile de las máscaras.*[93]

> All turned out to be the reverse, a mistaken reflection: for Russia what mattered in public was appearance. The lie as negation of truth. Those beings that I saw seemed to emerge from other tales, another literature, from, for example, *The Master and Margarita, The Brothers Karamazov, The Egyptian Stamp, The Village of Stepanchikovo, One Day in the Life of Ivan Denisovich* or *The Eternal Dance of the Masks.*

Armenteros's story suggests that the most powerful literature of dissidence portrays the Soviet Union more realistically than the socialist realism widely distributed by Mir and Progreso publishing houses.

In "*Souvenirs* de un Caribe soviético" (2008), Rafael Rojas explains this literary historiography and the anachronistic reproduction of Stalinist socialist realism in Cuba. "The reception of Soviet thought, on the island, passed through a filter of ideological correction, very similar to that which is reproduced in colonial situations."[94] Rojas reports that in the 1960s, Solzhenitsyn's writings on the forced labor camps and Yevgeni Yevtushenko's robust critique of Stalin were considered essential reading, but beginning in 1969, the Brezhnev era brought with it the promotion of socialist realism in Cuba:

> Although the cultural politicians of the Island did not explicitly subscribe to the theses of Mikhail Suslov, the principal ideologue of Brezhnevism, the intense reproduction of that literature was an alignment de facto with the most orthodox currents of Soviet culture. Said alignment, nevertheless, was not as perceptible in Cuban literature—although it does not lack examples of socialist realism.[95]

A critique of Cuban politics informed by the contemplation of dissident figures from the Soviet Union and Eastern Europe did not emerge in the mid-1980s with Perestroika, but rather before. As Juan Abreu, a "Marielito" writer born in Cuba in 1952, explains in "Deuda" (Debt), inheritance is not as related to influence as it is to debt. His essay catalogues the extent to which such writers impacted his generation—the one that came of age in the 1960s and suffered various repressions in the 1960s and 1970s, many attributed to the greater Soviet influence in the national sphere. Nevertheless, a vast cultural map also helped his generation cope with and ease its pain. In Abreu's words,

> In the decade of the 1970s, I lived in a country where, if it had not been for some writers from Eastern Europe, I (and the small group of writers I formed part of) would have given in and ended up as part of some group that wiggled its backside before power. Here are their names: Fyodor Dostoyevsky, Alexander Solzhenitsyn, Witold Gombrowicz, Sergiusz Piasecki, Isaak Babel, Mikhail Bulgakov.[96]

Abreu captured the contrast between nationalist imposition and intimate selection with the question, "Who said that Lenin does not serve any purpose?" Lenin Park was the place where, along with his companions, he had clandestine encounters with copies of Gombrowicz's *Ferdydurke* and Bulgakov's *The Master and Margarita*. Smuggled in by Reinaldo Arenas, these two texts possessed a potential for scandal that made them cult classics, especially for readers from former Socialist countries.[97]

To illustrate just how relevant this discussion is to today's extratextual experience, allow me to share with you an almost unreal resuscitation of the 1970s Soviet library for the purposes of the Russian-Cuban alliance, exemplifed in the 2010 International Book Fair of Cuba (whose guest of honor was Russia). The report from *Vanguardia*, a newspaper out of Santa Clara, Cuba, described Raúl Castro's tour of the fair's Russian Pavilion. Of central importance to this discussion of the Soviet archive is how the newspaper recounts the significance of Russian epic literature.

> In dialogue with the Russian Chancellor he remembered how the Russian epic literature accompanied the combatants that defended the conquests of the Revolution in the early 1960s, in middle of imperialist aggressions.
>
> Many of those who participated in the tour were reminded of titles like *The Volokolamsk Highway, A Story about a Real Man, We are Soviet People,* and *General Panfilov's Reserve*.[98]

This unrestrained relationship to a literature that diverse writers long ago revealed to be so charged is an indication of the complicated selection process that the Soviet memorialization in Cuba is taking on. It is as if Perestroika were being momentarily cast aside in order to embrace the old heroes.

In such texts, no evidence can be found of the suppression of the other, a constant within the "multinacional-racial masa soviética"[99] (Soviet multinational-racial mass), nor the prejudices Armenteros's darker-skinned Cuban characters are subjected to, who have brought to the USSR their own set of racial readings.[100] They are not blind to the violence enacted by their Soviet brethren, either. In "Misceláneas: Historias que rotan, trotan," the Afghani lover of César, one of the Cuban students, is anguished each time she thinks of the Soviet war in her homeland. By the end of the story, a 1980s temptress of late Soviet capitalism—whom César had told that he was the son of a Venezuelan magnate—drags him to a small village where she and her friends beat him up. The ideological narrative that he uses to plea with the gangsters, however, has been suspended. It seems that, as in the case of Manuel from Díaz's *Las cuatro fugas de Manuel*, Cuba remains viable as the hope of Latin America but, this time, in the protagonist's disfavor. When César attempts to retreat to the narrative of internationalism with these subjects, he falls on his face:

> Soy cubano, de Cuba, el primer país socialista de América Latina, y nada! Aquellos quince rublos que hallaron en mi bolsillo eran mi capital, pero mientras más se lo repetía, me zarandeaban y pateaban con más furia. ¡Marx y Engels sabían lo importante que es poseer un capital, yo lo olvidé y ya ves![101]

> I am Cuban, from Cuba, the first Socialist country in Latin America, and that's that! Those fifteen rubles they found in my pocket were my capital, but the more I repeated this to them, the more they shook and kicked me. Marx and Engels knew how important it is to possess capital. I forgot it and look what happened!

Such outright declarations, which counter what Cubans were taught about the Soviet Union, make *País que no era* a powerful testament to the lack of unity not just between two disparate worlds, approximately 9,550 kilometers away from one another, but also among the disparate republics that, as *La sexta parte del mundo* proves, supposedly formed one nation.

In another snapshot from Armenteros's "Misceláneas," the narrator/protagonist, now in love with a Russian, muses upon what Che Guevara would think about Cubans laboring in Siberia. The backdrop of this question is Guevara's critique of the Soviet Union in the aftermath of the Cuban Missile Crisis and of Cuba's increased dependence on the Soviet Union.

Usted, un estudiante insignificante y engreído de la ciudad, ya no sabes cuál: Moscú, La Habana . . . O al revés, entre tantas personas bravas, guapas, buenas de la geografía cubana, cortando madera, dando leña en la Siberia, otra Siberiada más. ¿A quién carajo se le ocurrió enviarnos a este infierno? Cómo explicarles a estos leñadores simples de Cuba que cuando el regimen zarista, aquí eran enviados los enemigos jurados del Zar. Y cuando el estado de obreros y campesinos del Padrecito Stalin — acero — quien solo creía en el brillo enceguecedor e indiscutible de sus propias ideas, aquí eran deportados y desaparecidos los verdaderos revolucionarios: los comunistas. Aquellos que se atrevieron a criticar el culto desmedido a la personalidad de Stalin.[102]

You, an insignificant and conceited student from the city. You don't know which one anymore: Moscow, Havana . . . Or, on the contrary, among so many fierce, handsome, good people from the Cuban land, cutting wood, giving lumber to Siberia, another Siberiada.[103] Who the fuck got this idea of sending us to this hell? How to explain to the simple woodcutters from Cuba that at the time of the czarist regime, the proven enemies of the czar were sent here. And at the time of the workers and peasants of Little Father Stalin — steel — who only believed in the blinding and indisputable brilliance of his own ideas, this is where the true revolutionaries — the Communists — were deported and disappeared. Those who dared to criticize the excessive cult of personality of Stalin.

Not unlike the impressions of *Siberiana*'s Bárbaro on Siberia, this passage is startling because the answer to the question of who sent us to this hell would likely be someone that could be compared to the csar or Stalin and who needed to pay for something or wanted others to pay for their wrongdoings through arduous labor. While neither Fidel nor a Soviet leader is named here, one can assume that the deviser of such a bizarre plan was himself a belligerent personality who made Cubans — often from the provinces — believe that they were heroic for realizing such monumental international missions in the East, missions that no one else was willing to execute.

Sergio Díaz-Briquets's illustrative 1983 "Demographic and Related Determinants of Recent Cuban Emigration" points out the importance of demographic factors for labor migration from Cuba, paying particular attention to the motivation behind Cubans in the Soviet Bloc.

The Cuban government has set in motion a third mechanism to ease the labor surplus: labor migration to Soviet bloc countries. In July 1981

Castro announced that 12,000 young Cubans were working in the German Democratic Republic, Czechoslovakia and Hungary. . . . Negotiations were underway for similar arrangements with other countries. This announcement followed earlier reports indicating that Cuba was in the process of negotiating labor transfers to Eastern bloc countries, including sending some 10,000 Cuban workers to assist with the harvesting of Siberian wood. . . . Supposedly, the availability of Cuban workers in Siberia would help accelerate deliveries of Soviet lumber to Cuba. Bottlenecks associated with wood shortages have been implicated in Cuba's low rate of housing construction.[104]

One of the latest cinematographic representations of Cuban workers in the Soviet Union can be seen in the 1989 documentary *Desde lejos,* directed by Guillermo Centeno. The film focuses on a community of seven hundred Cuban men and fifty women that went to the easternmost areas of the Soviet Union to cut lumber. Díaz Briquets's analogy between the Soviet Bloc's importation of Cuban labor and Western Europe's use of guest labor from poorer countries disrupts the way travel within the Socialist Bloc was often perceived. Education and training, in other words, were not the only reasons Cubans traveled to the Soviet Bloc.

The protagonist of Jesús Díaz's *Las cuatro fugas de Manuel* has little to do with Bárbaro. A white Cuban, Manuel Desdín speaks Ukrainian and Russian and is an insider in Soviet, Ukrainian, and Russian cultures, while Bárbaro is familiar with only the most basic Russian words. The novel is based on the actual experiences of Manuel Desdín, who met Jesús Díaz's son, Pablo, at a German-language class in Berlin in 1992, when Manuel finally successfully secured entry into another country after three failed attempts. To a large extent, *Las cuatro fugas de Manuel* can be considered a fictional testimonial novel, complete with an epilogue explaining the author's role in its creation. The fictionalized Manuel Desdín is studying physics in 1991 at the Institute of Physics of Low Temperatures, in Jarkov, Ukraine, when the acclaimed scientist Ignati Derkáchev presents him with an *atlichna,* or award for excellence. Manuel immediately realizes that his peers will be jealous, but he also knows that jealousy is only one of the many troubles that he is about to endure—in part for wanting to pursue his career in physics abroad rather than returning to Cuba, as he is told he must.

Both *Las cuatro fugas de Manuel* and *Callejones de Arbat* by Álvarez Gil end in the protagonists' having to renounce their nation's ideology on account of having been accused of betraying it. Yet, *Las cuatro fugas*'s Manuel and *Callejones*'s Mario think of themselves not only as patriots, but also as representatives of the Cuban Revolution abroad, until the day they must accept the verdict cast down on them by their superiors. In the 1970s and 1980s Cubans were supposed to admire the great Soviet narrative, but actually passing for Russian or Ukrainian in the Soviet Union, as this passage from *Las cuatro fugas de Manuel* elucidates, had consequences.

> El disertante había expuesto como un científico ruso, no como un estudiante extranjero. ¡Pero él era cubano, coño! ¡Él era un científico cubano! . . . ¿Iba a resultar, acaso, que los estúpidos que lo perseguían desde su infancia tenían razón al acusarlo de extranjerizante?[105]

> The speaker had presented as a Russian scientist, not as a foreign student. But he was Cuban, damnit. He was a Cuban scientist . . . Would it turn out that the idiots that had pursued him from his childhood were right to accuse him of being a lover of things foreign?

Being a lover of things foreign in Castro's Cuba has numerous, mostly pejorative, connotations.[106]

One of Manuel's main offenses was that of socializing with foreigners. This accusation reaches a new level when Erika Fesse, his former Bolivian girlfriend and a descendant of fascist Germans, with whom he studied in the Ukraine, leaves him in order to go to Sweden. He is reminded of the advice that Lucas Barthelemy, in charge of the Cuban students, often gave him:

> Por su bien, que no anduviera con extranjeras, que fuera a clases, que no estuviera por ahi repartiendo octavillas diversionistas sobre Ucrania independiente, que no hablara tanto del comemierda ese de Gorbachov, de la perestroika ni de la glasnost . . . Por su bien se lo había dicho . . . que asistiera a las reuniones del colectivo y a los círculos de estudio sobre los discursos de Fidel, que saludara a los compañeros, que se diera una vueltecita de vez en cuando por el Consulado, que no hablara más en ucraniano, que se pelara cortico como los hombres, que no usara sandalitas como las que tenía puestas.[107]

> For his own sake, that he should not hang out with foreign women, that he should go to class, not stand around passing out diversionist pamphlets about an independent Ukraine, not talk so much about that fool Gorbachev, about Perestroika or Glasnost . . . For his own good, he had told him . . . that he should attend meetings of the collective and the study groups about Fidel's speeches, say hello to his Cuban companions, come up and visit the Consulate once in a while, not speak in Ukrainian

any more, cut his hair short like men, not wear little sandals like those he had on.

The patronizing tone of the supervisor's message is magnified by the use of the *"ito"* diminutive suffix, usually an endearment, but here used to exert his power. Even though Manuel's passion is physics, with his language acumen, living in the Ukraine beside supporters of Gorbachev and of Yeltsin, he, like Pablo in Ulises Rodríguez Febles's *Sputnik*, cannot help but partake in conversations about Perestroika and Glasnost and Ukrainian nationalism, even though Cuban officials discourage him from voicing his opinions.

The painful conversion of Manuel Desdín into a counter-revolutionary is emblematic of the fight of many Cubans of his generation who similarly wished to adopt Perestroika-like measures within a Socialist Cuba and to remain faithful combatants of US imperialism. While the initial fate that Manuel wanted to avoid was that of being sent home to Cuba, the actions that he took in order to do so convert him into an enemy of the state. *Las cuatro fugas de Manuel* does not critique Socialist ideology per se, but rather shows the failures of the systematic rhetoric and operations that drive the Cold War. As Gustavo Guerrero states, "As extremely *atlichnik* as he may be, no one waits for him in the Occident with open arms."[108] As much as Díaz's narrative of Manuel's Sisyphean task leads readers to critique the Soviet and Cuban systems, it also implicates many who are guilty of hypocritical actions against individuals supposedly on the basis of their ideologies.

The protagonist's friends, most of whom had supported Communism and knew next to nothing about the Occident, urge him to leave: "Todos sus amigos lo habían animado a largarse a Occidente, aunque ninguno pudo darle una respuesta concreta acerca de él: no lo conocían, simplemente"[109] (All his friends had encouraged him to take off for the Occident, although no one could give him a concrete answer about it, they simply did not know it). Given that the Cuban protagonist of *Siberiana* was the representation of the West for his companions, it is interesting that neither Manuel nor his companions seem hardly cognizant of what exists beyond the confines of the "empire."

Manuel's possession of an official passport, the kind that Cubans who travel on government-sponsored programs carry, puts him in a complicated spot as he seeks asylum. Manuel's escape to Bern, Switzerland, is a failure because instead of asking for *political* asylum at the Red Cross office, he simply requests asylum, landing him back on a plane to Jarkov. Only after that misfortune does he realize that becoming a political asylum seeker — something he had resisted doing, as he did not wish to become a dissident "para agradar a aquellos capitalistas"[110] (to please those capitalists) — might save him from a bad end. The support that

Cuba maintains in the international sphere not only from Latin Americans but also from Europeans is a detriment to him. Manuel's experience in Sweden is altogether different from his experience in Switzerland—the Swedish official offers him unsolicited opinions about his desire to escape and the role of Cuba in the third world after the collapse of the USSR.

> Que usted es un gusano. Una rata que salta del barco y traiciona a su país ahora que la Unión Soviética se ha desplomado. Pero escúcheme bien, Cuba no se desplomará; no permiteremos que se desplome porque es la única esperanza del Tercer Mundo, y del nuestro.[111]

> That you are a *gusano*. A rat that jumps from the boat and betrays his country now that the USSR has collapsed. But listen to me carefully, Cuba will not collapse; we will not permit it to collapse because it is the only hope of the third world, and of ours.

Once again, Manuel's passport is returned with a stamp prohibiting his entry into the nation. To be called a "gusano" (worm, traitor) inclines him to use this derogatory epithet to his advantage—a strategic conversion that he painfully undertakes, "pensando que cubanos, rusos, suecos y suizos no le habían dejado otra alternativa"[112] (thinking that Cubans, Russians, Swedes, and Swiss had not left him another alternative). After his deportation to Poland, he goes to the US embassy, where he intends to seek asylum, only to face an equally frustrating situation. His only hope, that of becoming a "gusano," is not realized since, according to the officials at the US embassy in Poland, Poland was already considered the West. The "Americans" want more of Manuel—for him to divulge secrets about the enemy—but he refuses in order to remain faithful to his mentor, Derkáchev. Manuel finally finds refuge in Germany, having been helped by a German aid worker who recognizes his German ancestry. Between being just another refuge-seeking immigrant and confirming his German identity, he is exposed to the least friendly, yet not uncommon post-Communist experiences in the Eastern Bloc—a frightening encounter with fascist skinheads. In this way, *Las cuatro fugas de Manuel* also critiques the return of World War II phantoms in the no longer explicitly geographically or ideologically segmented post-Soviet East.

Manuel's existential turmoil can also be compared to that of Mario, the protagonist of *Callejones de Arbat*. As we have already seen, *The Master and Margarita* is a crucial subtext for Álvarez Gil's writing, but Bulgakov is not the only writer who suffered at the hands of totalitarianism and is resurrected by Álvarez Gil. Mario is a Cuban journalist on contract with the OCEI, "aquella organización que había simbolizado durante decenios la alternativa a la economía de mercado y la libertad de empresa como fuente de prosperidad y desarrollo material de las naciones en el mundo moderno"[113] (that organization that had symbolized for decades the alternative to the market economy and free enterprise as a source of prosperity and material development of nations in the modern world). When he travels to Moscow in 1989, he meets Dolores, a beautiful actress and the daughter of Santiago Álvarez, a Spanish republican translator who escaped to the USSR from Spain, and engages in an intense love affair with her, betraying his beloved wife Vera. A few months into their relationship, Dolores is offered the part of Margarita in a dramatization of Bulgakov's masterpiece. Mario's world opens up so much that he is forced to abandon his post and, by the end of the novel, ask for asylum in Canada for himself and his family.

*Callejones de Arbat* accuses the Cuban government of repressing the most prominent artistic and intellectual voices, drawing on Stalin's already-tested tactics. The heroic imitation described by Armenteros in 1970s Cuba acquires more pernicious dimensions in Álvarez Gil's novel, taking over the Cuban state apparatus. It is difficult to read Vera's tête-à-tête with the Cuban vice-minister about Soviet Perestroika without remembering Fernando Rojas's intervention in the debate on the fall of Socialism in Eastern Europe, published in *Temas* in 2004, concerning Stalin's centrality within the triumph over the Germans in the "Great Patriotic War." The novel's vice-minister states: "Todo eso que me estás diciendo es parte de una campaña de difamación contra el hombre que salvó a tu gran país de la invasión alemana"[114] (Everything you're telling me is part of a campaign of defamation against the man that saved your great country against the German invasion). Further on, he becomes even more impassioned: "Eran tiempos difíciles, de mucho peligro para la supervivencia del país, y que Stalin tenía que tener mano dura con la quinta columna enemiga que se le había formado en casa"[115] (They were difficult times, dangerous for the survival of the country, and Stalin had to have a strong hand with the fifth enemy column that had formed at home). This Cuban novel about Perestroika, Glasnost, and the present painfully reveals the consequences of the systems' logic.

Ariadna Efrón is the protagonist of the unnamed, unpublished, yet severely problematic novel within Álvarez Gil's novel, inhabited presumably by Marina Tsvetaeva, Boris Pasternak, Osip Mandelstam, Anna Akhmatova, Ivan Bunin, Vladimir Nabokov, Joseph Brodsky, and Nikolay Gumilev. A couple of these authors — Pasternak and Akhmatova — were actually published by Feijóo in his canonical *Poetas rusos y soviéticos* — a detail that reminds us that the divisions between what was read "officially" and "unofficially" are hardly as clear as they are sometimes made out to be. Most of these authors are the very same ones that are upheld by Cuban literati such as Reina María Rodríguez, from the island, as well as Juan Abreu and Jorge Ferrer, from Spain, who implement these figures as mechanisms of critique for their own nations.[116] The very thought that "la circunstancia de que el modelo cubano era un calco del soviético"[117] (the circumstance that the Cuban model is an exact replica of the Soviet model) leads Mario to his fate. The narrator expresses the crux of his problem:

> Ejemplos como el que acabo de citar en los casos de Pasternak y Mandelstam son una muestra de cómo el arrogante dictador se permite humillar al escritor rebelde. Los poemas laudatorios, las cartas de contrición y los reconocimientos públicos de culpa son sólo las aristas más visibles de vidas y talentos que se consumen y desaparecen en la artesa del poder totalitario. Desgraciadamente, la vida cultural de nuestro país no ha estado exenta de asuntos de esta guisa. Aunque no lo creo necesario, bien podría citar aquí varios casos de trato humillante y despótico hacia algunos escritores cubanos.[118]

> Examples like the one that I just cited in the cases of Pasternak and Mandelstam are a sample of how the arrogant dictator allows himself to humiliate the rebellious writer. The laudatory poems, the letters of contrition and the public acknowledgments of guilt are only the most visible edges of lives and talents that are consumed and disappear in the troughs of totalitarian power. Unfortunately, our country's cultural life has not been exempt from matters of this kind. Although I do not believe it necessary, I could well cite here various cases of humiliating and despotic treatment toward some Cuban writers.

Mario's outright condemnation of his own nation's manner of construing the limits of intellectual revolutionary practice is what gets him into trouble, since no system was being dismantled in Cuba. At no moment in the novel does Mario's awakening signify for him that he is against the heart of Socialist ideology—a crucial point for understanding *Callejones de Arbat* and *Cuatro fugas de Manuel*, as well as much current cultural production that reflects upon the Soviet period in Cuba as a means of thinking about the present. The force of *Callejones de Arbat* resides in its ability to depict the sensation felt by many Cuban intellectuals at the time of Perestroika—that Cubans could push forward within the Revolution through critical transformations.

### TIME IS MONEY ONLY FOR THOSE WITH MONEY

As we have already begun to see, no discussion of Cubans' memory of their contact with the Soviets and Russians can bypass José Manuel Prieto's oeuvre, the majority of which features a narrator whose nationality is difficult for others to pinpoint in addition to characters from the former Soviet Union and other parts of the Soviet Bloc, as well as from Europe and Asia.[119] Jorge Fornet is right on target when he suggests that "Prieto attributes to frivolity (a permanent theme in his texts) a devastating effect and a capital role in the 'explosion' of 1989."[120] Fornet's thesis draws heavily on *Nunca antes habías visto el rojo* (You've Never Seen Red like This Before), the only collection by Prieto that was published on the island, whose title Prieto appropriated from a *Vogue* magazine slogan. The structure of the story "Nunca antes habías visto el rojo" is distinctive; its footnotes and explanatory commentaries make it read like a kind of Borgesian-style philosophical treatise on the discovery of the joy of the commodity fetish. For instance,

> Salí a pasear a las diez de la mañana de un buen día de sol y tuve la suerte de encontrarme con Marina frente a los Grandes Almacenes del centro de la ciudad. Mi amiga lucía un magnífico vestido gris que le había comprado a unas gitanas durante un viaje a Tashkent. Era quizás la mejor prenda de su ajuar y le sentaba maravillosamente. Nunca sospechó que fuera del mismo Tashkent. Fui yo quien una vez descubrí la etiqueta verdadera bajo una falsa de la firma Dior.*
>
> > ... "*bajo una falsa de firma Dior.*" El mero contacto con ciertos objetos de una realidad no abandonada a su libre albedrío, sino organizada según criterio de calidad y nobleza estrictamente jerarquizados, inculcó en mí una fuerte noción de autenticidad, de segura valía; cambio mental que a la larga redundó benéficamente en la corrección de mis descuidados modales.[121]

> At ten o'clock on a fine sunny morning I went out for a stroll and, as luck would have it, ran into Marina in front of the big department stores in the city center. My friend was wearing a magnificent gray dress I'd bought for her from a band of gypsy women during a trip to Tashkent. It was probably the finest item in her wardrobe and suited her marvelously. I would never have dreamed that it actually was made in Tashkent. But I was the one to discover the real label beneath a fake one bearing the name Dior.*
>
> > *"beneath a fake tag bearing the name Dior." The mere contact with certain objects from a reality not left to its own devices but organized by strictly hierarchical criteria of quality and aristocracy instilled in me a strong notion of authenticity and solid value—a mental transformation which, over time, had a beneficial and corrective effect on my careless habits.[122]

Contact with the commodity lends the Socialist subject "a strong notion of authenticity" and restores his connection to the aura of the West—a relationship that may seem paradoxical given the extent to which authenticity is conventionally understood as a natural entity. The commodity circuit is based upon repetition, and here, "authenticity" is rendered through the subject's imagining of an external hierarchy.

Upon traveling to the East, Prieto takes home a tale that cautions Cubans against living only for the "future" and not appreciating the "frivolity" within life. In the novel *Enciclopedia de una vida en Rusia*, which indulges the theme of frivolity, the protagonist reflects upon the disintegration of the "Empire":

> Es decir, se evidenció un profundo antagonismo entre el quietismo de la Doctrina y el vertiginoso escándalo de los pañales desechables; entre la búsqueda de un reino de verdad en la Tierra y la "línea general" del siglo, que era consumir el presente, considerar el futuro una mera realidad mental. Los pueblos cautivos del Imperio se asomaban a la noche oscura y al mar cargado de gratos efluvios por el que avanzaba la nave iluminada que era el carnaval permanente de Occidente, y suspiraban pensativos: "Sí, está en vías de descomposición . . . Pero ¡qué bien huele!¹²³

> That is to say, a profound antagonism was evidenced between the quietism of the Doctrine and the vertiginous scandal of disposable diapers; between the search for a kingdom of truth on Earth and the "general line" of the century, which was to consume the present, to consider the future a mere mental reality. The captive peoples of the Empire came out to the dark night and to the sea loaded with pleasant effluvia through which the illuminated ship that was the permanent carnival of the Occident advanced, and they sighed pensively: "Yes, it is in the process of decomposition . . . But it smells so good!

This passage captures the essence of not only *Enciclopedia de una vida en Rusia* but also *Nunca antes habías visto el rojo*, *Treinta días en Moscú*, and to some extent, *Livadia*, wherein the imposition of the Soviet brand creates the libidinal desire for the prohibited—the Occident's brand.

In *Rex*, something else happens altogether: the protagonist does not suddenly yearn for the Soviet brand, but rather is antagonistic toward the overarching ideology of capitalism without limits (lived by Russians who are new to this game), and his position within this system as someone who relies on it, yet is only vaguely central to it. His need for money obliges him to write only "commentaries" and not "original" texts. Anke Birkenmaier brilliantly articulates the preceptor's relationship to money vis-à-vis his perception of his student, Petya, and authorship.

> Money is what distinguishes the preceptor from his pupil Petia: for lack of money he has to work as a teacher and worry about his salary, whereas Petia, thanks to his parents, is rich and will have the leisure to dedicate himself to writing and reading only. The Russian nationality of the family is here certainly an allusion to the new possibilities that Russians have had since 1989 to advance socially and materially, whereas Cubans are not yet in the same position. Consequently, their concerns and modes of writing are different. The preceptor himself is tied to the pastiche, whereas Petia will be the one able to write a book not in the manner of Proust or Borges, but a primary text, a text about time, not money: "Tú, Petia, que fácilmente podrías escribirlo, un libro real, un libro primario, sin comentarios ni citas en cursiva y sin que en página alguna de ese libro, en ninguno de los pliegues de tu memoria adulta, quedara y alumbrara desde allí, con el negro brillo de su nombre, el comentarista" (224–225).[124] This is the perspective with which the novel ends, with the preceptor correcting himself jokingly: "¿En búsqueda del dinero perdido? (no, vulgar y detestable. Mejor del tiempo). Tienes razón, Petia, del tiempo."*

> *In search of lost money? (No that would be vulgar and loathsome. Better to seek time.) You're right, Petya. Time.[125]

The ending of this passage is a wink at the author's positioning in the United States, wherein the phrase "time is money" is perfectly understandable for those who already have enough money. In a way, Prieto's trajectory is taking him closer to Cuba in the last novel of the trilogy *Rex*, where he ends up residing in what is supposed to be the antithesis of Cuban ideology—American capitalism, and it is from that perspective of late capitalism that he is able to explain to Petya why he should value time.

Cubans' present and future is often told through their anecdotes about life in the Socialist Bloc, what Jorge I. Domínguez in "The Political Impact on Cuba of the Reform and Collapse of Communist Regimes" calls "Aesopian language."[126] Britton Newman asks to what degree Russia may be read as a "stand-in for his native Cuba."[127] At the same time that Prieto's works ought to be read in conjunction with this body of Cuban literature as Aesopian, it forms part of a body of post-Socialist and late-capitalist twenty-first century literature written around the globe. Even Prieto's earliest writing catapults into a future wherein Cuba is decentralized and in direct dialogue with other peoples. Prieto's writing is also characterized by a post-Communist anxiety of inheritance and an obsession with private realms.

Prieto captures the rhetoric of memorialization of Soviet times in the days of the new Russian republic in a unique way. In *Treinta días en Moscú*, he describes reading in a metro train a newspaper article's recollection of the value of publicity in Soviet times. The account demarcates for its readers—citizens of the new Russian republic—the transformation from Soviet to Russian times. While in the past, national production was overvalued and omnipresent as exemplified in the slogan "'Soviético quiere decir excelente' . . . En los noventa la situación cambió drásticamente, la publicidad se ha convertido en parte insustituible del paisaje urbano"[128] ("Soviet means excellent" . . . In the nineties the situation changed drastically, and advertising has become an irreplaceable part of the urban landscape). This interpretive panorama contrasts sharply with that of Ulises Rodríguez Febles's *Sputnik*, whose characters are lost without the Soviet newspapers upon which they previously relied to explain their universe. Prieto's Russian newspaper reveals a present that is substantiated through the narrator's own observations of the world around him. His exit from the metro results in encounters with glossy magazines such as *Domovoi, Cosmopolitan,* and *Vogue,* the new visual language through which the protagonists of Prieto's *Enciclopedia de una vida en Rusia* and *Livadia* attempt to inscribe themselves.

One of the traveler's interviewees in *Treinta días* is Tom Klaim, who, having been born with the name Tolia Klimov, branded himself as Klaim in Canada. While much of the information provided in Prieto's character and location sketches corresponds precisely to extratextual reality, the company Tom Klaim was actually founded by a Russian named Anatoly Klimin, a minor discrepancy that makes it difficult to trust entirely in the narrator. Is Prieto really the narrator? The narrator's conversation with Klaim, the penultimate that he has in Moscow on his thirty-day journey, sets him over the edge. It is as if he has seen in Klaim, and in some of the other personages of the Russian capital, aspects of himself that he abandoned seven years prior when he left the country and abandoned the accelerated and chaotic transition from Socialism to capitalism. Referring to, among other antiquated habits, having sold contraband, the narrator of *Treinta días* says he no longer feels capable of negotiating with the same sorts of vulgar people.

The narrator of *Treinta días* asserts his tentative belonging to the West with his purchase of Smirnov vodka, an "empire" that transformed enormously after the disintegration of the Soviet Union. After the Russian Revolution forbade private enterprise, one branch of the Smirnov vodka company moved first to France, transformed into Smirnoff, and then moved once again, this time to the US. However, post-1991, the Smirnov family in Russia started its business up again. The narrator's fixation on the Smirnov bottle—like his unsuccessful search for authentic Russian goods at the market—denotes his distance from the source. He no longer needs to pass within a society that is itself bent on passing for the West.


CONCLUSION

These fictionalized accounts by travelers to the Soviet Union accomplish several tasks. Their transnational readings of race, projected onto Russian chauvinistic attitudes, reveal the persistence of prejudicial sentiments toward race within Cuba. They also establish highly attuned parameters of proximity and distance by way of mediating habits of reading Soviet literature, patterns of belonging to one's individual country and to the Socialist Bloc, and modes of punishment. The incorporation of Russian words (and, in the case of *Las cuatro fugas*, Ukrainian words as well) into their primarily Spanish-language texts is not as prevalent in the works of Cuban writers who did not live in Soviet territory and only accessed the Russian-speaking universe through translation and films, or in public realms, such as on city buses. This fiction suggests the extent to which linguistic worlds were penetrated by the language of empire. Furthermore, the fiction of Perestroika and Glasnost by Armenteros, Díaz, and Álvarez Gil illustrates the ways in which Cuban modes of punishment and dissidence were informed by Cuba's solidarity with the Soviet Union.

CHAPTER FOUR

# *"Made in USSR"*

$A$fter a presentation entitled "Intermediarios cubanos" (Cuban Intermediaries, or Brokers) that I delivered in April 2007 at the Torre de Letras in Havana, the space of literary and cultural encounters directed by Reina María Rodríguez and sponsored by the Cuban Book Institute, a debate ensued about the weight of the Socialist Bloc's influence in Cuba that rested on a confusion between the terms "influence" and "memory." Some of the older audience members could not distinguish memory, as an abundance of discrepant and illusory resonances, from influence, understood as a positive, integral acquisition, an authorized inheritance. They could hardly conceive of "youngsters" (already pushing middle age) truly assimilating Socialist Bloc cartoons—representative of the Soviet television aegis of the 1970s and 1980s—nor could they fathom that such a memory is not so easy to dismiss or exchange. For many who were young adults in the 1980s, zones of the "Great Soviet" from which they wanted to distance themselves in the beginning of the 1990s have now turned into objects of parody and intimate affection, even becoming signs of identity possessing many levels that are not easy to deconstruct.

Generations "become" generations for many reasons, one of which relates to sentimental attachment to cultural and fashion trends. Associations with particular cartoons are significant for identity formation, as Mario Masvidal Saavedra, the professor of the Instituto Superior de Artes in Havana, astutely remarks:

> In Cuba one could classify sociologically distinct generations in the twentieth century according to the cartoons that marked their infancy and adolescence. Accordingly, there'd be a first generation, born in the first quarter of the last century that grew up with silent cartoons—then later with sound—Mickey Mouse, Donald Duck, Felix the Cat, Snow

White, the clown Bimbo and Betty Boop, made by the famed North American artists like Walt Disney and Max Fleischer . . . Then come the generations born after 1959, a time in which the flow to Cuba of North American audiovisual material was abruptly interrupted as a consequence of the "dispute" (blockade, embargo, military invasion, economic sabotage, terrorism, etc.) of the United States against Cuba, a flow that was gradually substituted by the film and animation of Socialist countries. It was the period of the so-called *muñequitos rusos*, the generic tag with which both Soviet cartoons and those that originated in Eastern European were designated, such as *The Fröhlich Family* (GDR), *Gustav* (Hungary), *The Adventures of Aladar Mezga* (Hungary), *Pat & Mat* (Czechoslovakia),[1] *Bolek and Lolek* (Poland), among others. Much has been said about the omnipresence of the *muñequitos rusos* in the Cuban media, above all during the 1970s and 1980s. In fact, there is a surprising nostalgia, distinguished by "found" sentiments of attraction and avoidance, in a whole generation with respect to those cartoons; an adoration that approaches paroxysms of collecting and cultism among young Cubans in their thirties inside and outside of the island.[2]

According to Masvidal Saavedra, Japanese cartoons, which entered Cuba through official circuits at the end of the 1970s and into the 1980s, captured the imaginations of young artists and designers in the first decade of the twenty-first century. They were collected, downloaded, burned, and passed around in a manner that resembles the circulation of Soviet Bloc cartoons. The similarities stop there, first and foremost because of the prior omnisapience of the Soviets.

Unlike some other elements of Cubanness that possess distinct insular or diasporic components, fascination with *muñequitos rusos* manifests itself similarly on and off the island. It may come as a surprise that in Miami—a town in which the earliest of exiles blamed the Soviets for robbing them of their country—another generation of émigrés has actually sought out copies of *muñequitos rusos* in Little Havana, which end up forming part of an elaborate material culture in the Cuban exile community.[3] The commodity circuit in which they circulate in the US is actually comparable to Cuba's. Most of the DVDs on sale are pirated, and some of them may have even been acquired as cultural remittances not *to*, but *from* the island. In this gesture, perhaps, more than any other, the Soviet cartoons' substituting for the autochthonous sphere becomes most vivid. Duanel Díaz Infante has critiqued the significance of consumption of *muñequitos rusos* in Miami: "It's evidently about a significant sociological phenomenon: in Miami it has become customary to rent *muñequitos rusos* along with Cuban television programs from the past and from today, while in Havana what's offered in clandestine video shops are programs from 'over there' [that is, the US]."[4] Díaz Infante assesses well Cubans' desire to make their fragmented world whole again through keeping abreast of each other's television programs, but, as much contemporary fiction suggests, Díaz Infante also overestimates the difference between exiles and islanders regarding their relationship to *muñequitos rusos*, and in so doing, distances himself from those exiles who are dependent upon saccharine reminders of their homeland to feel Cuban—an assessment that is comprehensible, given that the craze was initially cast as such.

Díaz Infante relies, in part, on Ivette Leyva Martínez's 2003 report, published in *Encuentro en la red*, on the strange trend of renting *muñequitos rusos* at the start of the millennium in Miami, what she calls "little nostalgias of Castrism."[5] Soviet Bloc cartoons can easily be inserted in the following list of material culture delineated by Raúl Rubio as essential to the staging and commodification of Cuban culture:

> Stores like *Sentir Cubano* (http://www.sentircubano.com) or Little Havana-to-Go (http://www.littlehavanatogo.com) specifically target consumers of Cuban material culture or "cubana" and offer a variety of products from memorabilia to domino games to food products, including Conchita, Bustelo, Badía, and Goya brands. There are also female dolls available in three styles, all stylized after the traditionally-marketed women stereotypes: a *cubana santera*, a *cubana rumbera*, and a *cubana cabaretera* (cabaret dancer). A selection of T-shirts replicates vintage styles that bring to memory sporting clubs from the 1940s and 1950s such as The Havana Yacht Club and the Marianao baseball team.[6]

When Soviet cartoons are added to this inventory, the notion of replicating and staging Cuban identity is transformed, since Soviet memorabilia is identified neither with the old bourgeoisie nor with Afro-Cuban culture. The ideological component of the Soviets might appear to be "sent off the field" when the cartoons are sold alongside these other products, but that is not entirely the case.

The phenomenon of the *muñequitos rusos* is an important dimension of the Cuban zeitgeist of the last decade of the twentieth century and the first decade of the new millennium that links the children of the Soviet diaspora in Cuba to their Cuban peers of the same age. Antón Vélez Bichkov presented "¿Son rusos los muñequitos?" (Are the Cartoons Russian?), one of the earliest investigations on the cartoons, at the 2004 Koniec Conference of the Soviet Diaspora in Cuba, in which he argued against Cubans' erroneous grouping together of the cartoons under the rubric of Russia. For him, that inaccuracy reflects "a heavy inheritance from the era of capitalism and consequently from anti-

Communism that came to identify all of the Left with the Soviets and all the Soviet with Russia." Vélez Bichkov's assessment corresponds to Abel Prieto's notion about the lasting effects of the negative influence of the United States on Cubans' aesthetic taste and their definitions of entertainment.[7]

In *At Home in the World: Cosmopolitanism Now*, Timothy Brennan raises interesting questions about Socialism's ability to "offer pleasure," arguing that Carpentier was at the vanguard of forging a popular and mass Cuban culture through the continual reinvention of the "indigenous." According to Brennan, Carpentier's models for globally disseminating a mass culture that is not necessarily tied to capitalism are evident within the revival of 1940s *filin* in the 1960s, imperfect cinema, *nueva trova*, and salsa. Brennan's focus on the "relationship to fantasy associated in advance with the libidinal free play and spectacle of image capitalism" and the necessity of "unearth[ing] or explain[ing] more fully, the forms of alternative desire that socialist movements and societies have actually created, and are still creating" is fascinating for the discussion of *muñequitos rusos*.[8] Brennan is right on the mark when he asserts that "relief from consumerism (rather than escape from its lack) is what early Cuba represented."[9] The pleasure taken in the Soviet Bloc cartoons is easier to discern in retrospect, once those television viewers grow up. Most would agree that Cuba has not been able to deliver what, as children, they might have imagined it would. While it would be easy to posit an ideological division between the function of *muñequitos* within a Socialist island and a capitalist abroad, such a division would be unduly reductive. The *muñequitos rusos* craze can actually be viewed as another strange invention of the "indigenous Cubans" who "desire" to assert their difference from the rest of the globalizing world.

The sociological and political implications of the fascination with *muñequitos rusos* in the new millennium are far-reaching. Let us start with an intervention on a portal launched in 2007 by the name of "Generación Asere," which roughly translates as "Generation Mate," referring to the refrain popularized in the 1990s, "¿Qué bola, asere?" (What's up, man?). The portal envisions itself as breaking down distinctions between Cubans on the island and in the diaspora. However, its subtitle — "Blogoestroika Is Internet for Cubans" — is of even greater consequence, as it speaks to strategically intersected histories by appropriating the term "Perestroika" for a neologism that suggests the centrality of blogs to a more democratic Cuba. The documentary *Good Bye, Lolek* — the culmination of the *muñequitos* craze — captured the attention of Generación Asere.

> The documentary *Goodbye, Lolek!* (2005) by the creators Asori Soto and Magdiel Aspillaga (who recently arrived in Miami) retakes the pretext of nostalgia to dive into one of the mainstays of the Socialist education

that formed various generations of Cubans, beneath the crazy thesis of entertaining "ideologically" millions of little pioneers. Was it, by chance, an entertaining punishment? Or is Roly right, when he affirms in the documentary, "it was just a saying that it was obligatory to watch the *muñequitos rusos*"? The obligatory programming on Channel 21 on national television, of that material carrying a Socialist moral that could only be seen in "black and white" was a governmental attempt at transculturation by force. In the middle of those tropics of extroverted infantile wanderers, they almost made us crazy by obliging us to decipher the codes of that far-away Slavic identity.[10]

Generación Asere's questioning of whether the dissemination of *muñequitos rusos* in the 1970s and 1980s should be considered "transculturation by force" has its counterpart in Aurora Jácome's popular blog about Soviet Bloc cartoons, launched in Spain: *Muñequitos rusos . . . y otros: Para los cubanos que como yo, los siguen recordando con añoranza.*

In "The *Muñequitos Rusos* Generation," Jácome affirms that "these cartoons opened our eyes to that other world, toward those other ways of thinking and expression, which—even though it seems implausible—make us have more in common with someone from Poland than someone from Spain" (33). Jácome's blog, in which she goes by the screen name "Akekure," expresses similar sentiments. Jácome was born in Cuba but has lived in Spain, a country that shares both her native language and her family's genealogy, since she was sixteen years old, a combination of experiences that has shaped her awareness of the idiosyncrasies of her Cuban identity. She eventually came to feel more commonalities with former inhabitants of the Eastern Bloc than with her "new" compatriots. This admission is especially interesting, given Cubans' increasing claims to Spanish bloodlines during the Special Period and beyond as an attempt to escape the scarcities on the island and given the fact, too, that those who actually traveled to the Soviet Union manifested tremendously mixed visions, as has been shown, with regard to their own geopolitical affinities.

Displaying a specialized knowledge of Soviet visual arts, Jácome's blog has become a forum for her readers to dialogue about, yearn for, and rehearse the leftovers of the Soviet within themselves. Although many of the correspondents say they never truly liked the cartoons, it is impossible to doubt their function as symbolic glue in today's world. While the blog is not explicitly political, its implications are apparently conflictive enough for it to have inspired a parody. Using the screen name "Auroro Jacomino," another blog under the same title and logo, but with a different subtitle—"Para los comunistas como yo que seguimos recordando revolucionariamente" (For the Communists like Myself That Continue Remembering Revolutionarily)—mocks what it views as the political naïveté of Jácome's blog, a perspective that might be especially compelling for those who lived as adults through the most repressive years of Sovietization. However, a less polarized look at Jácome's blog might suggest that she is not blind to the political implications of the *muñequitos rusos*. "For our parents, the daily presence of Russian cartoons on the small screen at the designated children's hour was just another of the Revolution's impositions with regard to cultural politics."[11] The symbolic value of Jácome's blog is immense. Her first entry, on November 26, 2005, entitled "Compartiendo un 'trauma'" (Sharing a Trauma), generated hundreds of comments, many of which attest to the nostalgia that many Cubans—those in the diaspora but also those on the island—feel for some aspects of the Soviet epoch of their youth. While there is consensus that more than a generation lived in Cuba beneath a "Soviet television aegis," the emotions generated by that fact differ. Given that access to the Internet in Cuba was first ideologically and then economically restrictive, it is not surprising that more commentaries are written from outside of the island. Soon after Jácome launched her blog, copied and pasted entries from it circulated as e-mail among Cubans who live on the island, suggesting that the phenomenon is far from exclusively geographically demarcated. Furthermore, keeping abreast of the memorialization of the Soviets and Russians on the island, and not limited to the realm of animation per se, the blog has become a rich resource wherein geopolitical divisions are blurred. For example, the blog enthusiastically announced the 2010 Cuban book fair release of a new edition of *Cuentos populares rusos* (Popular Russian Tales), by Aleksander Nikolayevich Afanasyev, with illustrations by Cuban artists. Jácome also traces the popularity in today's Japan of Cheburashka, originally the funny little bear-like protagonist of Eduard Uspensky's Russian children's story of 1966, which became a widely disseminated children's series a few years later.

Jácome's blog is just one of many virtual spaces where the reaction to *muñequitos rusos* is rehearsed. The phenomenon has mushroomed, and in August 2008, just as the frequency of Jácome's posts was dwindling, Carlos R. Dueñas launched "Bolek y Lolek en la vía lacteal" (Bolek and Lolek in the Milky Way), a Facebook discussion group that is less honed and personal than Jácome's but that shows the power of these debates and the degree to which cartoons serve as cultural interrogators. One Facebooker, for instance, implicitly contests a refrain made popular by the Cuban comedian Enrique Arredondo in his role as Bernabé: "Si no te portas bien, te voy a castigar viendo muñequitos rusos" (If you don't behave, I'll punish you by making you watch the *muñequitos rusos*). She remarks in Spanish: "How many memories of *Bolek and Lolek*!!!! How they entertained me every day of my youth at six in the afternoon for an hour. There were times when they repeated them since there weren't many, but I always liked them" (May 22, 2010). A few other posts rejoice in the accessibility of Soviet Bloc cartoons through YouTube, which enables their children to get a glimpse into their parents' childhood. One of the heartiest of invitations to partake in the virtual community of fans is Yanelima's cartoon collection, dedicated to "all those older than thirty who grew up watching these cartoons, like myself and many Cubans, who anxiously waited for it to be 6 pm to sit down at the television and delight in the thrill of watching them."[12] Such unrestrained joy may be difficult to imagine upon recalling that Arredondo was suspended from his role as Bernabé on the television program *Detrás de la fachada* for voicing, in comedic fashion, people's bitterness toward the Soviet version of entertainment.[13]

### KONIEC(K) AGAIN

The song "Los músicos de Bremen" (Bremen-Town Musicians), by the controversial Cuban rock group Porno para Ricardo (Porn for Ricardo), and its accompanying video, directed by Ernesto René,[14] concludes with the word "*Koniek*," meaning "end" in Russian — the same word, with the difference of the final consonant, that was utilized by the Cuban-Soviet Mir Project, discussed in Chapter 1.[15] Porno para Ricardo garnered international attention when the group's charismatic lead singer, Gorki Luis Águila Carrasco, was sentenced to four years in prison in 2003.[16] Released in 2005, with immense support from abroad, Gorki was arrested again in 2008 on charges of "*peligrosidad*" (dangerousness). The band's message undoubtedly became more directly anti-Castrist in the aftermath of Gorki's first arrest, a process that can be compared to the conversion experiences of the protagonists in both Jesús Díaz's and Antonio Álvarez Gil's novels.

The band found its acerbic voice by combining references to the early 1990s US punk/metal band Porno for Pyros, Lou Reed, the Communist International, and Russian cartoons. Specifically, "Los músicos de Bremen" plays with the 1969 Soviet cartoon adaptation of the Brothers Grimm fairy tale of the same title, delivered punk-rock style in the language of this other idiosyncratic people whose cultural codes were so distinct from Cuba's that they could not communicate with one other.

While many renditions of "Los músicos de Bremen" exist, one of the earliest and most contestatory can be heard in the 1990s performance entitled "Los muñequitos rusos," by the Cuban comedy group Punto y Coma, which appropriates the melody of the famous theme song of the cartoon to critique Cuba's travel restrictions. Punto y Coma enacts a fictional travelogue of its journey to the numerous cities in what was once the Soviet Union. Not surprisingly, the group returns with stories ridiculing previous failures and present transforma-

*Still from the 2001 video* Los músicos de
Bremen, *by Porno para Ricardo; directed
by Ernesto René.*

tions. Punto y Coma comments upon the economy at the Ukraine Farmers'
Market, saying that in Chernobyl they encountered a sign that read "Estamos
para Tarará" (We Are in Tarará), referring to the area to the east of the Cuban
capital where victims from the Ukraine, Russia, and Belarus were sent after the
disaster in 1986. Without a public, they admit, they could not perform there.
Their observation of the change in ideology is simply put: the color "red" has
disappeared, the films have improved, and when you say hello to the people,
they respond in English with "yes, yes, yes." At the end of the song, the group
explains that the cartoon characters recycled themselves during the Special
Period and became tourism workers or small-time gasoline vendors. As we observed with the matrioshkas, which are used to tell Cubans' stories of transformation, Punto y Coma envisions the *muñequitos rusos* as exemplary of the
Cubans' post-Soviet plight.[17]

The video for Porno para Ricardo's "Los músicos de Bremen" is filled with
images of everything journalistic reports insisted Cubans were excited to see
go — Soviet pedagogy, red stars, the hammer and sickle. At the beginning
of René's video, which in 2002 was nominated for the national music video
awards, Los Premios Lucas, rapid clips ground spectators in cartoons that are
playing on an old Soviet television. The camera zooms in on a map of the Soviet
Union in a classroom, where the musicians pose as nerdy-looking Cubans. The
celebration begins once the band members get out of their school uniforms for
the *pre-universitario* Lenin school, the Russian school that included both *primaria* and *secundaria* — reflecting an imperfect uniformity reminiscent of the
1960s aesthetics of hunger — and refashion themselves as boldly diverse and
modern-day individuals in a Havana that belongs to the world.[18] These disguises
function as a means for the musical tourists in history to travel to the past and
reconnect with that world. Unlike Jácome, who rejoices in her difference from
the rest of the world on account of an exotic *muñequitos* sphere made her own,
Porno para Ricardo enters into the cartoons comedically in order to highlight
their absurdity.

In the video, a young girl's off-screen voice can be heard asking her father a

*Still from the 2001 video* Los músicos de Bremen, *by Porno para Ricardo; directed by Ernesto René.*

question, the response to which one expects to find in what at first sounds like a serious and patriotic Soviet anthem, but instead, the music turns into a punk-rock version of the theme song of the cartoon *Bremen-Town Musicians*. The video reflects the deterioration of the ideological dream through its portrayal of a run-down material culture. The abandonment and isolation that emerge out of an experience of insularity as well as out of the government's restrictive travel policies are easily read. In contrast to the more quaint beginning of the recording of the song on Porno para Ricardo's 2002 *Rock para las masas . . . (cárnicas)* album, sounds of static introduce the struggle to get reception. The video's principal female protagonist, who may be interpreted as the girl from the initial scene now grown up, stands on a rooftop talking on a cordless phone as she watches cartoon figurines of airplanes and birds fly away. Then she points the antenna toward the planes, desperately begging for a signal to communicate with the world, reminding spectators of the video's initial static. The video cuts to scenes in which she labors to traverse the city. Her appearance is exaggerated, cartoon-like; but the message is serious: the problem of transportation in Havana and, by proxy, that problem throughout the country and from the country to the exterior. Transportation has been one of the most pressing socioeconomic problems facing the nation, and only in 2005, with the support of Venezuela, did Cuba begin purchasing great quantities of buses from China, which has helped improve the situation.[19]

The possibility of travel to the Soviet Bloc for educational and professional reasons, or even as a reward for the most hardworking Cubans, is an ideological dream of the past, while the removal of these possibilities represents an acute sense of isolation. Both of these feelings are perceptible within the video's visual and musical pastiche. Superimposed cartoon-like images of the moon, birds, and airplanes point to an expansive temporal and spatial framework and to "cracks" in the legacy of Soviet history. Male subjects digging up the urban streets comment not only on the chaotic present, in which urban space is in such a state of disrepair that it looks like the countryside, but also on the 1970s

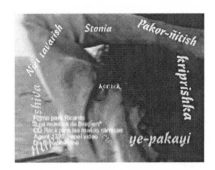

*Still from the 2001 video* Los músicos de Bremen, *by Porno para Ricardo; directed by Ernesto René.*

sugar harvests, remembered in a uniquely warm and empathic manner. This attitude toward these harvests, perhaps somewhat startling to outsiders, who are more familiar with the human oppression associated with such desired agricultural outcomes, can be explained partially by the temporal distance, but also by the last decade's less than sanguine experiences of a dual economy. As if in an ideological and aesthetic flashback, red paint is splattered in the room where the band is performing. The video stylizes the rhetoric of Cuban productivity that was so closely linked to the Soviet Union. The resulting differences between the haves and the have-nots undoubtedly temper the artists' recollection of their youth and of the universal, Soviet-style idealism with which they were inculcated. The gaze of the video's director reflects an element of insane harmony in the strange, collage-like experience. The video humorously concludes with a display of words, including *"Pashiva"* (thank you), *"Stonia"* (Estonia), *"Kroacia"* (Croatia), and finally *"Koniek."*

While stagnancy and immobility—thematic staples in representations of Cuba—are concerns of this three-minute video, so are cultural movements that contrast with the imposition of capitalism implied by the term "transition." The bubbly red and white letters that dance across one of the final segments of the video, declaring "esta guitarra es rusa" (this guitar is Russian), clearly allude to the principal trade relations with the Soviets. While this token of remnants could be taken as a sign that soon the Soviet past will dance off the stage entirely, it is important to archive this seemingly minor detail, prior to Gorki's own "dissidentization" and the Russians' renewed ties with Cubans. Furthermore, this video manifests competing pleasures: the musicians may look and sound like fools singing in a different language, one that their country had once appropriated, but the video also recalls national naïveté within such an aspiration of solidarity. The transition to modern-day world citizens is evidenced through the decor of the apartment where friends gather—a Marilyn Monroe poster is on the wall where the celebration takes place. A dark-skinned Cuban man is playing percussion on the beach. These two images allude to capitalist entertainment as well as identity politics, which had been cast aside in the Cuban cultural politics of the Soviet period.

To the likes of Heberto Padilla, Reina María Rodríguez, and Jorge Ferrer—a small sampling of the many Cubans who have echoed contestatory voices from the Soviet Bloc in their writing—can be added Ciro Díaz Penedo, Porno para Ricardo's lead guitarist and co-composer. Voices of Soviet Bloc dissidents pervade Díaz Penedo's music, particularly his side project, a band called La Babosa Azul (The Blue Slug). The story begins with his encounter with Gisela Delgado Sabión, one of the Damas de Blanco (activist wives of the political prisoners in Cuba), who encourages him to seek support for his music from the Polish embassy. The embassy tells him that it would consider doing so if his music can be linked to Polish culture.[20] Out of this came La Babosa Azul's 2007 album, *Cuando Amanezca el Día* (When the Day Breaks), inspired by Jacek Kaczmarski, one of the most renowned contestatory voices from Poland, whose hero was Vysotsky, already famous in Cuba. *Cuando Amanezca el Día* contains numerous songs by both Vysotsky and Kaczmarski, including Kaczmarski's "Epitafio para Vladimir Vysostsky" (Epitaph for Vladimir Vysotsky). This intentional recycling of protest voices from the East can be linked to the new alliances that have formed between Cuban dissidents and those from the former Soviet Bloc countries, especially the Czech Republic and Poland. The Czech Republic's involvement peaked with the creation of the International Committee for Democracy in Cuba (see http://www.icdcprague.org), led by former president Václav Havel, and the PIN (People in Need) project, both of which formed in 2003 after the Cuban government's crackdown on independent journalists. Poland's solidarity with Cuban dissidence is evidenced in the portal "Solidarity with Cuba" (see http://www.solidarnizkuba.pl/en/), which features communiqués from the former trade union organizer and president Lech Walesa to the Cuban people. The relationship between the Cuban so-called underground and Eastern Europe has been definitively shaped by the dissident voices of the past.

## TRAPPED IN CHEBURASHKA

If the imaginary and real travelers of Chapters 2 and 3 oscillate between their positioning within the East and West, these artists, born between the mid-1960s and the 1980s, deliberately fashion themselves on a symbolic geographic level, utilizing a product from the "East." Perhaps Wendy Guerra, born in 1970, is the most "fashioned" internationally as the spokeswoman for her generation, having been awarded in France in 2010 the Chevalier de l'Ordre des Arts et des Lettres. Interestingly enough, she confessed—an act with which readers of her fiction are familiar—to the interviewer of a Chilean magazine: "My problem is telling the truth. Perhaps no one is listening in on my phone call, and I am a psychopath. On the other hand, you say that you're going here and you're really there. I don't mean in Chile, but in the West. I don't live in the West, I live in Cuba."[21] This sense of displacement relates to the former ties between Cuba and Eastern Europe and their impact on the psychology of a subject who came of age in the 1980s. Guerra detaches Cuba from its "natural" position in the American continent.

For Nieve Guerra, the young protagonist in Guerra's first novel, *Todos se van* (They All Leave), the Russian cartoons are presented not just as important television programs, but as a requisite in her school curriculum. Nieve's teacher requires her to write a composition about them, and because her mother neither has enough money to buy a television nor the desire to do so, Nieve's classmate does her the favor of giving her a list of the cartoons' titles, the characters' names, and in addition, invites her over to see them. This detail leads us to question whether Cubans' feelings about the Soviets are as homogenous and benign as Abel Prieto makes them out to be. The division between public space (characterized by imposed obligations, for example, the need to possess a television to be part of the collective) and private space (characterized by creativity and the sensation that the very division is vital to survival) suggests that Cuban society was not entirely exempt from imitating the Soviet model.

Yoani Sánchez is undoubtedly the most famous Cuban dissident of the new millennium, and on her website, Generation Y, she expresses her own opinion of the impact of Sovietization in Cuba today.

> Many of our parents had studied or worked in the USSR, but we did not know of borsht soup nor did we like vodka, and everything "Soviet" seemed to us to be old-fashioned, rigid and passé. What paralyzed us about them was the bear-like power that emanated from their gestures and the veiled warning with which they sustained our Caribbean "paradise."
>
> The mixture of fear and mockery that the Bolos generated in us still remains. If today a tourist who wanders through the city does not want to be bothered by persistent sellers of tobacco, sex or rum, he only has to whisper something like "Tavarich," "Niet ponimayo" and the startled seller will melt away.[22]

While Sánchez's visceral and bitter tone toward the Soviet culture contrasts with Jácome's, like Abel Prieto, she typecasts the Soviets as members of a rudimentary world. It is difficult to believe, however, that Sánchez, born in 1975, could herself have been witness to so much bad taste and arrogance. More likely, she and her fellow companions of Generation Y assimilated their parents' sentiments and their society's posthumous publicized antipathy toward the Soviets.

The honorable mention of La Gaceta prize in 2006, the same year that Martínez Shvietsova won for "17 abstractos de una agenda," went to "Sobre Sovexportfilm" (About Sovexportfilm), a short story by Rubén Rodríguez, an author who, born in 1969, resides in Holguín, Cuba. Sovexportfilm was the state organization that dealt with the export and import of films, and Rodríguez's characters act as if they were within cartoons from the Soviet Bloc. Through its extraordinary intertextuality, the characters develop, and the contexts they inhabit are created.

> ¿Para qué quieren los ciegos la luz?
> "Para nada," se responde como el topo del muñequito ruso que ha visto cien veces, pues con otros pájaros suele reunirse a ver viejos dibujos animados soviéticos que les prestan en la cinemateca, en un proyector hurtado de un cine de barrio. Siempre los mismos.[23]

> Why do blind people want light?
> "For no reason," he responds like the mole from the cartoon that he has seen a hundred times. He often gets together with other fags to watch old Soviet cartoons that they lend them at the Cinemateca, on a projector stolen from a theater in the neighborhood. Always the same ones.

Once the cartoons are no longer used for the purpose of teaching a civic and ethical code, they return with a new function. A selected repetition occurs at the beginning of the story; that is, the "decision" to watch again and again the same old Soviet cartoons. However, this decision is somewhat faulty, because even in the aftermath, without the Soviets, the options for enjoyment for these aging homosexuals on the island are not limitless.

The imagination of the homosexual protagonist, Michel, is intimately and intricately involved in the Soviet cultural penetration within Cuba. Upon discussing his regular cosmetic habit of shaving his member in order to make it appear larger, he resorts to the Soviet cartoons, as if they were a remedy for his erotic antics: "Pero él es libre como el arroyuelo gozón y primaveral de aquel dibujo animado, producido por los estudios *Soyuzmultfilm* y doblado en los estudios *Filmexport*, con texto en español de Katia Olévskaya"[24] (But he is as free as the little joyful and springlike creek from that cartoon produced by Soyuzmultfilm studios and dubbed by Filmexport, with a Spanish text by Katia Olevskaya). Olevskaya, born in the Ukraine in 1917, spent time with her family in Mexico during her childhood and became the first female voice on the Spanish-language stations of The Voice of Russia.[25] Michel incessantly sexualizes cartoons, to the extent that they become "the book" through which to interpret the Soviet period within Cuban history.

"Sobre Sovexportfilm" symbolizes crucial aspects of life in the second and third worlds. "Camisetas rojas, azules, negras, blancas, grises y verde olivo con nombres cabalísticos, impresos al revés en el ojo de agua del espejo: *regifliH ymmoT, ekiN, nottiuV siuoL*; un triángulo troceado: *sadidA*; una efe de bordes romos: *aliF*"[26] (Red, blue, black, white, gray, and olive green t-shirts with cabalistic names, printed in reverse in the mirror's watery eye: *regifliH ymmoT, ekiN, nottiuV siuoL*; a triangular cut-out: *sadidA*; an F of dull edges: *aliF*). The narrator's description of the protagonist's clothing underscores the significance of being a mirror of the first world—an inevitable inversion that in the Cuban cultural sphere remains defiant.

The characters of "Sobre Sovexportfilm" express themselves by way of Soviet creators and seek their genealogy within them. Michel asks whether his grandmother could have been the crocodile—an allusion most likely to Gena, a character in "Cheburashka," a 1966 story by Eduard Uspensky.[27] Michel utilizes the Soviet imagined sphere as a guide for behavior, and what is even stranger is that, like Vladimir from Moscow in Ernesto Pérez Castillo's "Bajo la bandera rosa" (Beneath the Pink Flag), he arrives too late to be a witness or a participant. He is a "faggot" whose "único recuerdo del padre que nunca conoció" (only memory of the father he never met) was "un libro de Pushkin, en ruso" (a book by Pushkin, in Russian).[28]

> Michel se ha negado siempre a aprender una palabra de esa lengua; prefiere que el libro siga siendo un misterio indescifrable. Recuerda la ilustración: las ramas encadenadas del árbol por el que pasea un gato rayado. Se lo ha traducido su madre, quien vino de Rusia preñada por un apuesto *bogatyr* que siempre olía a arenques ahumados y se llamaba Mijaíl Gorbachov, lo que le hace cagarse de risa. Nunca supo de él, aunque le buscó desesperadamente en las películas y los dibujos animados soviéticos, mientras su mamá le embutía papilla de una cazuela esmaltada, tal como hacía la abuela burra en el televisor ruso. Y él pensaba: "¿Tal vez sea mi abuelita el cocodrilo?"[29]

> Michel has always refused to learn a word of that language; he prefers the book to remain an indecipherable mystery. He remembers the illustration: a tree with a chain of branches through which a striped cat walks. His mother had translated it for him. She had come from Russia

pregnant by a dashing *bogatyr* who always smelled of smoked herrings and was called Mikhail Gorbachev, which makes him die of laughter. He never heard from his father, although he looked for him desperately in movies and in Soviet cartoons, while his mother stuffed him with baby food from an enameled pot, just like the grandmother of the family of donkeys did on the Russian television. And he thought, maybe my grandmother was the crocodile?

Michel tries to compensate for the tragedy of his father's death in Angola by inserting himself into the cartoon entitled *La hija del sol* (The Daughter of the Sun), produced in 1963 by Soyuzmultfilm, the most influential Soviet animation studio. When, for example, he thinks about the necessity for order, he also reverts to *muñequitos*. To explain the behavior of his friend, a "flaming faggot" with little respect for authority, he says, "Él nunca vio el muñequito de 'Se puede y no se puede'"[30] (He never saw the cartoon of "You Can and You Cannot"), and as a result, the friend was frequently detained by the authorities. This declaration recognizes the prohibitive role played by the Soviet cartoons as well as their function within a sardonic reconstruction of family.

Rodríguez invents a monstrous bicultural product, a hybrid missing any integral cultural model that, unable to live within his own skin, relies on the *muñequitos rusos* to provide him with a framework. Nevertheless, judging by his mother, the *muñequitos* are poorly translated into Spanish. As if he were a colonized subject, Michel overdetermines the significance of his absent father, even attempting to seduce a classmate with "malas traducciones de versos rusos, figuritas de madera y postales con reproducciones de arte del Hermitage"[31] (bad translations of Russian verse, little wooden figures and postcards with reproductions of art from the Hermitage) — intimate objects that easily recall Solórzano's photo-essay. Even the seduction has its complication beyond societal homophobia. The Cuban father of his classmate, we are told, "[lo] mata si se entera"[32] (will kill him if he finds out). The "no" of the father not only relates to a latent homophobia, but also to a rejection of all things Soviet.

To rescue the protagonist from his classmates' taunting, his mother attempts to strengthen his character with symbols that for Cubans were typical of the Soviet spirit — such as the birch tree and the *komsomol*, as well as some new ones that are equally "used" in today's Cuban culture — such as Vladimir Vysotsky.

"¡Nunca!," aulló ella y puso a hacer té en la tetera esmaltada. Lo bebieron juntos en las hermosas tazas traídas de Leningrado. Ella sacó un libro en ruso y le tradujo algunos conceptos psicológicos elementales, que le hicieron sentir la fuerza de doce hércules. "¿Dónde era eso?", se preguntó, y no pudo recordar. La madre colocó en el tocadiscos una placa de Visotski y la sala se llenó de abedules y komsomoles.[33]

"Never!" she howled and went to make tea in the shiny teapot. They drank it together in the beautiful cups from Leningrad. She took out a book in Russian and translated some basic psychological concepts that made him feel as strong as twelve Hercules. "Where was that?" he asked himself and could not remember. The mother placed a Vysotsky record on the turntable and the living room was filled with birch trees and *komsomols*.

Is this the transculturation about which Fernando Ortiz speaks or a recitation of clichés that in the absence of vivid and transforming cultural legacies continue to possess value? These relics from the Soviet Union, like those within Adelaida Fernández de Juan's "Clemencia bajo el sol," continue to possess social value, albeit by way of the illusion of sentimental victory. Heroism in all forms is ridiculed. Upon talking to "la única mujer de su vida" (the only woman of his life) about his family, both reveal family secrets: "'Mi abuela fue puta', le contó ella. 'Mi papá es ruso', reveló él."[34] ("My grandmother was a whore," she told him. "My father is Russian," he revealed.) Michel's revelation indicates the perhaps momentary, and very negative, implications of being Russian in Cuba.

At the end of the story, Michel observes an orgy from the outside, imagining that he is within another cartoon in which toys attempt to reach "hasta la ventana alta, para ver el arco iris, pero no pueden. Menos el puerquito alcancía, que se la pasaba *luchando* monedas"[35] (up to the highest window, to see the rainbow, but they cannot. The piggy bank, which spent its time struggling to make money, had even fewer chances of reaching it). Rodríguez's story, bordering on fable, ends with a broken piggy bank and the impossibility of seeing the rainbow; that is to say, the tale ends with a bankrupt society. On one hand, the fact that an explicit moral is missing from Rodríguez's rewriting of *muñequitos rusos* is a poignant commentary about the exportation of Soviet Bloc cartoons to the Cuban sphere, but, on the other, this forced fictional emptying also illustrates the necessity for symbolic unloading. The characters of "Sobre Sovexportfilm" act out old episodes of history, as they are unable to integrate into a new social "superego," and so they remain, like "schizoids," lost in a Sputnik orbit, unsecured to their actual temporal and geographic surroundings.

It is difficult to read "Sobre Sovexportfilm" without thinking of the Lázaro Saavedra cartoon in which a gentleman who looks and speaks like a Cuban bureaucrat asks Cheburashka, "Después que dejastes la KGB, qué has hecho?" (After leaving the KGB, what have you done?) and the funny little animal responds, "Mucho dinero, negocios en Londres" (A lot of money, business in

*Illustration by Lázaro Saavedra, around 2006. Courtesy of artist.*

London). It is a cartoon that, like *Un rey en la Habana* and "Sobre Sovexport-film," highlights the discrepancy between Cuban time and time in the rest of the world by focusing on a genre that has elsewhere disappeared.

## DAMAGED DAMES

If Rodríguez explores the Soviet inheritance through parody and without outright blame, Wendy Guerra aims more directly at reproaching the Soviets in her second novel, *Nunca fui primera dama* (I Was Never the Leading Lady). *Nunca fui primera dama* evokes the impossibility of being a "leading lady" in revolutionary Cuba, since the individual is supposed to fight for the good of the collective. Not until I began confusing Guerra's title with Gustavo Pérez's *Todas iban a ser reinas* (They Were All Going to Be Queens) did I recognize their resemblance in the melancholic stance they share vis-à-vis female heroism within the revolutionary project. Nadia, the protagonist of the novel, is almost no one and yet almost the novel's grand dame. The secondary characters are her mother, who never "realized" her artistic self publicly and who requires her daughter to access the public sphere, and Celia Sánchez, the guerrilla fighter who is said to have been Fidel Castro's lover and the woman who is closest to being the grand dame of Cuban history.

Nadia shares with *Todos se van*'s protagonist the same last name and a mother whose biographical details and influence on her daughter are similar. In addition, that surname is the same as the author's; a quotation from a poem by Albis Torres, the author's mother, serves as the epigraph to *Nunca fui primera dama*—more than a wink at the novel's autobiographical elements. *Todos se van*—divided in two parts, the first, a diary from childhood and the latter, from adolescence—is a kind of autobiographical novel, while *Nunca fui primera dama* is a meta-*testimonio* that gives voice to a character without her own, Albis Torres. At the same time, *Nunca fui primera dama* comments upon the impossibility of the testimonial process, opening with a declaration that resonates with the exemplary *testimonio* by Rigoberta Menchú: "Me llamo Rigoberta Menchú. Tengo veintitrés años. Quisiera dar este testimonio vivo . . . No soy la única, pues ha vivido mucha gente y es la vida de todos."[36] (My name is Rigoberta Menchú. I am twenty-three years old. This is my testimony . . . It's not only my life, it's also the testimony of my people . . . My personal experience is the reality of a whole people.)[37] Guerra echoes these words in an ironic manner, immediately delivering to readers the intimacy of the protagonist: "Les habla la hija de todos, reportando desde el país de nadie"[38] (The daughter of everyone, reporting from the country of no one). This declaration illustrates Guerra's resentment toward a discourse that, viewing autobiography to be the principal domain of the capitalist world, tries to persuade writers into the collective voice of the *testimonio*.

If *Todos se van* draws readers' attention to the brain drain that Cuba experienced during the 1960s, 1970s, and 1980s, Guerra's second novel carries them to the time just after those years, when Cuba came to be defined as a country of leftovers. In *Todos se van*, the Soviets are the culprits of the disintegration of Nieve's family. Her stepfather, a Swedish man who may have abused her, works in a nuclear plant until one day in 1979 when he is fired and deported, which he blames on the Russians. The second part of *Todos se van* begins in the latter half the 1980s. Nieve construes a relation between her parents and the Berlin Wall, showing the pernicious effect of its disappearance on her mother and suggesting on a larger scale that the psychology and the behavior of Cuban citizens are directly conditioned by it.

The news reaches them in the winter of 1989:

> La noticia de la caída del Muro de Berlín. Se derrumban los muros,
> la gente le da con todo y ya parece una epidemia de comentarios que
> vienen en susurros, entran y salen de la casa a la escuela y de la escuela
> a la calle . . . Mi madre dice que un día ella se va a derrumbar como
> el muro, porque no tiene fuerzas para levantar otro, ella sin muros no
> sabe vivir, el muro es su barricada, en él se protege aunque lo odie, allí
> vive detrás de él. Si llegara el capitalismo . . . habría que aprender otra
> manera de sobrevivir. Mi madre no lo aguantará.[39]

> The news of the fall of the Berlin Wall. The walls are tumbling down,
> people hit it with everything and it already seems like an epidemic of
> commentaries that come in whispers, they enter and leave the house to
> school, and from school to the street . . . My mother says that one day
> she's going to tumble down like the wall, because she doesn't have the
> strength to erect another one. Without walls, she doesn't know how to

live. The wall is her barricade. In it she protects herself even though she hates it. She lives there, behind it. If capitalism arrives . . . she'd have to learn another way to survive. My mother could not endure it.

Nevertheless, the narrator informs us that they had been aware of the possibility of change for some time, because their friends who had studied in the Soviet Union long before used to say, "todo se derrumbó"[40] (everything fell apart). Nieve considers the consequences that this could have in Cuba. "No me imagino como podemos romper aquí un muro de agua, amorfo y profundo"[41] (I can't imagine how we can break here an amorphous and deep wall of water). In April 1990, Nieve is not able to track down a single copy of *Sputnik*, the magazine that her mother liked so much—the same magazine that sells like hotcakes at the beginning of Rodríguez Febles's *Sputnik*. The repetitive reproduction of this scenario in Cuban culture of the new millennium shows just how significant this depletion was and remains, at least within memory. Rubén Zardoya Loureda, a professor of social sciences in Havana, provides some rationale for this sentiment: "The influence of this media on Cuban public opinion turned out to be much more powerful than that exercised by hundreds of hours of counter-revolutionary radio propaganda that came to us from the U.S.A."[42] Zardoya Loureda's commentary reinforces the Soviets' ideological state apparatus for the purpose of encouraging Cubans to continue defending themselves in the face of Yankee aggression, while the sentiment Nieve's mother experiences is even more confused.

*Nunca fui primera dama* begins in the new millennium, approximately fifteen years after Nieve's last diary entry. Its protagonist, Nadia, expresses two opinions directly related to the influence of the Soviet Union in Cuba. Her mother abandoned her, her father, and Cuba to go to the Soviet Union when Nadia was just ten years old. In 2006 Nadia arrives in Moscow, following the lead of her mother's lover, who had seen her with a Russian art dealer and his two children in the Chanel shop—a reference to what readers of José Manuel Prieto's *Nunca antes habías visto el rojo* or *Enciclopedia de una vida en Rusia* know well: the frenzied capitalism that penetrates the former Communist sphere. In the end, Nadia succeeds in locating her mother "usando el poco ruso que aprendi[ó] en la escuela primaria de Cuba"[43] (using the little Russian she learned in elementary school in Cuba), a minimalism that suggests that the obligatory Russian language implemented in schools does not serve its initial idealist function, but rather consumes the individual in multiple ways. Nadia first explains to us, "No conozco esta cultura, coexistimos juntos 'allá lejos y hace tiempo', pero en realidad los soviéticos no nos dejaron casi nada y poco sabemos de ellos"[44] (I don't know this culture, we coexisted "faraway and long ago," but in reality the Soviets hardly left us anything and we know little about them). She continues:

Soy turista en un país que de algún modo, ya conozco. Ellos hicieron una gran intervención pública en Cuba. Dejaron huellas en nuestras memorias; mal aprendimos su lengua y ahora nos olvidaron. Por suerte, en un rapto de 'Amistad indestructible' pude arrebatarles la visa para encontrar a mi madre.

Koniec.[45]

I am a tourist in a country that, in a way, I already know. Their public intervention in Cuba was massive. They left traces in our memories. We learned their language poorly and now they forget us. Fortunately, in a rapture of "Indestructible Friendship," I was able to snatch a visa from them to find my mother.

Koniec.

The protagonist's reference to "La Amistad entre los pueblos" (the friendship among nations) when she utters "Amistad indestructible" (indestructible friendship) — which, we may recall, Abel Prieto suggested was not really an important genre of jokes in the Cuban world — stands out since the Cubans did not have a colonial status. At the same time that, according to the narrator, the Soviets did not leave anything, they did leave "traces in our memories." To some extent, she displaces onto the Soviets the bitter feelings she possesses toward the order that is still maintained in Cuba, even without the Russian language, the language of a nation that she blames in part not only for the dismantling of her mother but also for the breakdown of her nation. As can be seen, these two declarations are rather similar and, at the same time, contradictory both within and outside of the text.

There are innumerable instances of thirty- and forty-somethings memorializing the Soviet past, with the awareness that part of it is both strangely shattered and hauntingly persistent within the present. In a review of Guerra's *Nunca fui primera dama* entitled "Un diario desde el país caribeño criado con códigos soviéticos" (A Diary from the Caribbean Country Raised with Soviet Codes), Ihosvany Hernández writes:

> In the end it makes us think about our own past, and even about this twenty-first century, when that Soviet support no longer exists, although an indelible, penetrating mark remains that leads us to rectify past errors and bear the consequences of those errors in the middle of a shattered city . . . where, perhaps, new diaries are proliferating, between nostalgia and that which we lose without recourse.[46]

Hernández pinpoints the foundations of Guerra's textual modus operandi within a Soviet apparatus. Nadia goes to Russia in search of her mother, and in her place, she encounters a being stripped of memory. Once Nadia successfully reinstalls her mother in Havana, her mother becomes even crazier and eventually commits suicide. The protagonist explains: "Me llamaron Nadia, en honor a la esposa de Lenin. En ruso: надежда mi nombre y yo significamos 'la esperanza.'"[47] (They named me Nadia, in honor of Lenin's wife. In Russian: надежда my name and I mean "hope.") *Nunca fui primera dama* suggests that Nadia's mother became a victim of the system's lies—among which is hope itself, sustained in order to survive in Cuba. Nadia insinuates that oblivion is the tactic employed by her mother to escape reality. While her mother's madness has a physiological cause (Alzheimer's), it also possesses a sociological one.

> Mis verdaderos héroes son mis padres, víctimas de una supervivencia doméstica, callada, dilatada, dolorosa. Desintegrados en una secta de adoraciones y desencantos, ellos perdieron la razón.
>
> Derribados como el muro, al mirar del otro lado, quedaba el mar como único patrimonio; la bahía oscura y estrellada o el luminoso Caribe de todos los días. Y nada de eso les pudo salvar. Postergaron los proyectos personales para integrarse al proyecto colectivo.[48]

> My true heroes are my parents, victims of a domestic, silent, dilated, painful survival. Disintegrated in a sect of adorations and disenchantments, they lost their mind.
>
> Demolished like the wall, looking from the other side, the sea remained as the only patrimony, the dark and starry bay or the luminous Caribbean of every day. And nothing of that could save them. They postponed their personal projects to become part of the collective project.

The signifiers of the protagonists are an embarrassing loan to Nadia because the signifieds to which they refer have no place inside Cuba. As the loan's inheritor, Nadia Guerra continues playing with them. She inserts herself in the transnational history when she employs the word "Koniec" in the passage quoted earlier, without translation, to explain the strange experience of being a tourist in Russia, with a name like hers.

The same word, but this time defined to avoid confusion, infiltrates a poem by Guerra titled "De cómo los rusos se fueron despidiendo" (On How the Russians Left Saying Good-Bye), about the impossibility of an intercultural dialogue.

> Ellos nunca se integraron
> nos hablaban y nosotros contestábamos bailando

ellos nunca fueron parte
andaban visibles como su olor
ocultos como sus submarinos
no sé adónde puedo dirigirles esta carta
recuerdo que enseñé a mis amigos de Moscú fajarse sin llorar
pero ellos nunca se integraron quizás fuera el calor o las películas
poco a poco se fueron despidiendo y
KONIEC.*
Fin en ruso.[49]

They never integrated
They would speak to us and we would answer dancing.
They were never a part
They were visible, like their smell
Hidden, like their submarines
I don't know where I can send them this letter
I remember that I showed my friends from Moscow how to fight
    without crying
But they never integrated—perhaps it was the heat or the movies
Little by little they began saying good-bye and
KONIEC.*
End in Russian.

The lack of an addressee for Guerra's letter is symptomatic of the impossibility of communicating and understanding each other on account of extremely distinct codes of communication.

Heard repeatedly by Cubans of the *Muñequitos Rusos* generation, the word *"koniec"* is unforgettable. Upon mentioning the "Soviet smell," Guerra describes a visceral reaction to the Soviets that was seen in Díaz's *Siberiana* and in Yoani Sánchez's blog. In an era when the discourse on race, in some parts of the world, is circumscribed tightly by methods such as "political correctness," it is worth contemplating the reasons for such a poetic digression in a writer as acclaimed as Guerra. This poem could be interpreted as a vengeful jab at Soviet racism— something that travelers to the Soviet Union experienced up close, but that is not directly remarked upon by Guerra. Ernesto Hernández Busto is at least partially right when he says that Russian-Cuban biculturalism has not been sufficiently studied because of the "lost honor that is the fault of Criollo chauvinism."[50] Abel Prieto's attribution of the lack of interest in things Russian on the popular level to the persistent and powerful influence of "Yankee mass culture" also helps to explain the bold rejection of the Soviet sphere by Sánchez and Guerra. Their own chauvinism and rebelliousness are provoked by the fact that their early lives and nuclear families were permeated by an unachievable ideal that they themselves did not even have the right to choose.

For Guerra, Cubans are responsible for continuing to manufacture "forgetfulness" using, among other strategies, the tools imported from an already-disappeared Eastern Europe. Just like her mother twenty years prior, Nadia works at a radio station at the beginning of *Nunca fui primera dama*, but the moment arrives when she too decides to abandon it. The aesthetics of the goodbye deserve critical attention.

> Hice mi promenade visual: la oficina de cortinas color "curre mostaz", bustos de yeso con la cara de mártires desconocidos, varios trofeos de mármol y tarjas de hojalata un poco corroídas por el tiempo. Imitaciones de micrófonos de la RCA y, sobre todo, libros en perfecto ruso, imagino que sobre política radial, pensamientos de arte y socialismo, diccionarios de lengua española al ruso y viceversa. Fue ahí cuando recordé que esta mujer se había diplomado en una maestría de comunicaciones comunitarias en la Unión Soviética. Mi padre contaba que fue a Edelsa a la que se le ocurrió aquella idea de los cursos de ruso por radio. En fin, sigo vagando por el samovar de madera, las matriuskas empolvadas y sus fotos. La mulata cubana, entre puentes y monumentos nevados; la mujer con *shadka*, sonriente en instantáneas extendidas por el territorio de la oficina. Sitio detenido en el tiempo, con todo el frío de la estepa siberiana, el aire acondicionado al máximo y las postales rusas colocadas por orden de tamaño sobre la caja del aparato helado, ruidoso y también soviético, maltratado, pero ahí, en marcha. Dudo que los funcionarios rusos conserven un sitio parecido en su país.[51]

> I took a visual promenade: the office with mustard curry drapes, plaster busts of unknown martyrs, various marble trophies, tin shields a little corroded by time. Imitations of RCA microphones, and above all, books in perfect Russian about, I imagine, radio politics, ideas on art and Socialism, Spanish-Russian dictionaries and vice versa. It was then that I recalled that this woman had graduated with a master's in community communications in the Soviet Union. My father used to say that it was Edelsa who had the idea of airing Russian-language courses on the radio. In any event, I keep gazing over the wooden samovar, the dusty matrioshkas, and her photos. The Cuban mulatto, between bridges and snowy monuments, the woman with a *shadka*, smiling in Polaroids spread across the office. A place frozen in time, with all the cold of the Siberian steppe, the air conditioner on high, and Russian postcards arranged in size order on top of the frozen, noisy, and also Soviet appara-

tus, battered, but there, working. I doubt that Russian functionaries still have such a place in their country.

Although in Cuba it is prohibited to erect statues of national personalities while they are still alive, this atmosphere certainly resembles a mausoleum. The sensation of being trapped between different historical periods and dissimilar territories is common. It is as if the same Soviet air had been transported to the office's tropical atmosphere, where it cannot adequately circulate. The mulatto Edelsa, with her *shadka*, a Russian furry hat, is like an *objet trouvé*, emblematic of the reach of the Soviet "empire." A sampling of items from the Soviet Bloc was commonly used by Cubans to decorate their homes during the Soviet period in Cuba, especially by students who had studied abroad, but the weight of this inheritance of consumer products has more to do with their association, in Nadia's mind, with the hegemonic sphere. For her, Edelsa not only brought back travel mementos, but also assimilated the Soviet ideal to such an extent that she became a representative of their most oppressive mechanisms on the island.

This image is reminiscent of a painting by Gertrudis Rivalta Oliva (born in 1971) entitled *Quinceañera con Kremlin* (Fifteenth Birthday Girl with Kremlin) in which the mixed-race model, who is the painter's sister, sits with the Kremlin over her head like Carmen Miranda with her fruit basket headdress. The subject, however, is not smiling, but gazing up rather bitterly at the viewer. The exotic Carmen Miranda that captured the United States is transformed into a darker and more acrimonious other. *Quinceañera con Kremlin* portrays an encounter between American camp and Soviet kitsch. We are not looking at an experience of hybridity, but rather a strange and uneasy imposition whose uneasiness draws attention to the colonial aspects of the Soviet-Cuban fraternity. Rivalta, the artist, explains:

> It is the portrait of my sister Nildita at her fifteenth birthday party. There is an image of the Kremlin in the crown that she is wearing on her head ... I have reproduced it exactly as it is, but in perspective, and then I drew and painted ... the dress my sister was wearing for the party. The one is superimposed upon the other, in much the same way that we believe identity is constructed ... The title is "Fnimanief[,]" representing phonetically the Russian word for "attention." I took it from the Russian version of the story that tells of the competition between the tortoise and the hare, a fable also told in Cuba. You know these things left a deep impression on me since they make very clear what they wanted us to be and to do. In other words, they were important for the definition of who we are. You always have to look like someone, answer to the fashionable

Quinceañera con Kremlin, *by Gertrudis Rivalta Oliva, 2004. Courtesy of artist.*

model, an erroneous concept as far as being contemporary and functional are concerned.[52]

Imported models and their role in female subjectification, especially Afro-Cuban subjectification, is a definitive theme within Rivalta's oeuvre. Her riffs on Walker Evans's portraits illustrate the extent to which Cubans relied on the US sphere of influence for their own identification, but images such as *Quinceañera con Kremlin* suggest that the Soviets have had a lasting effect on the Cuban landscape.

In her article "*Fnimaniev! Fnimaniev!* The Tortoise and the Hare: The Black *Moña*," Rivalta notes the resemblance of the Soviet to the United States model with regard to its colonial implications.[53] The words "Fnimaniev! Fnimaniev!" (Attention! Attention!) accompanied the sound of the pistol signaling the start of the race in Irina Gurvich's 1963 animated adaptation of the Grimm fairy tale "The Hare and the Hedgehog." In e-mail correspondence I received from Rivalta on April 8, 2009, she explained their symbolic and sentimental meaning as "the sound of the pistol that initiated my return to the ideas and experiences of the USSR and Cuba." The second part of Rivalta's title, "The Tortoise and the Hare," entails an unusual substitution. Rivalta believed that her readers would not be able to pick out the hedgehog from Gurvich's short animated film, produced by Kiev Science Film, and so, instead, she subtitled her article with the internationally more recognizable title from the Aesop fable and Walt Disney cartoon, "The Tortoise and the Hare," containing a similar moral: do not underestimate the apparently weaker party. According to Homi K. Bhabha, the "discourse of mimicry is constructed around an *ambivalence*; in order to be effective, mimicry must continually produce its slippage, its excess, its difference."[54] It is as if Rivalta assumed that her previous incorporation of the categories of the Soviet empire must be replaced by those with which the West—the extant power—is more fluent. Rivalta positions herself alongside a wide range of female artists from around the world, including Cindy Sherman, Kara Walker, Mariana Botey, Elena del Rivero, Tania Bruguera, Charlotte Moorman, Yoko Ono, and Nan Goldin, as she analyzes the consequences of being a black Cuban woman who was obliged to at least attempt to assimilate to Soviet paradigms of beauty. If for Dmitri Prieto Samsonov and Polina Martínez Shvietsova the Cuban model of national identity—the *ajiaco*—is not as all-encompassing and tolerant as the hegemons make it out to be, because children of the Soviet diaspora attempt to diminish their Soviet inheritance in order to conform to the Cuban national identity, for Rivalta, the *ajiaco*, already compromised by Cuban racist paradigms of thought, was then "hijacked" by Soviet models from which she was left out. Although this chapter is particularly concerned with how Cubans today interpret the Soviets and how this interpretation in turn shapes their identity, Rivalta's work actually lays bare the diverse hegemonic processes shaped by slavery, colonization, imperialism, the Cuban Revolution, the Cold War, and globalization—all of which are incorporated within Cuban subjectivities.

SOVIET TEMPORALITIES

While Ricardo Alberto Pérez's poetry does not lay claim to history in the same way that Rivalta's visual works do, the exceptional tenor of Soviet and Eastern European references is noticeable. To take them away would leave much of Pérez's poetry without a temporal framework. They are not just far-away landscapes, nor are they singular impositions, but rather the lens through which the poet establishes temporal categories and identitarian relations. While the focus of this investigation is the Soviet Union, it is impossible to detach the complicated value of the Soviet and Russian in Pérez's poetry from his pre-occupation with international culture at large, and in particular with other cultures that were disseminated from the Soviet Bloc. Through the East German television series *The Clown Ferdinand*, Pérez describes the domination and the obligation of viewing exported entertainment, as well as what happens to that memory with the passage of time, in the absence of that obligation, encapsulating what Jácome reaches toward in her recognition of the *muñequitos rusos* for her parents' generation.

> Fabricado con un poco de bilis
> nos lo exportaron
> tocino a diario;
> semillas en los gestos,
> raíces.
> La esterilidad
> venía del seso de la res,
> contenido,
> apresado, prensado,
> Un abedul torcido semejaba;
> tres, o cuatro veces a la semana
> lo proyectaban
> a través de la programación infantil . . .
> un abedul torcido en el crepúsculo;
> y sin escrúpulos, regresaba,
> con su overol a cuadros,
> la tuba densa.
> Vacío, sin membranes
> copaba la pantalla
> del mueble ruso
> en la rosada seducción
> de la prima noche
> aún no instaurada.[55]

> Fabricated with a little bile
> they exported him to us

the daily bacon;
seeds in gestures,
roots.
His sterility
came from the brain of the cow,
contained,
imprisoned, pressed.
He resembled a twisted birch tree;
three or four times a week
they projected him
on a children's program . . .
a twisted birch tree at twilight;
and without scruples, he returned,
With his checkered overalls,
his dense tuba.
Empty, without membranes
he took over the screen
of the Russian set
in the pink seduction
of the exceptional night
not yet established.

In the penultimate stanza of "Ferdinando Prenom," the word "now" readjusts
and accommodates in a discrepant manner to the impact of a repressive international network on the poetic subject by suggesting unexpected gifts:

Un don de histerizar
que he dominado
gracias a su ausencia prolongada.
Otros vieron cicatrizar sus nacidos,
las rodillas rotas
ante este ser, o
silueta proyectada
gracias al CAME
(cerebrillo gomoso y conjunto de ciertos mandatorios).

Ahora contemplo,
y rememoro
la rumorosa disposición
de las ruinas;
sonrío.[56]

A gift of hystericizing
that I've mastered
thanks to his prolonged absence.
Others saw their pustules scar
their broken knees
before this being, or
projected silhouette
thanks to the CMEA
(slimy little brain and group of certain agents).

Now I contemplate,
and remember
the clamorous disposition
of the ruins;
I smile.

The grotesque injury, that irony that he calls attention to with the verb *"histeri-zar"* (to "hystericize")—borrowed from the Portuguese, as it is in English—undeniably marks Pérez's regard for this television series in the poem "Ferdinando Prenom," emblematic of the darkest decade of the Cuban Revolution.

If we understand "hystericization" to mean the subject's overdetermination of the realities that it confronts, then we can better appreciate the poem's description of the effects of Socialist culture on his individuation. This talent for dividing corresponds to having been subjectified through a distant yet powerful disciplinary discourse that permits the narrative subject to identify with the other and to splinter himself into pieces. The personal final smile emerges with bitter irony at the scars projected through the internationalist lens of the Socialist camp in which Cuba was deeply embroiled. Pérez's poetry specifies the elements of imposition and injury, as well as a perverse smile that is his own. The implications of Cuba's membership in the CMEA are grotesque for Pérez, but the poem also suggests that the final smile is not merely the result of the ideological failure, but of the odd meeting place of these two diverse cultures that creates in the poetic subject the ability to master a particular sense of hystericizing. The survivor's "now" knows the force whereby the dolorous ruins are converted into the charged energy of near madness, but also into artistic productivity.

Pérez's poem "Andréi Tarkovski," published in 2003, references the director of one of the first Soviet films to be shown on the island after the triumph of the Revolution, *Iván's Childhood* (1962). While Tarkovsky remains a source of inspiration for numerous Cuban artists, it was not until 2008 (perhaps in preparation for the 2010 book fair) that Tarkovsky, along with other new Russian and old Soviet directors, began to be reintroduced into the public sphere when the Cuban Cinemateca (Film Library) dedicated a film series to them. Joel del Río evokes the persistence of joy in a retro–Socialist Bloc aesthetics in post-Soviet times: "For nostalgics and Slavophiles, for those who believe that there can exist a good, solidly commercial cinema beyond Hollywood that is entertaining, well narrated, and rooted in generic keys, a Cinemateca Series has been put together for these first days of May."[57] The political undertones are evident in the simultaneous presentation of six recent films as well as films made during the Soviet period by Karen Shakhnazarov (a Soviet and Russian-Armenian director, screenwriter, and producer, and the director of Mosfilm studios since 1988). Also evident is the call to continue to oppose US hegemony on a cultural level. Dalia Acosta similarly picks up on these undertones in discussing the "return of Russian cinema to this island's big screen after an absence of about twenty years . . . The Cuban public again sees cinema by Andrei Tarkovsky with films like *Solaris* (1972), among other titles that made history, including *Moscow Does Not Believe in Tears* (Vladimir Menshov, 1980), *Siberiada* (Andrei Konchalovsky, 1979), and *Gypsies Go to Heaven* (Emil Loteanu, 1975)."[58] Acosta notes two important assessments made by these "Russian" guests in Havana: first, Shakhnazarov's contrast between Soviet and Russian film, esteeming the former for its humanitarian bent and embrace of Soviet identity, and second, the Russian actor Boris Galkin's comment, "How great that the movies that are going to be screened in this series don't smell of Hollywood film!"[59] This excitement accompanied the signing of a cooperation agreement between Mosfilm and the ICAIC (Cuban Institute of Cinematographic Art and Industry).

However, Pérez's musings on Tarkovsky and other disseminated Socialist Bloc cultural products made prior to these collective memorializations are more personal and more critical. The Soviet and Russian director Tarkovsky serves as an affective lens within Pérez's poem. While the first stanza of "Andréi Tarkovski" is conditioned by an obligation, performed in the imperfect tense, the second revives the poetry of a more intimate epoch, transforming it into another sort of prescription.

> Cada noche un soldado ruso,
> una mujer rusa
> llorando
> por un soldado
> ruso;
> después dormíamos
> un sueño ruso:
> sopas,

camaradas,

nieve.

Mas, cuando un polvo de metales
recuerda a los violines,
algo debe ser rescatado;
la música
de un hombre
entre discursos envejecidos.[60]

Every night a Russian soldier,
a Russian woman
crying
for a Russian soldier;
afterward we would sleep
a Russian dream:
soups,
comrades,
snow.

But, when a powder of metals
recalls violins
something ought to be rescued;
the music
of a man
among aged discourses.

This is to say that the present prescription to recall the poetry emerges almost organically from a past obligation, a seemingly boundless and monotonous habit that startles the reader by its insinuation that such unions not only yield fundamental totalities but also unexpected exceptions. Powders of metals recalling violins are not the subject of historical conjunctions, but those of artistic play that merits remembrance.

In Pérez's "Oficios de una bota" (Tasks of a Boot), a boot becomes the synecdoche of a historical epic. The poem begins by defining a boot as the heartbeat of an animal in the hour of its death as both intrahistorical and assonant. The boots are followed from the country to the city, but the journey is interrupted by two stanzas of seemingly superfluous experiences of aesthetics — Portuguese and cinema — that direct readers on a different path, taking them away from the labor of the most intimate boots. Within a cinematographic gaze, other boots are located, the boots of soldiers and also a trash can. Then the poem recalls the intimacy of an uncle's migration to the city and a new boot-donning job at a hotel in Havana. The last two stanzas of the poem are characterized by three phrases—"Convivencia textual" (textual cohabitation), "cenizas" (ashes), and "historias" (stories).

> Y, esa bota que viene
> de la convivencia textual;
> en Lorca ya la vi:
> bota de la guardia civil
> bota de la guardia fascista,
> un, dos, liebre
> un, dos, hiena,
> y *fumaça,*
> *muita fumaça.* Porque
> Querella, ya dejó el Puerto.
>
> También el Alabastro;
> y el ruso fuma
> mientras cae la ceniza
> encima de su bota,
> un, dos
> un, dos
> un, dos
> más un vodka,
> agua
> agua
> agua,
> entre los peces
> fluyen las historias.[61]

And, this boat that comes
from textual cohabitation;
in Lorca I already saw it:
boot of the Civil Guard
boot of the Fascist Guard,
one, two, hare
one, two, hyena,
and *fumaça*
*muita fumaça.* Because
Querelle, already left the Port.

Also the Alabaster;
and the Russian smokes

while the ashes fall
on top of his boot,
one, two
one, two
one, two
and a vodka,
water
water
water,
among the fishes
histories flow.

Boots weave together spheres of labor in which textual and extratextual can co-exist. The linguistic worlds of Russian, Portuguese, and Spanish cohabit. Pérez's years on a literary scholarship, not in the Soviet Union, but in Brazil, may help to explain his invocation of it, but the ashes of the Russian boots sculpt the poet's configuration of utopias and pain. In place of the initial solid definition of a boot, the final stanza yields the leftovers, wrought with a hybrid fluidity of vodka and water through which histories flow.

No discussion of the literary intertexts in Pérez's writing that speaks to the Soviet world can ignore the untitled poem appearing in his as-yet unpublished *Miedo a las ranas* (Fear of Frogs), in which it is impossible to confuse his impression of the 1970s with restorative nostalgia.

Los rusos fueron perdiendo el equilibrio
por el vodka ingerido
en más de sesenta años.
¿Qué pasa con el equilibrio
de los rusos?
No logran llegar en pie
a la plaza roja.
Ahora ingieren lociones de afeitar,
aguas de Colonia
(es decir, líquidos
que no pagan impuestos).
Los rusos son ese tipo
de gente
que de madrugada
se le ocurre despertar
al resto de la familia
y decirle que no se parecen

a Napoleón, a Mozart,
ni siquiera a Beethoven.
Ellos construyeron San Petersburgo,
los otros están agradecidos.

The Russians began losing their balance
because of the vodka ingested
over more than sixty years.
What happens with the Russians' equilibrium?
They are unable to arrive on foot
to Red Square.
Now they ingest shaving lotions,
waters from the Colony
(that is, to say liquids
that do not pay taxes).
The Russians are those kind
of people
who at dawn
decide to wake up
the rest of the family
and tell them that they don't seem like
Napoleon, Mozart,
not even Beethoven.
They built Saint Petersburg,
the others are grateful.

The somewhat affectionate and yet derogatory nickname "*los bolos*," which helps Cubans retain a sense of superiority over the Soviets, takes on a whole new level of critique in Pérez's verses. The Russians, about which the poetic subject speaks, also retain a sense of superiority, despite having already lost their empire. Pérez's Russians are not merely clumsy, but are colonialist drunkards who thrive on thinking themselves superior to the rest—better than "Napoleon," "Mozart," and even "Beethoven"—and who believe that "others" ought to be grateful to them. While the poetic voice does not establish an explicit "us" or "them" or incorporate itself into the "family," it is impossible to read this poem without acknowledging its intimate understanding of what sustained the Soviet empire and the current Russian impulse toward control and domination. While in Pérez's earlier "Andréi Tarkovski" and "Oficios de una bota" the repetitive model of loving, working, or viewing art is put to death, as it is in Ernesto René's videographic interpretation of "Los músicos de Bremen," in this unnamed poem, the violent tragedy of empire repeats itself as farce.

Like Pérez, the poet Juan Carlos Flores was born in 1962; his poetry evokes Cuba as another republic of the Soviet Union. He even calls himself the "last poet of the East." In "El selenista" (The Selenaist), Flores exhumes the laborer who wins a Selena radio for his good work. His repetition is not farcical but deeply dolorous. In this brief yet powerful "obituary" to the Soviet brand that no longer exists, the worker is entirely alienated, becoming the dead object that once defined him. The poem concludes with the tragic verse, "El hombre del radio receptor envejeció, enfermó, murió con el radio receptor junto a la oreja"[62] (The radio receiver man, he aged, he got sick, he died with the radio receiver next to his ear). One might associate this image with the old man guarding the incinerator while he waits for the arrival of Soviet parts in *Un rey en la Habana*, but the pain and beauty of Flores's poetry is without the comedic relief of Valdés's scene. In another poem, "Mea culpa por Tomás" (Mea Culpa for Tomás), Flores at first seems to talk back to Cuban chauvinism, only to reveal, in the last verse, the reason behind children ridiculing a Soviet child.

> Tomás, niño venido de la Unión Soviética, a quien nosotros llamábamos "cabeza de bolo." Porque se alimentaba mejor que nosotros, a golpear a "cabeza de bolo", porque se vestía mejor que nosotros, a golpear a "cabeza de bolo," porque tenía mejores juguetes que nosotros, a golpear a "cabeza de bolo", porque sacaba mejores notas que nosotros, a golpear a "cabeza de bolo", para que ninguna niña lo mirase, a golpear a "cabeza de bolo." Creo que frente a Tomás, todos nos sentíamos un poco checos.[63]

> Tomás, kid from the Soviet Union, whom we called "bowling-pin head." Because he ate better than we did, let's smack "bowling-pin head," because he dressed better than we did, smack "bowling-pin head," because he had better toys than we did, smack "bowling-pin head," because he got better grades than we did, smack "bowling-pin head," so no girl would look at him, smack "bowling-pin head." Next to Tomás I think we all felt a little bit Czech.[64]

Feeling "a little bit Czech" would mean that Cubans are not exempt from experiencing the Soviets as invaders, as did Czechoslovakia in 1968. Once again, an adult sentiment of envy toward what the Soviets could afford and aggression toward their presence in Cuba is displaced onto children.

No such bitterness toward the Soviet world is apparent in Ernesto René Rodríguez's 2005 short story "Solarística," wherein Andrei Tarkovsky becomes the tool through which the director of Porno para Ricardo's "Los músicos de Bremen" video frames a bizarre love letter to a woman, to a director, to a whole part of the Soviet imaginary, and to the city of Havana. In this story, which combines numerous genres, including the narrative poem and the epistolary, the characters do not insert themselves into Soviet Bloc cartoons, as they did in Rubén Rodríguez's "Sobre Sovexportfilm," but rather into cinema by both Tarkovksy and Larisa Shepitko. "Solarística" pays homage to Tarkovsky's 1972 film *Solaris*, about a psychologist who departs Earth and travels to the space station Solaris in order to understand why all there have gone mad. He, too, begins hallucinating and encounters in Solaris many whom he has loved and lost. "Recuerda, estábamos en octubre, bajo la égida de la balanza (palabra que le gustaba a Larissa—sí, tu nombre era Larissa) y te invité a Solaris. Dios mío, estaba lloviendo, el agua entraba en los zapatos, todo era un océano, pero había que ir."[65] (Remember, it was October, and we were beneath the aegis of balance [a word that Larissa liked—yes, your name was Larissa] and I invited you to Solaris. My god, it was raining, the water was getting into our shoes. Everything was an ocean, but we had to go.) Larissa is the name of Tarkovsky's second wife, and the ocean, an allusion to the ocean surface of Solaris. The narrator refers to his love interest's having just landed in this world and to his immense fascination with their different communicative codes.

> Pero, advertí que eran las menos cuartos y que las canchas estaban muy lejos, tal vez como tú, como los setenta, época que, por decirlo de alguna manera, hacía ratón y queso jugaba yo al quimbe y cuarta y tú (personita feliz), casi a las menos cuartos, en tercer aniversario de los Reyes 73, acababas de aterrizar en este mundo-jeroglífico.[66]

> But, I warned you that it was already a quarter of and the fields were very far away, maybe like you, like the 1970s, an era that, to put it another way . . . is long past. It's been forever since I played marbles, and you—dear happy person—at almost a quarter of, on the third anniversary of Reyes 73, you just landed in this hieroglyphic world.

Undoubtedly, this description corresponds to a time and place in which, unless readers happened to be insiders there, they would be lost by references to the popular children's marbles game *quimbe y cuarta* and the popular musical group of the 1970s, Reyes 73. It is as if Rodríguez, like Jácome, were resurrecting another dimension of the 1970s, not the monumental rhetoric that accompanied embittered struggles for greater productivity, or the immense repressions, nor even the figures of the Soviet countermemory, but the joyful gazes of a distinct Soviet humor and rhythm that was appreciated by some Cubans.

The narrator compares his beloved, an actress, to the Soviet/Russian film director Larisa Shepitko, a name that recalls a distinct era and horizons, and he compares himself to her husband, Elem Klimov, also a director, who finished her *Farewell to Matyora* when she died in a car accident in 1979.

> Te estoy llevando en tablitas por considerar que estas escapa a lo, digamos, Larissa Shepitco; por supuesto, salvando las distancias (9550 según el canal 6 . . . ¿en el 84? Dios mío, ¿20 años no son nada?) entre ambas actrices. Ya quisiera ser tu Elem Klimov.

> I'm giving you a hard time because I'm thinking you're going to get away like, let's say, Larissa Shepitko; of course, bridging the gap (9550 according to Channel 6 . . . In 1984? My god, twenty years is nothing?) between both actresses. I would like to be your Elem Klimov.

His grouping together of diverse Soviet iconography is relentless—it is as if the recitation of these names could somehow permit them to survive and combat the fear of contamination and fast technological advances within the protagonist.

The protagonist's subjectivity is tied to a youth that is free of a lover from the United States whose rhythm does not excite him. "No me había dejado en esas doremifasolasi en crescendo sostenido a través de su auricular con super-microchips de última generación"[67] (She had not left me with those do-re-mi-fa-so-la-ti's in sustained crescendo through her receiver with the latest generation of super microchips). With this story, Rodríguez holds onto a poetic and hallucinatory world inspired by a Soviet imaginary that does not correspond to the contemporary signifiers with which he is forced to live. In this world, "cualquiera tiene un chico, una chica extra-continental"[68] (everyone has an extra-continental boy or girl). But the most decisive moment in this story is when "la muchacha chejoviana más bella que ojos humanos han contemplado jamás"[69] (the most beautiful Chekhovian girl that human eyes have ever contemplated), in the company of her Chekhovian grandmother, asks him what movie will be screening at the cinema that night. Since he does not know, he asks another fellow, who answers, "*Solaris*." That response needs clarification. "'¿La rusa o la americana?', pregunté. 'No sé, ahí dice que es americana.'"[70] ("The Russian or the American?" I asked. "I don't know. Over there it says it is American.") His disillusionment with the response leads him to lie to them: "'*Despedida.* Es una peli rusa dirigida por la gran actriz Larissa Shepitko y terminada por su marido Elem Klimov.' KONIEC."[71] ("*Farewell to Matyora*. It's a Russian movie directed by the great actress Larissa Shepitko and finished by her husband Elem Klimov." KONIEC.) In so doing, he fulfills his wish and briefly restores the world. In a "especie de attachment opcional o carta-solaristica" (kind of optional attachment or solaristic letter) to readers, the "author" remarks, "Se recomienda (si lo desean) que cada lector haga su propia selección como más gustéis y logren su CD-Solarístico; pero antes les sugiero ver la película *Solaris* =made in URSS=, con el sello inconfundible de su realizador"[72] (It is recommended [if desired] that readers make their own selection as they please and get their CD-Solaristic; but beforehand, I suggest they watch the movie *Solaris* =made in USSR=, with the unmistakable stamp of its producer). The narrator's call is for readers to briefly inhabit the Soviet moment, which is distinct from the one in which they currently live. Strangely, Rodríguez's poeticization not only relies on the Soviet period, but also mixes it with the long-passed republic to which he refers when he speaks of "todos aquellos barrios que aún conservan la moderada elegancia de la República"[73] (all those neighborhoods that still conserve the moderate elegance of the Republic). The story's final ode to restoration—"Yo lo único que puedo hacer por ti en este universo es resucitar, resucitar, resucitar"[74] (The only thing I can do for you in this universe is to resuscitate, resuscitate, resuscitate)—is more in the vein of turn-of-the-century melancholy than other extratextual tendencies toward restoration that include persistent debates in Cuba over Stalin, the 2010 memorialization of figures of socialist realism such as Mikhail Sholokhov, or even the television programming that same year of diverse Soviet films from the 1970s and 1980s, such as Vladimir Menshov's 1980 *Moscow Does Not Believe in Tears*.

A clip of *Moscow Does Not Believe in Tears* actually also appears in Ernesto René and Jorge E. Betancourt's *9550* (2006), which pieces together in pastiche-like fashion other Soviet and Cuban films, documentaries, and cartoons.[75] In René and Betancourt's documentary, one of the first of what has turned out to be a handful on the topic realized by distinct filmmakers, the visual and affective universe of the Soviets is reflected upon by six seemingly random Cubans, including two children of Soviet-Cuban marriages, most of whom would be considered members of the *Muñequitos Rusos* generation. The imperfect documentary "matches" the emotions and attitudes conveyed in testimonies to scenes from Soviet cinema. It touches upon in a cursory and not at all controversial manner the mainstays of the Soviet legacy—film, cartoons, and food. The statement that most attests to the spirit of *9550* is delivered by Angelo Gotay, who as a child lived in the Sierra Maestra neighborhood of Miramar, mostly populated by members of the Soviet Bloc, since his mother was wed to a Polish man. While his commentaries sometimes give way to stereotypes (he enjoyed gatherings in which the Soviets started with great laughter and ended in tears), Gotay also conveys details that are not as stereotypical. His Soviets are generous, "always bearing fruit, drinks, or flowers at gatherings, and even without access to cellophane, wrap up their gifts in . . . newspaper." That beautiful yet somewhat archetypical spirit also penetrates the framing of the documentary within an actress's placing a record of Russian balalaikas on an old turntable, a bittersweet image that contrasts with Flores's more bitter "El silenista." Gotay also confirms what other moments of nostalgia within this book reveal—that Soviet products, whether liked or not, were far better known than Soviet people in Cuba and that they, in retrospect, are all the more appreciated now for having been affordable back then.

The exhumation of the Soviet Cuban 1970s and 1980s by the likes of Jácome, Rubén Rodríguez, Porno para Ricardo, Wendy Guerra, Gertrudis Rivalta, Ricardo Alberto Pérez, Juan Carlos Flores, and Ernesto René (Rodríguez) is filled with sentimentality—loss, anger, retribution, love—casting even more of what José Quiroga refers to as "palimpsests" onto the already-complicated beginning of the new millennium.

# CHAPTER FIVE

# The Phantasmagoric Sputnik

Cuban artists and writers of the 1990s and the new millennium cope with the symbolic displacement from the Soviet realm by reshaping their identities through the implementation of spare parts from the Soviet state and machinery within Cuba. A rich example of this process is found in José Manuel Prieto's *Livadia*, whose protagonist survives by trafficking in the spare parts of a recently dismantled Soviet army. However, the ramifications of many of this chapter's collages, composed of Soviet industries, are somewhat distinct in that their disillusionment and critique are directed back at the Cuban nation. Pierre Nora's discussion of the French revolutionary calendar as a site of memory is helpful for theorizing the creations.

> *Lieux de mémoire* are created by the interaction between memory and history, an interaction resulting in a mutual overdetermination . . .
> The *lieux* of which I speak are hybrid places, mutants in a sense, compounded of life and death, of the temporal and the eternal. They are like Mobius strips, endless rounds of the collective and the individual, the prosaic and the sacred, the immutable and the fleeting. For although it is true that the fundamental purpose of a *lieu de mémoire* is to stop time, to inhibit forgetting, to fix a state of things, to immortalize death, . . . it is also clear that *lieux de mémoire* thrive only because of their capacity for change, their ability to resurrect old meanings and generate new ones along with new and unforeseeable connections . . .
>
> The new calendar adopted for a time during the French Revolution . . . is a *lieu de mémoire* . . . since . . . the calendar was also supposed to stop the clock of history at the moment of the Revolution . . . What further establishes its claim in our eyes is its failure to fill the role foreseen for it by its authors.[1]

Nora explains that had the revolutionary calendar really replaced the Gregorian one, its purpose would have been transformed; it would have "fix[ed] the dates of other conceivable *lieux de memoire*."[2] For Nora, along with the formation of European nation-states came the need for subjective representations of memory, namely, history.

Like the French Revolution, the Cuban Revolution narrates a new calendar to remind the Cuban people of the important revolutionary dates and concepts. The recitation of phrases such as the year of "liberation," "agrarian reform," "productivity," and "the centennial of the fall of José Martí," among many others, is a strategy for ensuring that the Cuban people are held together collectively in the shared experience of time. Most Cuban publications these days simultaneously dictate time through both the Gregorian and the revolutionary calendar, and in this way, the Cuban revolutionary calendar is similarly converted into a "realm of memory"—a conversion that coincides with the melancholic tone of the 1990s. To such heroic displays of history, many Cuban artists respond with their own, more private, resuscitations of the past with words and visual objects.

Especially through the commodity circuit made possible through these virtual spaces, objects from the Communist world have acquired different value, as the *muñequitos rusos* make clear. As Andreas Huyssen asserts:

> Untold recent and not so recent pasts impinge upon the present
> through modern media of reproduction like photography, film, recorded
> music, and the Internet, as well as through the explosion of historical
> scholarship and an ever more voracious museal culture. The past has be-
> come part of the present in ways unimaginable in earlier centuries.[3]

The cultural critic herself, located outside of Cuba, in the academy sustained within the "belly of the beast," is complicit with distinct aspects of memorialization not only through the inevitable consolidating of disciplinary interests, but also through purchases of "minor" objects that once formed part of national patrimonies that are not her own. For instance, the Spanish-based online store Distribuciones Potemkin, which opened in 2006, only to fold about two years later, sold artifacts of Communist history, but they just as easily could have been relegated to the realm of relics from Communist countries, into which Distribuciones Potemkin grouped together the unlikely states of Cuba (itself not yet a relic of Communism), China, North Korea, the former states of the Soviet Union, Bulgaria, Vietnam, the German Democratic Republic, and Laos.[4] Although the site's consumer ethics were less alienated than, say, eBay or Amazon, evidence of its solidarity with the Communist cause, there's little difference between Distribuciones Potemkin selling off former patrimonies and these objects being sold on those other sites.

The function and value of mnemonic devices, discussed by Richard Terdiman, are crucial to understanding how artists transform and shape "realms of memory." These objects

> play a familiar triggering or anchoring role in the mnemonic process. Indeed, the nineteenth century institutionalized and exploited this connection between memories and objects in the form of a brisk trade in "keepsakes" and "souvenirs." So it is astonishing when somehow the mnemonic potential of the objects fundamental to an entire social formation turns up radically disrupted or disabled. Then the object — in its "metaphysically" enigmatic commodity form — mutates into a privileged icon symbolizing the crisis of memory and the sudden opacity of the past.[5]

In recent times, souvenirs from the Soviet period in Cuba have turned up in unusual places. Souvenirs are collected for all sorts of reasons, and in the Special Period, many objects, such as stamps, flags, newspapers, books, and medallions from the first three decades of the Revolution and from the Republican period were sold off to those with purchasing power. Those without the purchasing power are left to transform artistically the emblems once central to their nations into their own form of souvenirs.

### BACK AT THE SOVIET EXPO

Before examining how artists in recent years have recontextualized, imitated, and parodied memorabilia, let us engage a novel that accomplished these tasks even prior to the conclusion of the Soviet period. Manuel Pereira's *El ruso*, published in 1980, responded to the 1970s — a decade marked by the failure of the 10-million-ton sugar harvest in 1970, the Padilla Affair in 1971, the First Congress on Education and Development in 1971, and the creation of the Ministry of Culture in 1976, as well as by the Soviets' great technological and scientific achievements, the aura of which, at least, was exported to Cuba. As Juan Abreu recalls in his speech "Deuda" (Debt), slogans such as "writers are manual laborers, because they write with their hands" and "what is magical, what is really marvelous, is the outdated and picturesque vision that has been overtaken by a socialist, scientific, and revolutionary conscience" became the order of the day, suggesting that the 1960s exhortation to resist the socialist-realist style in literature, encapsulated in Che Guevara's concept of the "New Man," had been abandoned.

The process of Sovietization is frequently examined quantitatively, as does Silvia Pérez in her 1983 study on the relationship between Cuba and the Socialist Bloc. She estimates that between 1960 and 1972 technical and economic aid from the USSR to Cuba increased tenfold.[6] Mervyn J. Bain describes the Soviet-Cuban enterprise as having "impinged on virtually every part of life in both countries. By the mid-1980s, this had seen over 5,000 joint projects completed in Cuba and some 8,000 Cubans a year studying in the Soviet Union."[7] For Rafael Rojas, the philosophical penetration of the Soviets and their colonization of the social sciences, alongside Cuba's entrance into the Council for Mutual Economic Assistance, are crucial elements.[8]

These explanations all help to make sense of Manuel Pereira's parody of the overzealous appreciation of the Soviet Union in *El ruso*. Interestingly, when a new edition of the novel was published in Spain in 1982, Pereira explicitly linked "his autobiography of a generation of Cubans" to the 1960s: "It's a story about the young son of an old Communist militant during the crisis of 1962–63, when he was studying in the secondary."[9] The young man is an idiosyncratic Cuban who calls himself "el Ruso" and who quixotically mediates early revolutionary Cuba after the 1961 Bay of Pigs invasion, when the island nation, supported by Soviet and Czech weapons, began to develop closer ties with this "exotic" sphere. El Ruso, overheated in Havana for most of the novel's duration (due to an overcoat he always wears—a wink at Gogol's "The Overcoat"—that he claims is made of astrakhan but is really just remnants of wool), and his best friend "Peróxido," are an adolescent pair of scientists; el Ruso's field is the social sciences, and Peróxido's is engineering. Official Soviet discourse is ridiculed by the narrator's description of el Ruso's doodles:

> Comenzó entonces, frenéticamente, a dibujar monos y más monos sobre el mármol. Primero diseñó un primate colgando de un gajo. A eso siguió una retahíla de pitecántropos copiados de las ilustraciones de un libro de Darwin, y después del Cromagnon y del Hombre de Neandertal, dibujó la silueta de un cosmonauta y escribió arriba el nombre de Yuri Gagarin. Es su respuesta al Cristo de Casablanca. Era, en su febril imaginación, el monumento al materialismo erigido en la propia base del monumento al idealismo. Ésas fueron sus intenciones.[10]

> He then began to draw monkeys frenetically, more and more monkeys over the marble. First he sketched a primate hanging from a branch. He followed this with a string of pithecanthropi copied from the illustrations of a book by Darwin, and after drawing Cro-Magnon and Nean-

derthal man, he drew the silhouette of a cosmonaut and wrote above it the name Yuri Gagarin. It was his answer to the Christ of Casablanca. It was, in his feverish imagination, the monument to materialism erected at the very base of the monument to idealism. Those were his intentions.

This passage portrays a young susceptible mind that is able to imagine a connection between evolution and historical materialism, dramatizing the commensurability between the two systems of thought.

El Ruso's fanaticism for the Soviet Union is the result of his comradely relationship with his father, who shares his Sovietphilia. Although el Ruso was initially attracted to a young girl, Nieves, associating her name with the snowy Soviet climate, he loses his virginity to another young girl, and it is then that he withdraws from his idealist and nebulous state of mind. He finally strips himself of the overcoat, and temporarily, he is both el Ruso and Leonel Magín Hinojosa. However, as el Ruso's father's health worsens, he follows his father's last wish and departs for Odessa to study rocket science; there, he becomes Leonel. El Ruso's personal psychology, wrought by disassociations and delirium, both mirrors and magnifies that of a nation that struggles to be sovereign. As we recall Leonel and his ego ideal, it is difficult not to be haunted by the future as seen within the post-Soviet mirroring of José Manuel Prieto's *Rex*, where the new Russian — Sasha — no longer acknowledges his former "little brother." The years of political indoctrination behind him, Sasha advances within the spectacle, not of Socialism, but rather capitalism.

But let us return to more optimistic times, when, under the effects of Sovietization, Pereira's fictional Cuban adolescents become so delusional that they prepare to launch a household rocket from the beach to east of Havana, toward the cosmic ocean. Having learned everything about Yuri Gagarin and the little dog Laika's trip to outer space from the last Soviet exhibition in Havana and from the catalogues of spaceships that they stole from it, they are intellectually armed. The absurdity within *El ruso*, in some regards, more holistically represents the prism of the 1960s and 1970s than classics of socialist-realist novels such as Manuel Cofiño's 1971 *La última mujer y el próximo combate* (The Last Woman and the Next Battle) and *Cuando la sangre se parece al fuego* (When Blood Resembles Fire), published several years later, in 1975. These novels show the fight of good (born out of Socialist ideals) over evil (which is tied to the leftovers of a bourgeois neo-colonial society). In its representation of the 1960s and 1970s, *El ruso* also often rivals Lisandro Otero's *En ciudad semejante* (In a Certain City), a 1970 novel about the political and historical processes of overturning the society's moral corruption at the start of the Cuban Revolution. *El ruso* exploits the amazing reality of the bizarre imposition of Soviet ideals onto the new emerging nation.

There is no better site to consolidate and visualize this impact than at an exhibition. During Cuba's approximately thirty years of solidarity with the Soviet Bloc, two Soviet expositions took place in Havana. The first was the Soviet Exposition of Science, Technology, and Culture at Havana's National Museum of Fine Arts (February 4–13, 1960), which was inaugurated by the Soviet statesman Anastas Mikoyan. In a conversation with Norberto Fuentes, Mikoyan characterized it as emblematic of the Soviet Bloc's first entrance into revolutionary Cuba.[11] For example, *Lunes de revolución*, the literary cultural supplement of the newspaper *Revolución*, dedicated issue 46 to the event, which was followed by a Soviet film series some weeks later, as well as an important commercial accord.[12] Then, in 1976, an even more astonishing show took place. The Soviet Union covered fifteen thousand square meters of Havana's Academia de las Ciencias, Cuba's old capitol building, with another exposition, *Logros de la ciencia y la técnica soviética* (Accomplishments of Science and Soviet Technology).

The latter is installed in many Cubans' minds as exemplary of the period, and for many artists, it has served as a fount of inspiration. The Soviet expositions are remembered in Reina María Rodríguez's "Nostalgia," Jorge Miralles's "Una breve exposición: . . . fruto de la fantasía" (A Brief Exhibition . . . Fruit of Fantasy), and Esteban Insausti's 2005 documentary entitled *Existen* (They Exist), about the insane on Havana's streets, as well as, less explicitly, within the Vostok visual arts exhibitions of the first decade of the twenty-first century. Reina María Rodríguez contrasts the magnitude of the 1976 exhibition with the imprecise memories current city dwellers have of it:

> To write this piece I spent days asking everyone I came across what they remembered about the great Soviet exhibition shown in the salons of Havana's capitol building in 1970-something. No one could tell me the exact date or what they saw there. Some perhaps remembered the "Lunajod-16" for its lunar novelty, but how many things do we not recall from that fair thirty years later? Like the life-size rocket that did a mock takeoff, shooting artificial fire out of its tail. Would everyone else remember it?[13]

Haziness surrounding the "site of memory," however, does not diminish the exhibition's significance as a point of reference.

A flurry of newspaper articles documenting the exhibition substantiates Reina María Rodríguez's recollection of its significance. Luis López's "Tres horas en la URSS" (Three Hours in the USSR), published in *Verde Olivo* in July 1976, describes the positive impressions of members of the Cuban armed forces, the Ministry of the Interior, and the Youth Labor Party (Ejército Juvenil de Trabajo) regarding those pavilions that corresponded to their respective disciplinary realms. For example, an educator remarked: "The technical and scientific advances that the Soviet Union has had with respect to education is impressive . . . All this indicates to us what in the future we will be able to use and the technological level that we ought to reach."[14] As Rodríguez affirmed, it was the pavilion for science and the investigation of the cosmos that enchanted everyone. López assessed with fervor the section dedicated to Saliut (a space station), Lunajod (a lunar vehicle), and Luna 16 (the first lunar probe to land on the moon and return to Earth), where he encountered "cosmonauts' uniforms, and the equipment used for advanced satellite communications. It is the fascinating world of young science of our century: cosmonautics."[15]

Rodríguez's description differs from such journalistic pieces in her nostalgia and quiet disappointment that such a future never arrived and in her wish that the dream represented by the exposition had not vanished so quickly. In contrast, Jorge Miralles, born in 1967, hardly sounds disillusioned. He captures details about the transformations within the building for the event that went unremarked by the newspapers. "The sculpture highest up on the ceiling of a woman forged in bronze was replaced by a hologram of Vladimir Ilich Ulianov Lenin . . . The Soviet contraption replaced, paradoxically, the old symbol of the liberty of the Republic, with a new and even more extravagant one, the Socialist."[16] Bitterness over the effort to mold Cuban national identity to resemble Soviet identity for the purpose of "progress" seeps through Miralles's matter-of-factness. The actual displacing of the Republican imaginary with the Soviet one, we might recall, was absent from Ernesto René Rodríguez's "Solarística," wherein the two coexist, but only in the protagonist's imagination of a felicity that was replaced by the new global imposition. Reina María Rodríguez and Miralles's accounts of the exhibition, like Masvidal's story of the cartoons, illustrate how each generation's identity is asserted through the casting aside of a segment of history. This Revolution's future—not entirely distinct from the course that many emerging nations take around the world, though perhaps with more force, given how close to the United States the island is—depended on the erection of great Socialist causes and the categorical burial of those elements that would not benefit it.


A NEW SCIENTIFIC FAMILY

Pereira was questioning the ethics of such reductions as early as 1980. To what degree does Pereira's fictive exhibition in *El ruso* resemble the real one? While today the Internet is a virtual space where ideological and scientific battles can be carried out, in the early 1960s the fight for world domination was carried out in outer space. The Soviet-Cuban solidarity in outer space and the spirit of the Soviet exposition is transformed in the artwork of Antonio Eligio "Tonel" Fernández (born 1958). His exhibit, *Conversación con "La primera carga . . ."* (Conversation with "the First Charge"), which took place in July 2003 in Old Havana, is a parody of the heroic rhetoric within Soviet-Cuban solidarity. Tonel's influences in this exhibit are multiple, but it is impossible to skip over Manuel Octavio Gómez's film *La primera carga al machete* (The First Charge of the Machete, 1969), cited by Tonel as artwork with which he began a conversation years before. We can only speculate that a combination of the film's aesthetic approach (cinéma vérité) and its content (the war in 1869 between Cuban peasants and Spanish soldiers) was a seductive point of departure for Tonel's assemblage of objects, photographs of an international team of scientists, and etchings, into which the artist also inserted his "grandfather," Antonio Fernández, whose questionable link to these histories makes spectators wonder about the reliability of the artist's narrative. If the North American artist Joseph Cornell created boxes out of found objects in a surrealist vein, Tonel's cabinets—filled with Radar shirts (a Cuban brand popular in the 1970s and 1980s) and small metal pins with revolutionary themes, some evocative of Cuban-Soviet solidarity, including a metal monogram from the V. I. Lenin Vocational School—reflect the everyday but surreal life of Cubans.[17] In other words, the cabinets evidence the disparity between these cultures, whose juxtaposition is a surreal invention with which Tonel is strangely comfortable.

Tonel inscribes his "grandfather" Antonio Fernández into a vignette that forms part of his *Conversación con "La primera carga . . ."* He said that between 1962 and 1970, Fernández led a team of international rocket scientists, who, from a modest house in the neighborhood of Nicanor del Campo in Playa, investigated traveling to the moon and back, using the Soviet space launch facility in Baikonur (a city in Kazakhstan previously known as Leninsk) as a landing site. Like *El ruso*, Tonel's *Conversación con "La primera carga . . ."* leaves no doubt as to the paternalism of the nation when he exaggerates the phallocentric nature of the iconography of the Cold War's space race. In *Baikonur* (Before), a rocket explodes like an immense phallus. Similarly, the intersection of collective and personal fantasies are addressed in *Héroes de Baikonur* (Heroes of Baikonur), wherein in one part of the installation, an alternative family portrait includes, clockwise from top left, Vladimir Mayakovsky, Trotsky, Lenin, Rosa Luxembourg, and finally, Antonio Fernández. Tonel's instrumentation of such figures points to his critique of and homage to the Soviet past. As Juan Antonio Molina has remarked, in the early 1980s Leandro Soto subverted "the epical tradition of direct post-revolutionary photography" in his *Retablo familiar* (Family Altarpiece), but Tonel takes Soto's "tragicomic reconstruction of

Héroes de Baikonur *(detail), by Tonel, 2003, from the exhibit* Conversación con
"La primera carga . . . ," *La Casona Gallery, Havana, 2003. Courtesy of artist.*

official codes of representation"[18] to a new level when he envisions his grandfather within this bizarre international family. Salomon Berman's analysis of
the post-Soviet "search for an authentic Cuban brand of Marxism" elucidates a
context in which the dimensions of Tonel's artistic family can be apprehended.
For Berman, the search at the end of the 1990s and start of the millennium

> has expanded to figures and authors forgotten, ostracized, or banned by
> the Soviet Union and therefore of little or no diffusion in Cuba during
> the hegemony of the reverent view. These figures include Leon Trotsky
> and Rosa Luxemburg, but especially the so-called superstructure au-
> thors for their emphasis on the relative autonomy of human conscious-
> ness, among them Georg Lukács and, above anybody else, Antonio
> Gramsci.[19]

Mayakovsky's fate is similarly fascinating. Although Spanish translations of
his poetry of the workers are well disseminated in Cuba, access to his satiri-
cal poetry, critical of "diverse social phenomena of Soviet society," written between 1922 and 1932, is limited. According to Desiderio Navarro, the selection
of poems included in Lila Guerrero's 1943 anthology (published in Buenos
Aires by Claridad) showed a more "benign" face. Navarro was contracted to

publish a broader selection in the 1980s, but that project has yet to be completed, a delay that speaks not only to the complicated legacy of the Soviets in Cuba, but also to the complicated nature of Cuban cultural politics.[20]

The union of Tonel's grandfather with these Russian revolutionaries nuances this historical quest for progress, captured within the Soviet exposition, and makes spectators feel almost as if they were traversing a family photo album linked to the fading moments of a nation's history. It familiarizes history by substituting first names for surnames, and makes it seem as if Cuba's involvement in the Soviet exploration in outer space were the culmination of the October Revolution.

What is the point of this artistic mnemonic rendering in today's world — why not simply bury it within the annals of foolishness? Tonel unfastens the logic of history, recasting aspects of it in a manner that he deems fit. In 1967, *Islas* published Samuel Feijóo's travelogue of his journey to the Soviet Union alongside a chronicle of Vladimir Mayakovsky's trip to Havana. The issue was dedicated to the October Revolution and was evidence of the historical basis for Tonel's fantasies. In "Mayakovski en la Habana" (Mayakovsky in Havana), Juan Hernández introduces the poet's twenty-four hours in Havana on his way to Mexico and the United States in 1925. The Russian poet was impressed by "el antiguo y exótico *folklore*" (the ancient and exotic folklore)[21] and by the "alimentos . . . desconocidos, pero sabrosos" (the food . . . unfamiliar but delicious).[22] In "La novela es el género . . ." (The Novel Is the Genre . . .), the text that accompanied Tonel's exhibit, the artist experiments with the genre of testimony, fantasizing about a fortuitous encounter that takes place on a streetcar in 1925 between his "grandfather," a streetcar driver who also happened to be a poet, and Mayakovsky. Out of that brief meeting Tonel claims that his grandfather became the "primer poeta castellano de su generación en ser traducido al ruso, al kirguíz, al tártaro y al armenio (de todas esas ediciones príncipes, por suerte, se han salvado copias en los archivos de la familia)" (the first Spanish poet of his generation to be translated into Russian, Kirghiz, Tatar, and Armenian [of all these first editions, copies have luckily been saved in the family archives]). With a tone evocative of Jorge Luis Borges and Witold Gombrowicz, both origins and legacy are construed as overdetermined by history. Tonel ridicules the links between family and national pride, rendering humorous "his grandfather's" entrance into Soviet internationalism.

Tonel's 2009 exhibit, *Cosmos: Feeling the Pull of Gravity* (Chelsea Galleria, Miami), manifests how definitions and explanations mirror the desires of those in power. *Lunajod-1* and *Lunajod-2* exemplify the dream of robust Soviet machinery and the superficiality and frailty that characterize the present. *Lunajod-1* evokes the greatness of the Soviet machinery, while *Lunajod-2* all but erases it and leaves the spectator with a golf cart that oddly resembles one of the

Lunajod-1 *and* Lunajod-2, *by Tonel, 2009, from the exhibit* Cosmos: Feeling the Pull of Gravity, *Chelsea Galleria, Miami, Florida, 2009. Courtesy of artist.*

more unusual modes of transport in Havana, those doorless two-seater yellow motorized vehicles carrying tourists paying in hard currency one year, and nationals the next. Fantasies of greatness in the form of photographs of the moon are fast sinking from the frame of Tonel's *Lunajod-2*. The golf cart's reappearance on the Cuban scene represents the return of the ideology that the Revolution sought to abolish.[23] In his statement on the exhibit, Tonel links the first Lunajod to the second.

> The show tries to connect the events taking place miles away and above the earth with some of the realities of the post–Cold War period, from the expansion of suburban life with its quintessential golf courses and golf carts to the triumph of neo-liberalism, free-market ideology and world (or perhaps cosmic) trade. The effects of the gravitational law have clearly played a role in all of these developments, affecting the rockets that are still being launched from Baikonur in Kazakhstan as well as the golf balls that fly over the artificial green grass of North American golf courses, not to mention the ups and downs of mighty superheroes.

Tonel's cynicism reveals not only the underside of the spectacle of the Soviet phantasm, but also a web of intellectual, familiar, and sexual intimacies of which it forms part. He illustrates the ways in which one cosmos can sublimate an-

History (Always Wraps Itself in Red Fabric), *by Tonel, 2009, from the exhibit* Cosmos: Feeling the Pull of Gravity, *Chelsea Galleria, Miami, Florida, 2009.* *Courtesy of artist.*

other and insists upon remembering the processes of these sublimations. His *History (Always Wraps Itself in Red Fabric)* catches viewers off-guard by turning Stalin into a giant beside Little Red Riding Hood and Superman. At first glance, the three figures wrapped in red could be a novel rendition of a fairy tale or superhero story, rather than a fairy-tale-like packaging of Communist history. Frivolity and play—the same qualities that are upheld by José Manuel Prieto and that are said to be absent from the Soviet Bloc cartoons—are central. These qualities, predominantly cast aside by monumental narratives of progress, are the mainstays for Tonel's humorous and dramatic rereading of the twentieth century, which foregrounds the importance of the space wars and scientific competitions.

## SPARE PARTS OF THE SOVIET MACHINERY

Tonel is not the only artist to present reincarnations of the Soviet machinery within Cuban families. The diptych drawing in pencil and felt pen entitled *Valentinas Tereshkova*, by Gertrudis Rivalta, the same artist who painted *Quinceañera con Kremlin*, points to Cubans' ironic distance from the foreign narrative of a Soviet woman launched into outer space in 1963. In the drawing, ten women, most of them seemingly fair complexioned, though two or three of them are likely of mixed race, are grouped together with the female cosmonaut in the background. The aspiration of being like Tereshkova, reflected in the phrase, "Todas queremos ser como Valentina Tereshkova" (We all want to be like Valentina Tereshkova), sublimates the phrase "Todos queremos ser como el Che" (We all want to be like Che). In fact, it takes several viewings to realize that the words "el Che" are present in the image. In the second part of this diptych, there is an implicit reply: "Que fue de nuestras Valentinas Tereshkovas" (What happened to our Valentinas Tereshkovas). The remains are artificial eyelashes. Suset Sánchez's analysis of Rivalta's appropriation of history is crucial to understanding the weight of a figure such as Tereshkova within these visual representations.

> This palimpsestic warp that Gertrudis creates within her work, starting with the accumulation and overlapping of figures from the History of Cuba, and along with it, of historical times, destroys, through fiction, the reality of a teleological project sustained as an inexorable destiny toward which the progressive forces that have participated in the nation's becoming are directed.[24]

To a large extent, artists such as Rivalta inject new meaning into contestable memory sites. As is well known, Vostok (meaning "east" in Russian) was a Soviet spaceflight project whose goal was sending people into orbit around Earth; it used the Vostok spacecraft, designed for human spaceflight. Launched from Baikonur in 1961 with Yuri Gagarin onboard, Vostok was the first space flight with a crew. The spacecraft's last flight, with Valentina Tereshkova on board, was in 1963. The Vostok program manifested the excellence of Soviet political, economic, scientific, and technological command — excellence that in

Valentinas Tereshkova, *diptych by Gertrudis Rivalta, 2004. Courtesy of artist.*

the aftermath of the Soviet Union's disintegration was overshadowed by Cuba's embarrassment over its history having overlapped with this failed superpower.

That cosmonaut past can be identified not only by the number of Cuban Yuris and Laikas these days (fewer Laikas than Yuris, given the life span of dogs), but also by the numerous artistic interventions that reflect upon Vostok, starting with Manuel Pereira's *El ruso*. On an even more concrete level, besides the Taller de Reparación de Aviones Cosmonauta Yuri Gagarin (Airplane Repair Workshop of Cosmonaut Yuri Gagarin), founded in 1966 by Raúl Castro, the word *"Vostok"* throws *habaneros* back to another repair shop of a different, more tedious order, which does not specialize in military airplanes, but rather in Soviet appliances. In November 2007, the Taller de Reparaciones de Equipos Electrodomésticos Vostok (Vostok Appliances Repair Workshop) was transformed into an exhibition space, one of two sites of a collective exhibition entitled Vostok: Proyecto de exposición colectiva (Vostok: A Collective Exhibition Project), by the curators Frency Fernández and Victoria Gallardo. For being an award-winning exhibition, it is surprising that one of the few places that acknowledge it is its own blogspot (http://www.proyectovostok.blogspot .com). Before the exhibition's inauguration, it was briefly announced in *La Jiribilla*, a Cuban cultural journal, and Rafael Grillo published a substantial article about it in an online publication. Little public discussion ensued around the event, however, and those intellectuals based in Havana who I knew to be interested in the artistic and sociocultural phenomena related to the remains of the

Valentinas Tereshkova, *diptych by Gertrudis Rivalta, 2004. Courtesy of artist.*

USSR on the island said that they had not even heard of the project. Regarding the meaning of artwork, Hans Haacke affirmed in his discussions with Pierre Bourdieu that "the problem is not only to say something, to take a position, but also to create a productive provocation. The sensitivity of the context into which one inserts something, or the manner in which one does it, can trigger a public debate."[25] However, with Vostok, seemingly no public debate ensued, and in line with Haacke, the meaning of the exhibition is put into question.

While few knew anything, one source, attributing the information to a rumor, said that some of the works had been censored or destroyed and that the exhibition at the Vostok workshop in Centro Havana (an impoverished neighborhood in the city's center) was actually closed early. Another spoke of not understanding the youngest participating artists' anger toward the Soviet Bloc when they were too young to have lived through Cuba's solidarity with it. In response to my question about the technique he utilized, one young exhibitor provided a little extra information, saying that his work "was disappeared by political authorities," and that another artist's was partially so—an act that he said greatly affected the entire exhibition. Like many Cubans before him, he attributed this occurrence to the most repressive legacies of the Soviet Union.

The majority of the artists who showed their work were born in the 1960s and early 1970s and came of age at about the time of the disintegration of the Socialist camp. The world they inhabit is distinct from that which informed a previous generation of artists, such as Cosme Proenza, Arturo Montoto, Rocío

García, and Manuel Alcalde, all of whom were children at the height of the Cold War (a war that was fought, in part, through scientific experiments such as Vostok) and who, as young adults, studied in the USSR. For all of Vostok's exhibitors, the actual Vostok program was, for all intents and purposes, only inherited memory: Jairo Alfonso was born in 1974, Tessio Barba in 1975, Alejandro Campins in 1981, Diana Fonseca in 1978, José Fidel García in 1981, Hamlet Lavastida in 1983, Ernesto Leal in 1971, Jorge Luis Marrero in 1970, Gertrudis Rivalta in 1971, Lázaro Saavedra in 1964, Ezequiel Suárez in 1967, and Ulises Urra in 1972.

With the 2007 Vostok exhibition in mind, let us briefly recall some of the other moments of the artistic panorama of the 1960s and 1970s that were recycled and resignified between 2005 and 2008. In December 2006, just five months after Raúl Castro took over command of the island for the first time, debate around the Gray Period of the 1970s and the resurgence of one of its biggest figureheads, Luis Pavón, ignited both in virtual Cuba and in Cuba's capital.[26]

In April 2007, approximately four months after "Pavóngate" and just six months prior to the Vostok exhibition, Los 70: Puente para las rupturas (The 70s: Bridge for Ruptures) opened at the National Museum of Fine Arts in Havana. Its core rationale was to show that the 1970s was not as artistically repressive and monolithic as it is often conceived. The national museum project was actually in the making for some time. Its curator, Hortensia Montero Méndez, argued that the art of the 1970s possessed commonalities with both the art of the hopeful 1960s and the critical 1980s. That is, Cuban artists — many of whom came from the countryside to take advantage of the new national initiatives — may have created works that reflected the period's principal official rhetoric in favor of the pedagogical value of art, but they did not imitate Soviet socialist realism. Quoting Pedro Pablo Oliva, Montero Méndez asserts: "The 1970s was a world full of dreams linked to what in politics they now call utopian socialism. It meant dreaming of a better world, a lovely and beautiful world, which led many people to attempt to transform it, so they could improve it, so they could make it much more lovely."[27]

With that spirit of the decade in mind, the exhibition showcased a return to nature, the myths of Cubanía, as well as photorealism. On the one hand, the extent to which the Soviet Union peopled the imaginary of 1970s Cuba is not explicitly apparent in any of the works, although Montero Méndez points out that many of the artists did, in fact, study there. On the other hand, the emphasis upon utopianism can be viewed either as the product of Soviet influence or simply as tendencies common to both countries on account of shared ideologies.

As Juan Carlos Betancourt details, "an ample catalog of images attests to the presence of Perestroika on the island."[28] In a discussion of the praxis of artists such as René Francisco, Eduardo Ponjuan, Glexis Novoa, Lázaro Saavedra, and José Angel Toirac, Betancourt "proves the critical connection of their poetics to the socialist realist aesthetic whose corpse had been buried formally in Havana at the beginning of the 1980s."[29] Cuban travelers were not the only ones to insert themselves into Perestroika; so did Cuban artists in the late 1980s and early 1990s, who painted portraits of the most important of Soviet figureheads. Alexis Esquivel's 1990 *Retrato escultórico de Lenin* (Sculptural Portrait of Lenin) portrays a monumentally bodied Lenin seeming to be hitchhiking on a Cuban street, and his 1992 *Retrato de Gorbachov en pose romántica* (Portrait of Gorbachev in a Romantic Pose) places a giant Gorbachev with a hammer and sickle on his red t-shirt in front of a mountain range (miniscule by comparison) and a stormy sky, demonstrating the leader's struggle to maintain his ideology in a transforming landscape. Esquivel not only plays with soon-to-be-ousted Soviet figures, but also places autochthonous heroes in unheroic poses. Che Guevara, for example, leans back on a toilet, his legs extended, monsterlike, reading a newspaper; the whirlwind of Fidel Castro eats a strawberry ice cream cone (rather than pontificating on a microphone). Betancourt describes similar parodies of socialist realism in the works of René Francisco and Eduardo Ponjuán:

> The numbers in "Composición 26753" (1989, Composition 7/26/53) allude to the date of the battle when a group of young soldiers led by Fidel Castro attacked the barracks of a Batista military regiment. It marked the beginning of the July 26th Movement . . . It also depicts the red and black flag of that movement in the form of a square, reminiscent of the Russian vanguard, but placed in a kitsch background as found in the sort of cheap ever-present reproductions on the walls of Cuban homes.[30]

Raúl Cordero's 2001 mixed-media piece *Lo que pasaba en el banco de abajo mientras yo pintaba el retrato de Yuri Gagarin* (What Happened on the Bench Downstairs While I Painted Yuri Gagarin), realized about a decade after the parodies just discussed, is a minutely realistic reproduction of the most disseminated photograph of the mythical figure in his spacesuit with the letter "C" of "CCCP" visible. The video installation, however, picks up on the partial representation of the name of the nation and grounds the cosmonaut on the street below the artist's Havana studio. Cristina Vives describes the contrast as almost Brechtian: "The video breaks the 'spell' and Yuri Gagarin—the theme—loses prominence in order to yield it to the bench—the circumstance—that is Cordero's center of interest."[31] A curious aside is that the actual, up-close monumentalism of Gagarin was as unknown to Cordero, who was born in 1971, as it was to the participants in the Vostok exhibition.

While some works in Vostok utilize comparable strategies, others apply a myriad of techniques to excerpt objects and moments from the imported Soviet world and recast them within a new Cuban twenty-first-century topography. For instance, snowy landscapes of small villages characterize Alejandro Campins's work, but there is something strange and out-of-place within these otherwise idealistic images. In *Todo se cocina en la misma hoguera* (All Is Cooked in the Same Bonfire), a flock of birds flies in a churchlike building, and the text reads: "Entran por la izquierda, Escapan por la derecha" (They Enter at the Left, Escape at the Right). It is difficult to read the artist's statements as descriptions alone, without taking into account political ideology. In another untitled piece, Campins places what could be an Eastern European landscape in the foreground with a sea behind it and, in the background, a tropical island.[32] The image is reminiscent of the kinds of blurry, surrealistic landscapes evoked in Ulises Rodríguez Febles's play *Sputnik* and Jorge Miralles's "Fotos de boda." Through naïve stylization, Campins suggests an encounter between a dominant territory and a faraway place under its sphere of influence. In *Es tan grande que aplasta* (This Is so Big That It Crushes), a red cloudlike figure monopolizes a light blue sky and splatters something red onto the landscape below. Handscripted in black, with the second word scratched out in red, with only part of an "I" and an "Ó" remaining visible, is written: "ESTA ——IÓN ES TAN GRANDE QUE APLASTA" (This ——ion is so big that it crushes).

In a 2007 interview, Abel Prieto, Cuba's cultural minister, characterized the nation's bittersweet reflection on the Soviet Bloc by referencing his book-long essay from a decade earlier, *El humor de Misha* (The Humor of Misha). "What I was interested in, obviously, was to discuss always in a humorous, ironical tone if the link with the Soviets meant something 'backward' or 'advancement.'"[33] Likewise, Campins's bittersweet oil paintings suggest that repression is part and parcel of ideological constructions, even if they are construed idealistically, as in his palette of childlike colors, which obliges viewers to feel empathy for the dreams of solidarity.[34]

In a similar vein, Jorge Luis Marrero's work imparts an old pedagogical lesson wherein Lenin instructs a Cuban who is placed in the role of the child. In *Ya es hora* (It's Time), for example, the image of Lenin appears alongside a child's scribbles, as if the artist were narrating the evolution of the "national" into the "international." In another of Marrero's works, cut-outs of film reels display a medley of Soviet Bloc cartoons, the emblem of *Sovexportfilm*, and V. Borisov and Y. Seguei's *Como fui mono* (How I Was a Monkey).[35] Marrero's paintings, even more directly than Campins's, allude to a form of colonization. In fact,

*Es tan grande que aplasta,* by Alejandro Campins, *from the exhibition Vostok: Proyecto de exposición colectiva, Havana, 2007.*

Marrero explained to me that *Ya es hora* is comprised of enlarged reproductions of little drawings he did as a child within a Russian schoolbook translated into Spanish, which told stories about the October Revolution. The originals can be seen in the upper corners of the adult paintings. Undoubtedly, Marrero's childhood paintings and those of Pereira's "El Ruso" form part of the same universe, which is construed through the tenets of Marxism-Leninism. Marrero's many images evoke childhood and transmit an odd lightheartedness within this process. International revolutionary solidarity, like evolution, entails a definitive line of progress; the starting point is the monkey, and the endpoint—an author of one's own destiny.

Subjugation of the personal to collective politics is the concern of Tessio Barba's montage of the Kremlin shown above the emblem of a Zil automobile[36] (the Soviet/Russian brand driven by the Cuban government), engraved on a naked body. In another Barba collage, a militaristic Fidel shouts "Todos somos uno" (We are all one) beside a military parade. Like other exhibitors in Vostok, Barba recalls another pleasurable part of the Revolution and his own infancy

Ya es hora, *by Jorge Luis Marrero, 1999. Courtesy of artist.*

through a reference to the Soviet circus and a school notebook that reads, "La educación es el futuro del país" (Education is the future of the country). The Russian circus, in fact, returned to Havana during the Cuban book fair in 2010.

In a more acerbic interrogation of militarism and solidarity, Hamlet Lavastida engages an undoubtedly inherited memory with graffiti-like stencils of Castro and Khrushchev on the city's walls, along with "Partido del Pueblo

Cubano" (Party of the Cuban People), and the saying "unidad monolítica de pueblo, ejército y partido" (monolithic unity of the people, military, and party). Lavastida's work is immediately exposed to the elements—as soon as it is elaborated on the streets of Havana, it is erased, as it aims to challenge the dominant semiotic codes. As Rafael Grillo aptly asserts in his coverage of the exhibition, "if irony and even a certain cynicism predominates, both readings are present in the work of the gathered artists." For Grillo, Hamlet Lavastida "represents the most radical of the critical visions with his installation and video projection duet titled *Microfracción o Macrofracción* (Micro-fraction or Macro-fraction), a collage of images and press headlines that not in vain includes the phrase 'Return to Colonialism' among its most disturbing messages."[37] "*Microfracción*," we remember, was the term used by Raúl and Fidel Castro in 1968 to refer to the supposedly pro-Soviet and treacherous faction led by Aníbal Escalante. By calling his installation and video projection *Microfracción o Macrofracción*, Lavastida challenges the limits of this memorialization of a Soviet past. Can artistic defiance be so explicit as to cast these new street semantics over a "revolutionary tribunal" led by Raúl Castro, the head of the Cuban state when this artistic piece was executed?

Lavastida's approach to critiquing the Gray Period involves a semiological encounter with the past in a project that he calls "UMAP." This is the acronym for Unidades Militares para la Ayuda de Producción (Military Units to Aid Production), the highly repressive and internationally criticized camps established in 1965 and closed sometime between 1967 and 1969. Lavastida resignifies the acronym by assigning new words to each letter—Unión Militante de Agitación y Propaganda (Militant Union for Agitation and Propaganda)—and using it to refer to the street art he creates and soon after erases.

Lavastida proposes to transform the visual universe of Havana's streets through defamiliarization and recontextualization. In his works, made on walls six meters wide and three meters high and displayed in miniature on the Vostok blog, expressions of commitment to social and political causes are depleted of their original significance. No longer solely part of a national patrimony, objects such as the Cuban edition of *Manual básico del miliciano de tropas territoriales* (1981) (Basic Manual of the Militiamen of Territory Troops), are now housed among other found objects. The Vostok project illustrates the desire to work through multiple narratives of "spare parts" originating in the Soviet Bloc.

As suggested by the Vostok exhibition as well as by the artwork of the late 1980s and early 1990s to which it already harkens back, some of the strategies utilized by Cuban artists to represent the post-Soviet situation are comparable to those employed by artists of late Socialism in other parts of the world. Among the traits that Aleš Erjavec calls characteristic of the art and culture of late Socialism are "profuse employment of socialist and Communist imagery,"[38] the result of the "specific conditions of possibility"[39] shared by Socialist countries. While Erjavec goes on to say that the 1990s witnessed "very little of the previous interest in such art and culture,"[40] the postmodern strategies of recycling and recontextualizing Soviet realities are identifiable within Cuban art, not only immediately after the fall of the Berlin Wall, but within the new millennium.[41]

Cuban visual artists are not the only ones to intentionally disrupt the monumentalism of Soviet science. The cosmonaut Yuri Gagarin is *choteo*-ized by Ramón Fernández Larrea (born 1958) in a letter published in *Cubaencuentro's* humor column. According to Damián Fernández, who elaborates upon Jorge Mañach's fundamental term within Cuban studies, the *choteo* "deauthorizes authority by debunking it and constitutes a form of rebellion . . . In the world of choteo individual exceptionalism and personal attachments are valued above the personal rules and distant norms of bureaucratic order."[42] A leading poet of the generation of the 1980s and well-known radio host, Fernández Larrea embraces the epistolary form in his publications for *Encuentro de la cultura cubana*, the leading journal of the Cuban diaspora. Whether he writes to a tin can of condensed milk or to a suitcase for the school in the countryside, he focuses on the most mundane details of collective experience through parody and personification, the very strategies he implements in his "Carta a Yuri Gagarin" (Letter to Yuri Gagarin), a letter that looks back at the idealism and foolishness of the 1960s through bits of anecdotes about Gagarin in light of what happened to Cuba in the subsequent decades. The letter's opening salutation, "Ingrávido y cosmopolita Yuri Alexeyevich Gagarin" (Weightless and cosmopolitan Yuri Alexeyevich Gagarin), implements the lofty language characteristic of official communiqués to mock the Soviet legacy in Cuba. Fernández Larrea reveals at the start that his initial impression of Gagarin — "vestidito de blanco, junto a una cosa grande, verde, barbuda, desaliñada y con boina, saludando con cara de ruso alegre a la multitud por toda la calle 23" (dressed in white, next to a big green thing, bearded, scruffy, and with a beret, waving with the face of a happy Russian to the multitude on Twenty-Third Street) — is exceptionally early (from 1961), long before he even needed to shave — "aún no había probado las cuchillas Astra" (I hadn't yet tried Astra razors). Astra razors, manufactured in the Czech Republic, form part of the Socialist brand imaginary for Cubans. Artists' recitation and recycling of such objects in the post-Soviet era, however, are means to exert power over the Cuban destiny. For Fernández Larrea, Gagarin represents the Soviet yoke that inspired his own and Cuba's youth, as well as a young Castro, with dreams of fortitude through the invention of a spaceship only big enough to fit a homunculus (Gagarin was five foot two, Fernández Larrea informs) — a spacecraft named "Vostok" whose size the author compares to the decrepit dwellings in Centro Havana. By calling attention to the novel form of mediation of the post-Soviet world—the Internet—Fernández Larrea perhaps too easily dismisses the geopolitics of the Cold War.

> Más allá de aquella imagen imborrable que guardo, de tu uniforme blanco y tu sonrisa de guajiro estepario, al lado del lobo estrafalario, he tenido que buscarte ahora en otros lugares. Como Internet, por ejemplo. Internauta cosmogónico yo, listo y nada aniñado, he buscado de galaxia en galaxia, ahora que cosmo todos los días y mi órbita es más desorbitante. Internado en Internet he hallado datos tuyos que no cesan de darme vueltas en el globo del ojo y que surcan mi descosmunal imaginación como un *sputnik* fantasmal.[43]

> Beyond that indelible image that I keep of you in your white uniform and your smile, like a hick's from the steppes, beside the outlandish wolf, I've now had to look for you in other places. Like on the Internet, for example. Me—a cosmogonical Internaut—sharp and far from childlike, I have looked around the galaxies, now that I traverse the cosmos every day and my orbit is more exorbitant. Interned in the Internet I have found facts about you that never stop turning in my eyeball and that plow into my enormous imagination like a phantasmagoric sputnik.

Remembering Gagarin's death in a 1968 flight accident, Fernández Larrea makes it clear that nothing is sacred. He wishes that Gagarin had landed on Fidel Castro, and thus, through what at first seems to be a benign use of apostrophe of a Soviet hero becomes symbolic regicide. Furthermore, Fernández Larrea's remarks about the Internet's lack of reliability—the very medium through which his writing is disseminated—also render a strange nostalgia for the era of his childhood, when he was too naïve and trusting to detect the idiosyncrasies of Gagarin, the person that turned into a cult figure. Fernández Larrea foregrounds the difference between the galaxy of the 1960s and the virtual space of the new millennium through which the author is linked to other Cubans who have been, like himself, let loose in the intergalactic diaspora, alone and yet virtually intertwined through their memories of the miniature Soviet hero on the Cuban street.

## SOVIET WANDERING SIGNIFIERS

The condition of the phantasmagoric sputnik is exploded within Estebán Insausti's 2005 documentary *Existen*, which recovers old *noticieros* footage to explain Cubans' deterritorialized condition. The documentary shows sociological, cultural, and political transition by demonstrating what happens when a principal element within the symbolic order is dislodged. It is as if *Existen's* subjects have been traumatized and desire the restoration of the symbolic order.

The documentary's frame is the 1960 Soviet exhibition in Havana, which, having taken place one year before the first manned spacecraft, Vostok, highlighted the same aspects of Soviet greatness. *Existen* documents the most recognizable insane people on Havana's streets. Like the exhibition Vostok, which transforms Cuba's topography by exhibiting artists' memories of their country's relationship to the East, *Existen* foregrounds certain elements of a recent past that still haunt Havana, that are unforgettable within the discourse of the "crazies." As a portrait of Havana, the twenty-five-minute film can be seen as a counterpoint to Fernando Pérez's 2004 *Suite Habana*, where the actors live their lives articulated through provocative silences, dreams, and disillusionments that compose Havana's revolutionary topography of social habits, dependencies, and aspirations. In *Existen* the camera focuses on a handful of insane men who are recognizable to Habaneros precisely because they consistently situate themselves in the same public spaces. However, it is not the city's landscapes that are recalled in *Existen*, but rather the faces and words of those who inhabit it. Spectators merely get glimpses of the places that they occupy. The speech of the "characters" in *Existen* is captioned below in the original Spanish, as if their disoriented argot were in need of translation. Besides having screened at a number of international festivals, *Existen* received the Coral Prize for the best experimental documentary by the Twenty-Eighth International Festival of Latin America Cinema in Havana.

Thanks to the use of montage and a velocity of cuts reminiscent of a music video, spectators can hardly distinguish between the past and the recitation of it by the mentally ill in the present. What is especially interesting to me is the extent to which the globalizing present infringes upon how the Soviet past is remembered and represented, and what the future consequences of this growing archive may be.

From the beginning of the documentary, the music, provided by the Cuban groups Nacional Electrónica and X Alfonso, is a protagonist in the exploration of arrested sociopolitical development. Nacional Electrónica, composed of a diversity of styles, is influenced by German and British techno music, but they make it clear that their sound is "'poor', rudimentary, dirty, homemade."[44] Nacional Electrónica's contribution to the film is particularly significant in the context of examining Cubans' memory of the Soviet machine age. Permit me an interwoven tale about the video, directed by Eduardo Benchoam, for one of their songs, "¡Llegamos al futuro!" (We've Made It to the Future!), in which an actor, reminiscent of a character from Fritz Lang's *Metropolis*, contemplates an issue of the magazine *Sputnik* whose cover headline reads "Gagarin: Apertura de la era cósmica" (Gagarin: Opening of the Cosmic Era). The next frame focuses on a vinyl record of Soviet music. From a small workshop space, typical of today's makeshift Havana, the video's protagonist—a cosmonaut, apparently—is propelled into outer space. As the lyrics place him entering Soyuz and leaving Moscow behind, he walks in slow motion, finally making his way to the top of an unidentified Havana building, and presses the button. The *Sputnik* cover appears to be from 1981, while the landscape into which the protagonist is first projected seems deserted. Might we once again be in Tarará, the area to the east of Havana in which the victims of Chernobyl were sent (and Polina Martínez Shvietsova situated the encounter of her *polovina* protagonists)? Or perhaps it is Alamar, the Russian neighborhood that once accommodated Russian technicians, most of whom left many years before?

Upon examining the cosmonaut, we observe that his oxygen tank hardly resembles one; it looks more like an intravenous catheter, as if the video's director could not locate the precise part within his own workshop to fit the post-Soviet cosmonaut, and perhaps preferred this more gruesome apparatus. The outcome is an image more evocative of Lázaro Saavedra and Rubén Torres Llorca's 1989 exhibit, *Una mirada retrospectiva* (A Retrospective Gaze), comparable to the post-Soviet realm elsewhere: the matrioshka and Elpidio Valdés, the hero of the cartoons who fought against Spanish colonialism, are linked—not by the embrace of solidarity, but rather by an intravenous catheter, pumping blood into Elpidio. In fact, what makes Enrique Colina's fifty-two-minute documentary *Los rusos en Cuba* (2008) especially provocative are its final scenes, in which Saavedra speaks about this installation as Los Van Van's song "Se acabó el querer" (Wanting Is Done With) plays, and a young, modern-day Cuban girl dances in front of a mural of Cuban and Soviet flags, with cuts of old footage from the years of the Soviet-Cuban solidarity in the background. At once, Saavedra cuts the catheter in the foreground.[45]

*Existen* suggests that the insane are enslaved by the empowered discourse of so-called sanity, in line with the postmodern theory of Foucault and Deleuze and Guatarri, among many others. The most critical aspects of Vostok, such as Lavastida's *Microfracción o Macrofracción*, suggested that the Soviet and Cuban alliance placed Cubans in the roles of apes. In *Existen* the Soviets are portrayed as the principal architects of the colonization and hijacking of present-day Cuba by numerous powers, but the words of the marginalized themselves suggest that the US blockade and certain Cuban governmental policies are all complicit in the endeavor. It is as if Nacional Electrónica's music leads into the very decapitation of a human cartoon figure. The captions below read: "¿Por qué perdemos la cabeza?" (Why do we lose our minds?).[46]

At this point viewers are referred to answers contained within a catalogue of distinct transnational relationships. While the Vostok spaceflight project epitomizes the first part of the story, where the Cuban youth still has the potential of embodying the Soviet ideal, in *Existen* the Soviet ideal is already transformed into Cuban disfigurement. It is precisely this juxtaposition that is the focus of many narratives of the last ten years, making the film's initial voice-over particularly illuminating:

> Given the ideological characteristics of the exhibiting nation, we ought to declare that, in some way, the fact that the determined state in use and its perfect right to expand its economic and commercial horizon and exhibit its products before another country does not necessarily imply that we have to incorporate this ideology.

The statement leads spectators to wonder about the extent to which that claim was validated or exceeded. Answers are found within the portraits of the insane inhabitants themselves. The historical indentations of the Soviet legacy left on individuals born after 1960 — which includes all of the film's "actors" — are immense, even if, or precisely because, Cubans collectively and aggressively cast aside the Soviet past in the early 1990s.

A cut from the 1960 Soviet exposition in Havana introduces one of the madmen of Havana speaking about the Special Period. As Antonio José Ponte indicates in his positive review of this film:

> *Existen* could be understood as an exploration of nationalism in madness. And it's not a coincidence that *Existen* begins with images of the great Soviet exhibition celebrated in Havana in 1960. That exhibition of technological and scientific successes sought a rapprochement between both nations. The voice of the newscast from which the images come warns that what is on display there is not forcefully the fruit of the virtues of a political regime that is so remote from the Cuban one. And, judging by that meeting, it seems that a case of alienation is being spoken about. The country is in danger of remaining outside of itself, given into a destiny that is not its own, driven crazy.[47]

Ponte's own analysis of the degree to which historical events and normalized nationalistic discourse penetrate psychotic speech is especially fascinating upon considering a parallel within Ponte's short fiction. For instance, in "Corazón de skitalietz," the condition of alienation needs to be expressed in the idiom of the previous provider — "*skitalietz*," a Russian word for "wanderer." Published in Cuba in 1998, the story takes the word from Dostoevsky's 1880 address on Pushkin, in which he describes Pushkin as having discovered and traced that unlucky *skitalietz* in his own native soil. Although Dostoevsky was not favored by the Soviets, many of his works were, indeed, published in Cuba from the 1960s to the 1980s. As in the Soviet Union, where *Notes from the Underground* and *The Possessed* were viewed as the darkest and least easily assimilated of Dostoevsky's work, in Cuba they were not read as much during the Soviet period as *Crime and Punishment*, *The Idiot*, *The Gambler*, and "White Nights" were.

Abandoned by the Soviet Union, all the characters in Ponte's story are perpetual orphans. Through the utilization of Russian to describe the contemporary Cuban situation, "Corazón de skitaliez" re-creates the disinherited nation's link to the Soviet Union. Russian is the language of the country upon which Cuba depended, but it is also alien and other.[48] The epilogue of the 1998 edition of *Corazón de skitalietz* provokes the reader at the same time that it explains the title, stating that Dostoevsky viewed

> universal happiness to be indispensable for the *skitalietz* to calm his or her spirit . . . Some years later, the young Gorky speaks passionately to Vladimir Korolenko about the searchers for truth . . . Korolenko listens with a smile and then makes him see that these same searchers for truth on various paths are great egomaniacs and lazy bums. For good or bad, the word "skitalietz" appears within quotes. Why did I choose this Russian word? Unlike Scorpio, I was neither educated in Russian, nor can I read Russian directly. It must then be for the same reason that I called them by these names — Scorpio, Veranda — nicknames more than names for this pair of characters. Because fiction seems to me to be a foreign land. Because it doesn't take place in the language I write.[49]

Ponte's biography is by now well known. His critical approach toward top-down prescriptions of truth within the Cuban nation, expressed in essays such as "Las comidas profundas" (1997; Profound Meals) and "El abrigo de aire" (2000; The Overcoat of Air), and his service on the editorial board of one of the most controversial and well-circulated journals of the Cuban diaspora, *Encuentro de la cultura cubana*, led to his expulsion from the Cuban Writers' Union in 2003. Shortly thereafter he went into exile in Madrid and became the co-director of *Encuentro*. The equivalence of the terms "searchers for truth" and *skitalietz* (the word used by Dostoevsky to describe those Europeanizing intellectuals that thought themselves superior to the Russian village) emphasizes the instability of meanings and the importance of context for anchoring signifiers. To Ponte's explanation of his appropriation of *"skitalietz,"* we can add that the sense of strangeness cannot be narrated within the realm of the national, nor in a random foreign language, but instead in the language of the empire that supposedly anchored the Cuban people to their country for about three decades.

In "Corazón de skitalietz" the characters that wander are in charge of transforming the capital of their nation into another. From the beginning, the blackouts of the Special Period function as natural forces that shape the narrative's development, provisionally authorizing the characters to reinvent not only themselves but also the landscapes around them. While Rafael Rojas affirms that Ponte's fictions are peopled by "Cuban students that went to the Soviet Union and Eastern Europe" and not by the diaspora of the 1990s, primarily codified as economic (those that fled the hunger and blackouts on the island), I would say that "Corazón de skitalietz" portrays a bridge between the two. Deserted by the Soviet Union, they live continuously in the condition of an orphan but, still, like many of the authors who are analyzed in this book, also under the immense debt of Russian language and literature, which provides them with the linguistic code with which to express that sentimental reality.

In "Corazón de skitalietz," the character of the historian is baptized "Scorpio" upon losing his job at an institute. The loss of his status resonates with the complete collapse of the Historical ideal promulgated by the Revolution — the collapse of an ideology that tied Cuba economically and politically to other parts of the world in the struggle against imperialism. Scorpio is joined by an astrologer, a Cancer whose name is Veranda. Havana is no longer a city in which the two find themselves in a boring routine; rather, it has become a place where they are wanderers: *skitalietz*. After their phone lines cross, they reunite to cope with the lack of movement, which we have already seen performed in Porno para Ricardo's *Los músicos de Bremen*, by imagining themselves as tourists in a foreign country. When Scorpio ends up in a home for vagabonds (as an aside, there is no sign of such a place in *Existen*) and he is asked for his occupation, he answers: "De ocupación skitalietz. Es en ruso, deletreó."[50] ("Occupation skitalietz. It's Russian, he spelled out.")[51] Asked if he is Russian, he says, "Quieren hacer un loco de mí"[52] ("They want to make a nut out of me"[53]). Without the power to gaze directly upon the exotic sphere, these characters attempt to invert the structures of internationalism, social vigilance, and tourism. They can hardly fathom their contemporary situation without referring to the Soviet/ Russian inheritance. What Scorpio refers to as the "Logia de las Vidas Paralelas"[54] ("Lodge of Parallel Lives")[55] also refers to the experience of wandering in what could be called a foreign language of the disinherited. In the words of the protagonist, first "nadie podría ser libre si existía un solo, un único aquí, y tantos infinitos allá que reclamaban"[56] (no one could be free if only one single here existed while so many infinite elsewheres were beckoning[57]). And second: "La libertad puede consistir en un espacio cerrado un poco más grande"[58] (Freedom can consist of a closed space that's a little larger[59]). Ponte's fiction examines the simultaneous, almost schizophrenic, dissonant, and discrepant sounds of languages through which spaces can be creatively amplified. The *skitalietz* is one manner of enlarging this space and converting dependence into liberty. When Scorpio, the protagonist of Ponte's novella, is released from the home for vagabonds, he recognizes that "la ciudad estaba llena de skitalietzs"[60] (the city was full of skitalietzs[61]). "Corazón de skitalietz," like *Existen*, manifests Cuban protagonists whose memories entrap them within *skitalietz*-like lives. Left only with Soviet signifiers, even further unanchored from the signified than they were in Pereira's *El ruso*, these memories also protect them from an unknown future.

Within *Existen*, a delirious man in his thirties provides a possible solution for the Special Period, pontificating next to the cafeteria La Pelota on Twenty-Third Street—one of the few cafeterias in Havana's El Vedado neighborhood that does business in the national currency:

> Buscar todos los requisitos recaudables de dólares, hacer convenios
> con otros países menos con Rusia . . . hasta que Rusia no sea parte de la
> Unión Soviética otra vez y depende si nosotros no damos combustible a
> ellos . . . que sea por préstamo . . . creo que no podemos fallar más.

> To look for the collectible requisites of dollars, to make agreements with
> other countries, except with Russia . . . until Russia is not part of the
> Soviet Union again and depending on whether we don't give them fuel
> . . . it should be as a loan . . . I believe that we can't fail again.

Hardly any effort has to be made to piece together the order of his madness since it keeps intact the collective sphere through its collective voice. The subject is overly invested in the symbolic order, in Cuba having distanced itself from the newly formed Russia, the effect of which he links to his life almost as intimately as the poor quality of the food at La Pelota.

The effectiveness of Insausti's critique is due, in part, to Angelica Salvador's brilliant editing, a montage-like technique that blurs distinct temporalities, and a selection of official declarations through which spectators can easily measure the nation's progress and its discontents. As Antonio José Ponte states:

> It's interesting to examine how much subjects related to the country in-
> habit these monologues. Of course, Insausti, screenwriter and director,
> could have selected fragments that dealt with the same thing. However,
> if that were the case, the coincidence of so many actors with identical
> themes still stands.[62]

Ponte's response to the documentary encourages us to reflect upon the film's similarities to a 2002 issue of Benetton's magazine *Colors*, on life in mental institutions around the world and especially in Cuba. Both interweave strategies of avant-garde photography, video, and marketing. *Existen*, financed by the Spanish embassy in Cuba, the Spanish Agency of International Cooperation (AECI), El Ingenio, the Ludwig Foundation, Producciones Sincover, and the Cuban Institute of Cinematographic Arts and Industry (ICAIC), mixes the fast rhythms of the short music video with the technique of montage to create an incongruent sensation in spectators. The combination leads to the question of whether the techno music ends up accommodating outside spectators or creates an uncanny feeling about the Cuban national sphere.

What I said about the representation of one of the insane in *Colors* could also be said about many of the people interviewed in *Existen*: "The changes within her discourse extend to a game whose referents are outside of the mental institution, in the very nation: she confesses, then cries, her voice becomes infantile, she mentions something very powerful (exiting the country), she cries again, she affirms her nationality, and then—within the frame of categories constitutive of adversity—she seduces."[63] Another intern within the Camagüey asylum portrayed in *Colors* declares: "Quise suicidarme dos veces, las dos veces con un Sputnik, una navaja rusa" (I tried to commit suicide twice, both times with a Sputnik, a Russian razor).[64] Soviet Sputnik razor blades, after Yuri Gagarin's 1961 Vostok flight, were uniquely packaged with CCCP letters and a spaceship. The fact that they become an instrument of self-destruction for this insane Cuban intern speaks to the reproduction of social relationships in the form of the appearance of the Soviet figure. These days, such razors are sometimes auctioned on eBay and, until recently, on the more specialized Distribuciones Potemkin. The world's collectibles have slightly different functions within the Cuban asylum and in Havana's streets. Even the delirium denotes that the Soviet Bloc continues to undergo mystification for Cubans.

The rest of the speeches within *Existen* similarly imitate dominant revolutionary discourse. One of the witnesses, the film's subtitles indicate, went mad because he left Cuba. After revealing all the cities he came to know abroad, he states: "Todo eso es mío pero mi Cuba es mi Cuba" (All this is mine but my Cuba is my Cuba). Another madman declares: "Bueno quiero tener que querer a Cuba pero soy verdaderamente español" (Well, I want to have to love Cuba, but I am truly Spanish)—a statement suggestive of pervasive social politics in the 1990s and in the new millennium. Proving how particular is, in fact, the perspective of Aurora Jácome, creator of the principal *muñequitos rusos* blog, on the strength of her Soviet cultural affiliations, this "insane" perspective alludes to the failure of "ideological affiliations" with "Our Soviet Brothers" and to Cubans' claiming filial ties with Spain and its autonomous regions in the prospect of acquiring dual citizenship and immigrating to Spain. A black man who we are told went crazy after going to war in Angola delivers one of the film's most fragmented speeches, concluding with, "Y el de la bolchevique negra 'bing

bang'" (And the one of the black Bolshevik "bing bang"). Finally, another declares: "En la Unión Soviética había una equivalencia del que ganaba poco o
menos, ¿no? A nosotros lo que se nos bloqueó eso, porque, aquí todo el mundo
iba en Lada a la playa . . . Aquí 100 pesos eran 100 pesos, ¿era así o no es así?"
(In the Soviet Union there was an equivalence of the one who earned little
or less, right? For us, what was blocked was that, because here everyone went
to the beach in Ladas . . . Here 100 pesos were 100 pesos. That's how it was,
isn't it?) The interrogatives throughout the discourse suggest his desire to be
understood and affirmed. He expresses indecisiveness about his position—
responsibility for the blockade is left in abeyance. Is equality "here" as equal
as the Soviets'? In his words the nation's recent past, which coincides with his
early adulthood, seems far away but still in need of the collective sphere to make
sense of it.

The last madman speaks of linking Cuba to other lands:

> Ya Cuba tiene un promedio de 375 mil "shopping" . . . hacen falta unas
> 400,900 shopping más para que totalmente ya Cuba sea un capital total.
> ¿Me entiendes? . . . y que uniremos, unamos, esta tierra con otra tierra
> . . . que sea desconocida esta, unamos esta con la otra . . . y que sea un
> país grande como el Japón, como Norteamérica.

> Cuba already has an average of 375 thousand shopping centers—it
> needs about 400,900 more so that Cuba can totally be a total capital
> now. You understand me? . . . and that we join, let's join, this land with
> another . . . that this one's unknown, let's join it with another . . . and it
> can be a big country like Japan, like North America.

Like the film's beginning, its conclusion suggests that the inability to adapt
to the capitalist system contributes to conditions of national schizophrenia.
Statistics are flashed on the screen: "En el año 2000, hubo un 45% más de
esquizofrénicos que en 1985" (In the year 2000, there were 45% more schizo-
phrenics than in 1985).

The parenthesis that was the fragmented representation of the insane on the
streets is then closed with a sequence about the all-wise Soviet Union: the 1960
Soviet exposition and the discourse of expansion, once explained to Cubans
through the rhetoric of fraternity and solidarity, returns. "Hay que romper fron-
teras que impiden conocerse y ayudarse a los hombres . . . Cuba, aislada como
isla, alza sus brazos . . . en cordial saludo para todo el que quiera venir a sus
lares . . ." (It is necessary to break borders that prevent knowing each other and
helping people . . . Cuba, isolated as an island, raises its arms . . . in a cordial
greeting for all who want to come to its lands . . .) In the frame's background, a

poster that cannot be read completely announces, "En la URSS está creada una potente industria de construcción de tractores" (In the USSR a strong industry of tractor construction is created). Finally,

> El progreso que exhiben los productos, la capacidad técnica de sus obreros y la admirable organización demostrada en esta exposición nos dicen, del adelanto que goza este pueblo, cosa que celebramos pero que mantenemos intacto nuestro sentido nacionalista informado del humanismo que tiene como filosofía, nuestra formidable revolución.

> The progress that the products exhibit, the technical capacity of its workers and the admirable organization demonstrated in this exhibition speak to us about the advancement enjoyed by these people, something we celebrate, but at the same time we keep intact our nationalist sense, informed by the humanism that our formidable revolution takes as its philosophy.

As did the *Colors* issue on madness, *Existen* inscribes itself within the language of the World Health Organization by presenting a discourse on solidarity and production that concealed inequalities and hid repressions. Through rapid cuts and techno music, *Existen* represents a Havana plagued by schizophrenia; the World Health Organization's universalizing statistics reflect back on the madmen's obsessions with lists and numbers—the keys to a nationalistic and heroic discourse. Representing the discourse of the insane in Havana becomes a useful method for revealing the experiences of this nation's inhabitants.

### THE SOVIET CYBORG, OR THE MAD SANITY OF THE POST-INTERNATIONALIST SUBJECT

If for Fernández Larrea the decay of the great Soviet machinery is projected onto a marginal neighborhood in the center of the city, Centro Habana, in the writing and installations of the previously discussed young binational Polina Martínez Shvietsova, the aftermath of the Soviet-Cuban alliance manifests itself as a war on the gendered body. However, this war is not filled with disappointment. Dislocated by the machinery of the state, the fictional narrator and her visual counterpart embody a schizophrenic subjectivity comparable to that of Rubén Rodríguez's protagonist in "Sobre Sovexportfilm." Martínez Shvietsova deploys the body as a device to challenge diverse iconographies, including those originating from the Soviet Union, Russia, Cuba, the East, and the West (which is often manufactured in the East). As seen in Chapter

1, her naked body is adorned with some of the symbols that composed the fictional unity of Soviet-Cuban solidarity. In Martínez Shvietsova's 2008 Cortázar award–winning short story "Skizein (Decálogo del año cero)" (Skizein [Decalogue of Year Zero]), she brilliantly narrates the impact of disinheritance and disassociation on a female subject who sustains herself by imagining travels to the landscapes of literature from other parts of the world.

Originating from the Greek word *"skhizein,"* to split, the title of the story evokes failed transculturation.[65] As in *Existen,* where the insane are confused by individual desires and national demands, in "Skizein" the narrator mixes up humanitarian and military trade, as the following phrases suggest: "pasaportes de la CCCP y carnecitos vencidos del PCUS" (passports from the CCCP and expired identification cards from the Soviet Communist Party) and "colchones y bastidores de IL-62" (mattresses and frames from the IL-62). "IL-62" stands for the Ilyushin-62, a Soviet long-range jet airliner. Out of such irreconcilable parts, coded in an incoherent manner in Soviet militarism, Martínez Shvietsova forges a post-internationalist subjectivity. The world the narrator dreams of is both spatial and aerial, but her illusions are marked by Cubans' inability to travel and the Soviet Union's militaristic encroachment on territory.

> Un rugido de IL-62 o de MIG-15: son miles, millones; son moscas, abejorros barzuk: este es un país de mamíferos aéreos. Semejante ingravidez sólo la viven los que habitan en un aeropuerto, como yo. Los nómadas de la stalinofilia y toda esa mierda perestroika del corazón.[66]

> A roar from an IL-62 or from a MIG-15; there are thousands, millions; they are flies, Barzuk bumblebees: this is a country of aerial mammals. A similar weightlessness is lived only by those who reside in an airport, like me. The nomads of Stalinphilia and all that perestroika shit from the heart.

Martínez Shvietsova rejects conventional logic in her depiction of the schism in which she resides, and in fact, the story's second epigraph, from Julio Cortázar's *La prosa del observatorio* (1972; Prose from the Observatory), speaks directly to existential interstices: "Esa hora que puede llegar alguna vez fuera de toda hora, agujero en la red del tiempo, esa manera de estar entre, no por encima o detrás, sino entre"[67] (This hour that can arrive sometimes outside of all hours, hole in the web of time, this way of being between, not above or behind but between[68]). By approximating the internal logic of the story through the clues given by the epigraphs, readers can piece together the disparate parts.

Martínez Shvietsova's story captures the vexed memories of the Soviet Bloc in Cuba.

Cuando salen las maletas, una viene soltando plumas de kolokol por la esterilla. Yo sé. Yo soy Dios, soy Vladimir sin Iliushin-62. Soy una Revolucioncita Mundial piloteada por quince MIGS. Ese paquete de plumas viene cargado con infinitas e ínfimas alas de kolokol, el pájaro mudo de la Siberia: la mejor música es su silencio. Esa maleta es un contrabando. La madrecita patria rusa que quiere emigrar de la Nueva Rusia y aterrizar otra vez aquí. Como en los ochenta. En la misma olla de presión termonuclear.[69]

When the suitcases come out, one arrives trailing kolokol feathers on the baggage claim. I know. I am God, I am Vladimir without Iliushin-62. I am a little World Revolution piloted by fifteen MIGS. That pack of feathers comes filled with endless and meager wings of kolokol, the mute bird of Siberia: the best music is its silence. That suitcase is contraband. The little Russian mother country that wants to emigrate from the New Russia and land here once again. Like in the 1980s. In the same thermonuclear pressure cooker.

Martínez Shvietsova does not enact the breakdown of hierarchies utilizing *choteo*; rather, she disturbs conventional generic categories through incessant poetic phrases that run counter to historic linearity. The narrator of "Skizein" ends up rehearsing a "desmemoria tangible del desierto" (tangible unmemory of the desert) that is not "loca de remate" (totally crazy) but rather "cuerdo de remate" (totally sane), implying what Esteban Insausti already has—that the truths about the Soviet-Cuban alliance need to be told in the language of those who are categorically insane.

*Existen* is crucial for envisioning the collective memory of the Soviet Bloc's presence within Cuba today. A similar debate may appear on a wall momentarily within Havana's streets but may not remain so within Vostok. These insane inhabitants of Havana are contemporaries of many of the artists whose work is collected in Vostok and also of *Existen*'s director, Insausti, who was born in 1971, and who, like them, came of age in the 1980s. However, Tonel's revised Baikonur and Fernández Larrea's recollection of a gaze upon Gagarin illustrate that the memory of the Soviet machinery does not solely belong to the generation of the *muñequitos rusos*. Soviet objects foreground past and present failures within Cuba. They portray both the new geopolitical order, which rapidly advances the substitution of hegemonic powers, and the imperial aspiration of the past for international and ideological solidarity.

# The Soviet Theme Park

*En un cruce del ferrocarril transiberiano descansa una gallina de aspecto indeciso.*

*El porvenir le reservaba tres destinos: ser devorada, cuando corriera a la taiga, por un zorro—que perseguido por un mujik, cayó en un cepo cuyos dientes le destrozaron el cuello—; ser cocinada, cuando regresara a su gallinero, en la olla de un mujik—que en persecución de un zorro fue triturado por un tren cargado de uranio al cruzar la línea del transiberiano—; o ser aplastada por un tren cargado de uranio a ciento diez millas por hora—que está descarrilado a dos kilometros de allí, pues sus maquinistas frenaron bruscamente para evitar sin resultado despedazar a un mujik que cruzó sin mirar.*

*La gallina del cruce del transiberiano no está indecisa. Es el porvenir, que no sabe qué hacer con ella.*

At a trans-Siberian railroad crossing rests a hen with an indecisive look.

The future reserves three destinies for it: be devoured, upon running to the taiga, by a fox—that chased by a muzhik, fell into a trap whose prongs destroyed its neck; be cooked, when it returned to the coop, in the pot of the peasant—who, upon chasing a fox, was crushed by a train loaded with uranium upon crossing the Trans-Siberian line—; or be squashed by a train loaded with uranium going 110 miles per hour—which is derailed two kilometers from there when its drivers brake abruptly to try to avoid, unsuccessfully, tearing a muzhik, who crossed without looking, into pieces.

The hen at the trans-Siberian crossing is not indecisive. It is the future that does not know what to do with the hen.

"GALLINA" (HEN), KEVIN FERNÁNDEZ DELGADO

$K$evin Fernández Delgado's "Gallina" won the Dinosaurio prize for mini-short stories in 2008, awarded by the Centro Onelio Jorge Cardoso. In this difficult-to-decipher tale, in two out of the three scenarios, the muzhik dies, although the hen remains "decisive." The fable is impossible to read without asking if the hen at the trans-Siberian crossing is not Cuba, no longer able to envision itself through the progress of a faraway empire since its derailment twenty years before. It faces the obstacles of an orphan (abandoned by a not always benevolent patron), of the sort that has already been interpreted in numerous texts throughout this book, especially within Ponte's characteristic story of the Special Period, "Heart of Skitalietz," wherein Cuba's destiny, unhinged from the geography and vocabulary of the Soviet world, is at stake. However, in Fernández Delgado's fable, the hen will not succumb to the geopolitical and economic implications of this trap; clues to this transformation are located in a distinct moment of what we may call, provisionally, Cuban post-post-Soviet culture, which emerged around the time that the Special Period likely ended, around 2005. This coda tries to decipher this moment, primarily through visual clues that point to the refabrication of old bonds—on the road toward derailment or restoration, it is difficult to determine—as well as the molding of new ones, and their echoes within the arts. In *Dreaming in Russian*, the hen casts its multiple narratives upon the previous derailment.

The rehearsal of Cuba as a Socialist Bloc junkyard has entered a new stage altogether. It is now almost standard for Cubans to delineate the Soviet physical remains on the island before they dig deeper into a discussion of the Soviet legacy. The award-winning 2007 exhibition of cutting-edge artists, Vostok, re-codified a workshop of spare parts into a radical visual arts experiment, challenging that gesture to recite the list while, at the "Último Jueves" (Last Thursday) roundtable of the journal *Temas* in May 2009, the esteemed critic and translator Zoia Barash began her presentation on the influence of Soviet cinematography in Cuba with the phrase "Russian traces exist, and at times, they are perceived not only in the form of nostalgia for Russian meat or for the Aurika washing machine." It was an anecdotal nod to which Julio Travieso, another respected translator who was in the audience, added "vodka" and "Russian women."[1]

Enrique Colina's documentary *Los rusos en Cuba* (2008) does a great job at picking up on the plethora of consumer items from the Soviet Bloc that the masses continue not only to recall, as in those cans of Russian meat and powdered milk, but also to use, albeit against all odds, as the documentary's magnificent close-ups of an Aurika washer and Orbita fan prove.

A somewhat fairy tale–like version of the Soviet-Cuban alliance can be found in Daniel Díaz Torres's *Lisanka* (2009), which was produced by Spain's

Ibermedia, the ICAIC, and Mosfilm Studios, the first result of the agreement formed in 2008 between Russia and Cuba.[2] Using the stylistic strategies of fables—an omniscient narrator, animation, archetypical characters who live in a picturesque village—this feature neatly assigns the 1962 Cuban Missile Crisis a backseat in order to focus on the more sentimental consequences of the arrival of a young romantic Soviet to a nearby military base and his interrupting the love triangle between an ebullient young Cuban lady, Lisanka; her revolutionary lover; and her reactionary lover.

The new, balanced climate of Cuban revisions of the Soviets must be understood as dimensions of many recent strategic collaborations, of which the 2008 cinematographic accord is only one; others include a series of visits by Russian officials (Prime Minister Dmitry Medvedev in 2008 and Foreign Minister Sergei Lavrov in 2010), the inauguration of the Russian Orthodox Church in 2008, and offshore oil concessions in 2011.

However, some things still escape such choreography. By far, the act of memorialization that best displays the multiple loyalties, complexities, contradictions, and opportunisms that come into play around the topic of Cubans' memories of the Soviet Bloc was the 2010 International Book Fair of Cuba, wherein Russia was the guest of honor. On the grounds of the Morro Castle and La Cabaña Fort, unique material installations in the form of replicas (as opposed to ruins) took temporary root. Perhaps none was comparable to the oddly placed replica of a rocket from the CCCP (the acronym for Soyuz Sovetskikh Sotsialisticheskikh Respublik, or USSR), which contained within it a photograph of the cosmonauts Arnaldo Tamayo and Yuri Romanenko. This ambiguous object was positioned in the back of the "Russian"-themed restaurant on the fairgrounds and within the visual panorama of the crosses of a number of churches. Had this replica of greatness and solidarity been situated more centrally, it could have been a major highlight of the theme park. The ambiguity as to whether to call the theme park "Russian" or "Soviet" has not perished with the disintegration of the Soviet Union. On the periphery of the grounds, the installation could very easily have passed for a ruin.

That said, it is difficult to assess this "found object" and not wonder who was behind such an idea. Depending on the answer, it could be a symptom of Russian imperial nostalgia or an expression of Cuban aspirations for the future laid out through a visual ode to a previous solidarity.

Before examining the book fair's "Russian" restaurant, let us consider the actual restaurant presented in Zoe García's documentary *Todo tiempo pasado fue mejor* (2008; Everything in the Past Was Better). The documentary, an interview with four intellectuals and artists about the topic of the Soviets in Cuba, is structured around the story of Havana's Moscú restaurant, which opened in 1974, two years after Cuba's entrance into the COMECON, and burned down

*Photograph of cosmonauts Arnaldo Tamayo and Yuri Romanenko inside Soviet rocket, part of Ode to the CCCP Program in Outer Space, 2010 International Book Fair of Cuba. Author's photograph.*

in January 1990. The premise is evocative of the shifting perspectives on the incipient Revolution that were prompted by the arson attack on the glamorous department store El encanto (The Enchantment) in April 1961.[3] Moscú restaurant, which once showcased the triumphs of the USSR's kitchen, is a perfect metonym for Cuba's relationship with the Soviet Bloc. The title of the documentary, tellingly scripted in Latin letters in a Cyrillic font, is portrayed as a national shield crowned by the PCC (the acronym for Partido Comunista de Cuba) and supported below by "CCCP." For a whole minute, spectators can study the shield and listen to a conventional version of the song "The Bremen-Town Musicians"—the same one that Ernesto René rendered so brilliantly in the 2001 music video, which was used by Asori Soto in the 2005 *Good Bye, Lolek* and again by René and Betancourt in their 2006 documentary *9550*. Of the song's repetition, one may conclude that the *Muñequitos Rusos* generation either suffers from a lack of originality or, more likely, that no other song captures quite as well the anxieties of that generation to not end up merely as the characters of Soviet Bloc animation.

The documentary's establishing shots render the disorientation characteristic of aging inhabitants whose world has changed before their eyes. Gray, stormy skies above buildings that look as if they have been bombed suggest parts of the former Socialist Bloc, yet close-ups showing Havana's residents trying to indicate the location of Moscú restaurant undoubtedly place the documentary in Cuba. The documentary's focus on a restaurant and its culinary offerings distracts viewers from some of its more problematic remarks, such as the warning by film critic Gustavo Arcos: "The Soviet Union failed for many reasons. But attention: the reasons the Soviet system failed are the same reasons that could make our own system fail because it is structured—I repeat—on the same schemes, the same principals." Such an admission captures a fundamental contradiction raised by this book—Cubans act out nostalgia toward Soviet commodity culture and yet simultaneously critique Soviet ideology, some of which remains well anchored in Cuba.

It is within this contradiction that we must consider the "Russian" restaurant, re-created solely for the purposes of the 2010 book fair. The menu, like the majority of the products sold at the fair, was priced in national currency and featured tartar soup, borsch, *salianka*, and *sashik*, as well as a slew of other archetypical meals, replicated in post-Soviet Cuba with the palates of nostalgic Cubans in mind. No matter that Russians and other foreigners with access to the same menu in the capitalist world largely did not recognize the dishes being served, and that, on more than one occasion, Cuban patrons complained that

*Ode to the CCCP Program, 2010 International Book Fair of Cuba. Author's photograph.*

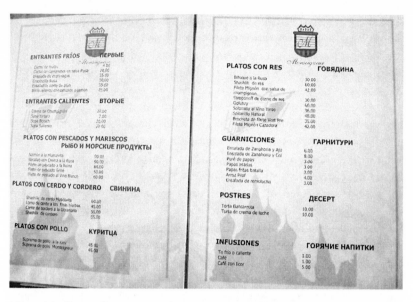

*Menu of the "Russian" restaurant at the 2010 International Book Fair of Cuba. Author's photograph.*

the food would have been more authentic had those "matrioshkas" remaining on the island prepared it. The seasoning lacked some of the ingredients to make it taste Russian, but fortunately, many of the diners' memories were sufficiently "informed" that the missing ingredients did not significantly disturb the overall set design. The atmosphere was pleasant and even reminiscent of the 1980s heyday of equanimity.

The multifaceted and ambiguous presentation of the Soviet-Cuban alliance at the book fair reflects the varied impulses that inspired it. First, Russians and Cubans alike sought to bring to light pre-Soviet ties between Cuba and Russia, from the nineteenth and early twentieth centuries. Second, they sought to rescue from the Soviet mirage the nineteenth- and twentieth-century Russian classics. Third, they tried to uphold the positive aspects of the Soviet period. Finally, they wanted to distinguish between the old Soviets, who served as Cuban big brothers, and the new Russians, who have moved far away from the Soviet period. All these goals serve to articulate possibilities for future cultural collaborations.

Corresponding to a similar impulse of historicizing the Russian-Cuban friendship seen in Alexander Moiseev and Olga Egorova's book *Los rusos en Cuba* is the publication of *La cultura rusa en José Martí* (2010), by Luis Álvarez Álvarez. An even more remarkable dimension of the quest for a renewed friendship on the part of the Russians is the fact that in 2010, their writers' union awarded the Cuban Jaime Abelino López García the Gold Pen prize for his translation into Russian of a chapter of Álvarez Álvarez's book.[4] In 1992, some eighteen years prior to these occurrences, at the time of the restructuring of the Cuban "autonomous" constitution, a book about Russian traces within the nineteenth-century apostle would have been almost inconceivable. "As is obvious," Álvarez Álvarez concludes, "the Russian culture was for Martí a magnetic pole of attraction: poets, novelists, scientists, plastic artists, playwrights, monarchs and politicians, but also its language, its popular customs, its folkloric heritage magnetized his attention."[5] For Spanish American modernists, foreign cultures were indeed exploited, and Álvarez Álvarez situates Russian culture within this universal panorama; nevertheless, the tremendously convenient timing of this scholarly exploration is impossible to deny.

Translation is of utmost importance to the project of new ties, as it was during the Soviet period. In 2010, López García impressed the Russian judges with his fluency in Russian; one year prior, this purportedly nostalgic admirer of all things from the former Soviet Union—where he had studied mechanical engineering—actually won the Gold Pen's honorable mention for his translation into Spanish of popular tales about the Mari people in the former Soviet Union. What is particular about the case of López García is his desire to transmit knowledge of Soviet diversity to the young people of Cuba, as reflected in the volume's title, which pays homage to his daughter, Laura: *Cuentos para Laura: Relatos populares maris* (Stories for Laura: Popular Mari Tales). This book can be understood as a flashback to López García's own youth, which was populated by the kinds of tales published in Cuban-Soviet editions from the 1970s and 1980s.

Like the exploration of Martí's Russian influence in two languages, the publication of numerous translations of Russian nineteenth- and twentieth-century classics into Spanish signals the resuscitated political vigor of Russian culture in Cuba. The anthology *Cuentos de grandes escritores rusos* (Stories of Great Russian Writers), edited by Julio Travieso and published by Arte y Literatura in 2009, includes stories by Alexander Pushkin, Nikolai Gogol, Mikhail Lermontov, Ivan Turgenev, Fyodor Dostoevsky, Mikhail Saltykov-Schedrin, Leo Tolstoy, Boris Pilnyak, Eugene Zamiatin, Nikolai Leskov, Vladimir Korolenko, Anton Chekhov, Maxim Gorky, Alexsandr Kuprin, Ivan Bunin, Isaac Babel, Mikhail Bulgakov, Vladimir Nabokov, and Mikhail Sholokhov, among many others. The collection corresponds precisely to the new trend. With the exception of the translations by Travieso, the translations are anonymous.

Although the volume's prologue (another contribution by Travieso) is far from extensive, it does point out a few central issues whose significance goes beyond the volume. Travieso describes a process of increased institutionalization between 1934 and 1953 that resulted in prescriptions of how to write "gray

En la tierra del "Don Apacible" *(In the Land of "And Quiet Flows the Don"),* an exhibit in honor of Mikhail Sholokhov, 2010 International Book Fair of Cuba. Author's photograph.

and flat literature."[6] That period, he continues, was preceded by the golden age of Russian literature and followed by transitional years. An example of how the more problematic of writers is treated by Travieso is his explanation of his selection of, among other realist writers, Sholokhov, whom he calls a practitioner of "psychological realism" as opposed to "socialist realism."[7] Travieso mentions that Sholokhov won the Nobel Prize in 1965, but does not mention that he also won the Stalin Prize (in 1941). Travieso's treatment of Sholokhov in his collection, along with the Soviet writer's resuscitation at the 2010 book fair—which honored the 105th anniversary of his birth—is a way of ensuring that Sholokhov remain every bit a hero in the international sphere as he once was.

In addition, by deflecting the more critical aspects of the Soviet-Cuban relationship onto the lesser known pre- and post-Soviet/Russian ties, the book fair symbolically elongated the span of time that Russians and Cubans have been interested in each other. For instance, in 2010 the Russian embassy published a magazine entitled *Rusia: Los libros que hacen sabio al hombre* (Russia: The Books That Make Man Wise), whose content virtually bypassed recent history: one short piece dedicated to the wealth of the Cuban journal *Unión's* cultural collaboration during the Soviet period was placed within the scope of an article about the first Russian teacher in Cuba, named Fiodor V. Karzhavin, first published in *Granma* in the significant year of 1989; an exposé on contemporary Russian literature; an excerpt of Travieso's translation of *The Master and Margarita*; a text on the monumental nature of Russian libraries such as "la Léninka"; translations of popular Russian stories; and to top it off, a final section of translated Russian jokes, which is perhaps the most significant contribution for understanding the future of Russian-Cuban relations. A caricature of President Obama with a bottle of Vodka in one hand and a cocktail glass in the other appears at the top of the page; below, the phrase "¡Hola, vamos a hacer amistad!" (Hello, we are going to make friends!) This humor ensures that Cuban readers do not forget that while the United States may possess a friendlier guise these days, it remains naïve, at best, and as Dmitri Prieto Samsonov's chronicles point out, for Russians, foolishness is dangerous. The Cold War antagonisms endure.

The prolongation of the Soviet-Cuban friendship also affected the book fair's display of military, diplomatic, and cultural collaboration. For example, a section of the Russian Pavilion was dedicated to the sixty-fifth anniversary of the victory of the Second World War and, in particular, honored Enrique Vilar Figueredo (born in 1925 in Manzanillo, Cuba), the Cuban internationalist who, having enlisted in the Red Army in 1942, died in Poland in 1945 in the fight against fascism.[8] Some photographs commemorating the Soviet-Cuban friendship were never hung, but instead were leaned up against the walls of the exhibition hall: images of Fidel skiing in Russia, of Fidel meeting the Russian ballerina Maya Plisetskaya, and of Fidel holding hands with leaders Nikita Kruschev and Leonid Brezhnev, along with military ships with the word "Cuba" written in Cyrillic.

The 2010 exhibition of "things Russian" did not by any means take on the proportions of the grand 1976 Soviet exposition in Havana's capitol building. The book fair's Russian Pavilion was a mere 450 square meters; yet three hundred publishing houses were present, and thirty-five hundred books were on display.[9] Computers were on-site with advanced programs to teach Cuban youth about life in Russia. As if this weren't enough, the Russkiy Mir Foundation donated approximately thirty thousand euros to the José Martí National Library to inaugurate the Cultural Center of Russia, one of forty-six similar centers worldwide and the first to open in the Americas, with plans for Nicaragua, Guatemala, and Mexico.

One of the most provocative strategies for ensuring the persistence of things Russian in Cubans' future manifested itself through the efforts at teaching Cuban children about Russian and Soviet history and culture and, at the same time, reminding their parents, members of the *Muñequitos Rusos* generation, about their own sentimental ties to the Soviets. Cubans also had the chance to become reacquainted with Vladimir Vysotsky's poetry, translated by Juan Luis

*San Basilio Church at Children's Pavilion, 2010 International Book Fair of Cuba.*
*Author's photograph.*

Hernández Milian, which was published by Ediciones Matanzas in 2010. Accompanying the display of children's books from Russia was Vadim Levin's collection of handmade models used in Soviet animation. Eduard Uspensky, the
author of the stories about Cheburashka and the Crocodile Gena, along with
other children's book authors, returned to visit these once unusual brethren to
try to charm the Cuban people, but Uspensky already seemed to be on a different plane, in which "time is only money for those with money." Having expected to address an audience of children, he found himself in front of a group
of parents who came of age with his cartoons and who were eager to inquire
about old topics such as ethics and aesthetics, upon which he appeared not to
wish to remark.[10] More than with any other group, it was with the *Muñequitos
Rusos* generation that the book fair engaged in a subtle conversation. The pathway through the Morro Castle to the Children's Pavilion was decorated with
Soviet cartoons, and on the other side, above the children's stage, was a cut-out
of another "castle," San Basilio Church, placed there almost as if it were the
crown in Gertrudis Rivalta's *Quinceañera con Kremlin.*

The children's sections at the Book Fair were the spaces in which the restorative impulses of the Cuban and Russian regimes were most evident. The Russian aspirations for Cuba translated into a stunning exhibit entitled *¡Cuba, eres mi amor!* (Cuba, You Are My Love), which represented Russian children's fantasies about the island and decorated the walls of the pavilion and was reproduced in a small but beautiful magazine catalogue.[11] After having read some of the most canonical texts of Cuban literature, such as Regino Eladio Boti, Nicolás Guillén, José María Heredia, José Martí, and Juan Marinello Vidaurreta, Russian children painted what they imagined of the island. In some cases, Cuba resembled Gauguin's Tahiti in the sense that dark-skinned bodies and primitive landscapes reigned. Cuban children, in turn, participated in a contest at the book fair entitled "Pintando Rusia" (Painting Russia). Even though the contest, properly titled "Los niños cubanos dibujan Rusia" (Cuban Children Draw Russia), was actually organized by the Russian publishing house Veselye Kartinki (Merry Pictures), the fact that the announcement for the contest was handwritten in a makeshift manner, instead of printed out in an attractive design in advance, suggests something similar to what was seen in the infamous Sasha-protagonist episode in Prieto's *Rex*, that is, the discrepant temporalities that are involved within the current Russian-Cuban mirroring. Cuban children's imaginary of Russia today did not differ so much from the replicas of Soviet families seen in Adelaida Fernández de Juan's short story or even in Lissette Solórzano's photo-essay. Snowy landscapes, samovars, matrioshkas, and the San Basilio Church somehow effortlessly leaped into the drawings by the contest's participants.

The makeshift sign also contrasts sharply with the series of postcards, printed on paper of a quality rarely seen in Cuba, released for the book fair. The cards, representing monumental scenes in Soviet-Cuban history, were disseminated to child visitors of the Russian Pavilion. These images with text, written primarily in Cyrillic (as opposed to the Cyrillic font of *Todo tiempo pasado fue mejor*), resuscitate sites of remembrance, utilizing a classic pedagogical tool of challenging children to stimulate their curiosity. For people who are eager to possess frivolous objects from abroad, these postcards were a hit for their opulence alone. One day in the future these children may come to penetrate the foreign words and discover their meaning. Postcard 6 reads "All Cuba is a military post, the lines of the combatants grow. The heroes of Cuba will defend liberty, land, and work." This militaristic slogan captures the fervor of the year following the establishment of economic and trade relations between Cuba and the Soviet Union and Castro's pledge to align Cuba with the domestic and foreign policies of the Soviet Union. However, that the postcard is in Cyrillic without translation suggests that its original intention was to augment fervor in the Soviet world toward the incipient Cuban Revolution, utilizing the image of a Sovietized Cuban farmer that might remind Soviet onlookers of their October

*Postcard 6, "All Cuba is a military post, the lines of the combatants grow. The heroes of Cuba will defend liberty, land, and work," by Oleg Masliakov and Efim Tsvik, 1961.*

ДА ЗДРАВСТВУЕТ ВЕЧНАЯ, НЕРУШИМАЯ ДРУЖБА И СОТРУДНИЧЕСТВО МЕЖДУ СОВЕТСКИМ И КУБИНСКИМ НАРОДАМИ !

*Postcard 12, "Long live the eternal and indestructible friendship and cooperation between the peoples of the Soviet Union and Cuba," by Y. Kerchin and C. Turari, 1963.*

Revolution. Postcard 12 from 1963 renders a familiar image of Fidel Castro and Nikita Khrushchev and the oft-heard slogan "Long live the eternal and inde-structible friendship and cooperation between the peoples of the Soviet Union and Cuba." Postcard 7, also from 1963, reminds spectators that Cuba and the Soviet Union are "always together." These last two cards are reminders of spe-cial importance in the aftermath of the Cuban Missile Crisis. It would have been difficult to imagine back in 1991 that in 2010 such recitations would be disseminated to Cuban children, albeit in a language unknown to them, since these new, yet old, injections of solidarity were believed to have been buried.

The children's extravaganza had many other dimensions, some with mes-sianic overtones. Numerous copies of a 2004 book entitled *Niños del milagro* (Children of the Miracle), by the journalists Katiushka Blanco, Alina Perera, and Alberto Núñez, were placed in a box in a central place at the book fair, free for the taking. The cover features a child's eyes behind a book entitled *Dime como es Venezuela* (Tell Me What Venezuela Is Like). Beginning with a short saga about José Martí's arrival in the land of Bolívar in 1881, the book is struc-tured like a travelogue through Venezuela, featuring the testimonies of benefi-ciaries of one of Cuba's successful humanitarian projects, Operación Milagro (Operation Miracle); that is, it focuses on the real and beautiful stories of Vene-zuelan children who returned to their country after having been cured of ocu-

ВСЕГДА ВМЕСТЕ!

Postcard 7, "Always Together," by V. Ivanov, 1963. Copyright Estate of Vladimir Ivanov/ RAO, Moscow/Vaga, New York.

lar illnesses in Cuba. The book's rhetoric makes it seem as if Operation Miracle were the realization of a historical solidarity between Martí and Simón Bolívar. Russia distributed for free its own children's magazine—*Veselye Kartinki* (Merry Pictures)—to entertain Cubans. At first glance, the Russian messiah was much more traditional: Santa Claus. The explicit message of friendship only slightly transforms those messages from the "olden times" of the Soviet-Cuban friendship. Translated by someone with a limited knowledge of Cuban Spanish, indicated by the use of the peninsular second-person plural, the following declaration most relives the prior heroism: "Despite Russia and the precious island of Cuba being far from one another, our peoples have always been friends. Now we want you to get to know our culture, history, [and] country today, and about how Russian children of your age live today."[12] The message could not be clearer. However, the Russian-Cuban attempt to teach children about the long history is more distanced from the real accomplishments of the two peoples, and instead, represents for Cuban children a cartoon about the Christmas and New Year celebration in Russia, as well as a sampling of watercolor paintings depicting Russians imagining Cuba that seem more like stereotypical portraits than the documentation of any real collaboration.

The other group of Cubans with whom the book fair subtly dialogued was a bit older than the *Muñequitos Rusos* generation; between forty-five and sixty years old, some of them had traveled to the Soviet Union and served as translators on the fair's bilingual panels. They sought to mingle with the Russian visitors, to get closer to the people with whom, in retrospect, they felt an affinity that did not have purely nostalgic dimensions, as the words of the renowned Russian-Spanish translator Julio Travieso at the 2009 *Temas* roundtable convey: "The important thing for me, more than to remember the past . . . are the traces that today's Russia will leave on Cuba. And I ask myself if some of the thousands of us that went to the Soviet Union will someday be able to return to Moscow, Volgograd, the different regions where we studied."[13] Once again, Svetlana Boym's categories of "restorative" and "reflective" nostalgia prove useful for analyzing these distinct gestures, where reflective nostalgia allows for "the meditation of history and the passage of time" and is about "individual and cultural memory,"[14] processes with which Travieso's words negotiate.

But it is Yoss's outspoken intervention at that very same *Temas* roundtable in 2009 that uncovered a general strategy of imitation that directly challenged restorative nostalgia.

> I believe that this concept of "we hide the truth" still has an extraordinary influence on Cuban society: the politics of verticality is one of the worst traces that the Russian presence has left here. Other traces, one could say, are the military degrees and theory that is studied, and upon which our army operates, and that is based on, according to my criteria, completely dislocated concepts. Does someone remember what the "War of All People" was? It is a strategic concept that has meaning in a country of great territorial extension, that can give itself the luxury of presenting a strategy of elastic backward movement . . . that would not make much sense in Cuba, and that nevertheless, had been mechanically copied from the Russian military manuals, as they copy some other things.[15]

The "War of all People," a strategy initiated in 1980 involving all citizens' involvement in a potential fight against aggression, Yoss remarks, was an example of an unfortunate copy of Soviet military strategies on the island. The "War of all People" was executed by Raul Castro, who was at that time the minister of the Cuban armed forces and largely responsible for the military collaborations—both the successful and the fraught—with the Soviet Union. To blame the Soviet big brother for the strategy of concealing truths, an accusation which is at least partially valid, is audacious in its admission of the extant remains of the negative dimensions of Cuba's reliance on the Soviets, especially so given that the recent cultural interactions are part of an initiative toward new Russian investment on the island.

Leave it to this renowned, primarily science fiction writer not only to critique but also to exploit the comic element of the new encounters between the Soviet past and Russian present in Cuba. In Yoss's short story "Ivana Ivanovna y la peste a grajo" (Ivana Ivanovna and the Stench of Armpits), published in *El cuentero*'s "red" issue (March 2010),[16] the narrator, a writer by profession, observes a man named Igor watching a sexy, foreign-looking redheaded woman and her companion, a slight Cuban "mulatto" man, Yosvany (of Generation Y), at a drinks stand in Havana while Dmitry Medvedev is making a speech in the background. In the meantime, Igor approaches the narrator offering to entertain him, to forego the long speech of the "gran jefe ruso"[17] (great Russian chief), volunteering the story of his own interaction with the redhead, Ivana Ivanovna, in Alamar some twenty years before. Igor reveals that Ivana is actually a Russian born in Cuba to a Soviet colonel who lost his wife to Dengue fever in the tropics soon after she gave birth to Ivana. Yosvany, Ivana's companion that day, is her friend from years before. Igor claims that even though she was as stunning then as she is today, he avoided her romantically since she smelled so bad, until the day she announced that it was time for the Soviets to return to their homeland—the moment of "*bye bye asesores soviéticos, bye bye Bolilandia*"[18] (bye-bye Soviet advisors, bye-bye Bololand). Ivana then offered herself to Igor, and he gasped for a deep breath before diving into a passionate affair. The story elucidates the by now familiar stereotypes that have emerged out of Cubans' contact with the Soviets: Igor recollects the food, the gorgeous and smelly redhead who as an adolescent betrayed her Soviet legacy by not properly memorizing Mayakovsky and Lermentov, and even dancing like a Cuban. Igor and the narrator's conversation is overheard by the folkloric kiosk attendant, a large woman who concludes the tale. The thin "mulatto" is her brother, who lost his sense of smell after contracting pneumonia during his first winter in Moscow in 1988. When the Cuban students and workers were called back home at the time of Perestroika and Glasnost, Yosvany stayed, only to reencounter his redheaded friend in 1991 while he was working as a translator at the Cervantes Institute in Moscow. And, why are they in Havana? For the book fair, "siendo Rusia la invitada"[19] (Russia being the invited one). Yoss's "Ivana Ivanovna" carnivalizes the new bonds between Russia and Cuba, highlighting the bizarre nature of the fast reconciliation that is friend to the serious collective forgetting which Yoss combats in other contexts.

More than Cuba's being a wasteland or museum solely for Soviet material products, in post-post-Soviet times, Cuba persists in many ways in a performance of a Soviet theme park. Cuba was codified already in similar terms by Ivan de la Nuéz, who called it a "theme park" in the sense of its being a "watering trough of nostalgias," and by Antonio José Ponte, who specified it as a "theme park of the Cold War."[20] However, *Dreaming in Russian* also shows that donning an astrakhan coat or erecting a minor CCCP monument to rocket science on occasion and doing so in a manner that exceeds even the original is not the only way that Cubans remember the Soviet and Russian past. Creative attempts at reckoning with the Cuban-Soviet alliance translate a very Cuban reality that escapes commitments to transitions, at the same time that they show numerous and complex layers of forward- and backward-looking tensions and movements. The collective filter of the world that the Soviet Union provided Cuba has disappeared, but just because the Soviet Union has disintegrated hardly means that it has departed from the imaginations of Cubans. In its very disintegration, the Soviet Union has expanded and morphed in contemporary Cuban culture.

# Notes

INTRODUCTION

Unless otherwise indicated, all translations are my own.

1. Prieto, *El humor de Misha*, 45.

2. Ibid., 56.

3. The 1901 Platt Amendment was composed of clauses appended to the Cuban Constitution by United States secretary of war Elihu Root that, among other privileges and restrictions, gave the United States control over the Guantánamo naval base and the right to intervene in matters of Cuban independence.

4. Isabel García-Zarza, "Cuba aún guarda huellas de la era soviética."

5. Buck-Morss, *Dreamworld and Catastrophe*, 68.

6. *Nueva trova* is a movement that emerged in the 1960s, with roots in *trova* folk music and influences from international folk music, popular music, and rock music. Following is a translation of the lyrics of Frank Delgado's anthem (the original Spanish is available online at http://www.cancioneros.com/nc/4504/0/konchalovski-hace -rato-que-no-monta-en-lada-frank-delgado):

> I'll no longer be able to read any book of those
> Published by Raduga and Progreso.
> I won't be able to enjoy that Tío Stiopa
> With his incredible stature and horrible clothing.
> I can't deny that my eyes burn.
> Mayakovsky lets the cowards cringe nowadays
> And I will not be able to drink black tea in the afternoons.
> The Bolshoi theater still has not been plundered
> There are Nights of Moscow, organized crime
> Surely, the Mosfilm Studios have closed.
>
> I won't get excited again by *Siberiada*.
> Konchalovsky hasn't ridden a Lada in a while.

I won't be able to enjoy those Olympics
With the Soviets winning all the medals.
Kasankina shouts: Don't leave me alone.
Serguei Bubka gets revenge, drinks Coca Cola
With Salenko, who plays in the Spanish League.

Someone asked me if I'd read *Capital*.
Yes, but I didn't like it, since the heroine dies in the end.
Anyway, I don't like so much fictionalized economy
That some Karl Marx wrote.

Now that the censors don't pitch low
We can laugh at their cartoons
Now that the ministers changed flags
We can speak badly about their light industry.
Now that I carry on my forehead the stamp of loser
And they accuse me of walls that have finally fallen down
I can be post-modern, lose meaning.
I can renege on the utopias I believe in
Or become passionately enraged
By Lenin's mummy and his Mausoleum.

Now that the only thing left from the vodka is the hangover
I refuse, my love, to become a turncoat
Now that the Komsomols don't care about a thing
Hug me, my sweetie, and don't leave me alone.
And while Fukuyama repeats in rage
That we're at the end of world history
My friend Benedetti opens the second volume.

Someone asked me if I'd read *Capital*:
Yes, but I didn't like it, since the heroine dies at the end.
Anyway, these little three-volume novels that Karl Marx wrote
Don't serve me anymore.

7. Buck-Morss, *Dreamworld and Catastrophe*, 208–209.

8. Acanda, "Racapitular la Cuba de los 90," http://biblioteca.filosofia.cu/php
/export.php?format=htm&id=34&view=1.

9. Strangely, one of the earliest texts that directly engages the leftovers of the
Soviets on the island at any length is not by a Cuban scholar but by the North American Martin Cruz Smith in his novel *Havana Bay*, wherein a Russian detective, Arkady
Renko, travels to Cuba to reckon with the mysterious death of a colleague, as well as
with the remains of the Soviet Union in Cuba. The point of departure is Cuba's embittered feelings toward the Soviets, and as such, it is a quasi-anthropological study that
serves as a screwball precedent to my own.

10. Boym, *Future of Nostalgia*, 41.

11. Ubieta Gómez, "Prólogo," 5. Ubieta Gómez's anthology is a response to the anthology compiled by Iván de la Nuéz, *Cuba y el día después: Doce ensayistas nacidos con la revolución imaginan el futuro*, whose point of departure is the day after Fidel Castro's death.

12. Bain, "Gorbachev's Legacy," 214.

13. Rojas, *De lo efímero*, 15.

14. Rojas, "El triunfo de Stalin," http://www.caimanbarbudo.cu/caiman321/especial1 .htm. (This link no longer works.)

15. Rojas participated in the *Temas* debate; see Brown, Dacal, Díaz Vázquez, et al. "¿Por qué cayó el socialismo?" 99.

16. Francisco Brown Infante and Arial Dacal's *Rusia: Del socialismo real al capitalismo real* analyzes the reasons and the consequences of the fall of the USSR. In Allen Woods's preface, available at http://www.elmilitante.org/content/view/3033/74, he reminds readers of Russia's backwardness before the Revolution and of the discrepancies between Marx and Engel's vision and the actual Soviet experience, as well as the problem of the USSR's isolation, signaled by Lenin and Trotsky. He concludes by calling for the destruction of bureaucracy, "the terrain where pro-bourgeois tendencies can put down roots and grow." For Woods, Venezuela is a beacon for a future in which Cuba is less isolated. Also see Gerardo Arreola's "Debaten en Cuba la renovación del socialismo" for more on the twenty-first-century re-evaluation of Trotsky.

17. Rojas, "De lo efímero," 14. *P.M.*, directed by Sabá Cabrera Infante, is a short 1961 film that features Havana's nightlife. It was censored, and *Lunes de revolución*, the cultural supplement edited by Cabrera Infante's brother, Guillermo Cabrera Infante, was subsequently shut down. This controversy resulted in Fidel Castro's 1961 "Palabras a los intelectuales" (Words to the Intellectuals), the most memorable part of which is frequently quoted: "Dentro de la Revolución, todo; contra la Revolución, nada" (Within the Revolution, everything; against the Revolution, nothing).

18. Rodríguez, "Carta para no ser un espíritu prisionero," http://www.cubaencuentro.com/cultura/articulos/carta-para-no-ser-un-espiritu-prisionero-29675.

19. Hernández, "Cuban Transition," http://news.uchicago.edu/multimedia/latin -american-briefing-series-cuban-transition-imagined-and-actual-rafael-hernandez.

20. La Fountain-Stokes, "Trans/Bolero/Drag/Migration," 194.

21. De la Nuez, "Llega el 'eastern,'" www.elpais.com/articulo/portada/Llega /eastern/elpepuculbab/20100508elpbabpor_3/Tes.

22. By far one of the most outlandish works is Luis Manuel García's *Aventuras eslavas de Don Antolín del Corojo y crónica del nuevo mundo según Iván el terrible: ¿Novela testimonio?* (Slavic Adventures of Don Antolín del Corojo and Chronicle of the New World According to Ivan the Terrible: Testimonial Novel?). Using a postmodern mixture of Cuban argot and seventeenth-century Castilian, the epistolary form, and "authentic" materials from the characters' voyage, this work exploits the bizarre scenario of young Cubans' discovery of Russia and a Russian's travel to Cuba, bringing immense humor to the consequences of the Cuban-Soviet solidarity.

1. Bain, *Russian-Cuban Relations*, 83.

2. Dacosta, "New Miscegenation," 24.

3. Ibid., 24–25.

4. Ibid., 28.

5. See Martínez Shvietsova and Prieto Samsonov, ". . . So, Borscht and the *Ajiaco* Don't Mix?"

6. Moiseev and Egorova, *Los rusos en Cuba*, 135.

7. Dacosta, "New Miscegenation," 2.

8. Martínez Shvietsova, "¿Koniec? 2004–Asere, Nu pogogy," unpublished text.

9. Prieto Samsonov, "Jurel en pesos," 49.

10. Ibid.

11. Ibid., 49–50.

12. Prieto Samsonov, "Military Bases," http://www.havanatimes.org/?p=12727.

13. Prieto Samsonov, "Moon Landing," http://www.havanatimes.org/?p=12782.

14. Prieto Samsonov, "Descubrir 'el agua tibia,'" http://www.esquife.cult.cu/primera epoca/revista/56/13.htm.

15. Prieto Samsonov, "The Pravda of Reggaetón," http://www.havanatimes.org /?p=8363.

16. Ibid.

17. Only in May of 2008 did artists gather in Espacio Aglutinador (Agglutinating Space), in the home of the plastic artist Sandra Ceballos, to celebrate a pornography exhibit entitled *We Are Porno, Sí* that implemented the language of the enemy—English— with a brief and affirmative nod to Spanish—to say something forbidden in the domestic sphere.

18. Martínez Shvietsova, "17 abstractos de una agenda," http://www.centronelio .cult.cu/index.php?option=com_content&task=view&id=241&Itemid=90.

19. See Armengol, "Unas 24,000 víctimas de Chernobil atendidas en Cuba en 19 años," *Cuaderno de Cuba*, April 1, 2009, http://www.llarmengol.blogspot.com/2009/04 /unas-24000-victimas-de-chernobil.html, for more on the massive humanitarian project that Cuba initiated in 1990 to help the victims of Chernobyl.

20. Allatson, *Key Terms*, 67.

21. Young, *Colonial Desire*, 175.

22. Martínez Shvietsova, "17 abstractos de una agenda," http://www.centronelio .cult.cu/index.php?option=com_content&task=view&id=241&Itemid=90.

23. Ibid.

24. López-Cabrales, *Arenas cálidas*, 76.

25. Vega Serova, *Ánima fatua*, 33.

26. Ibid., 34.

27. Ibid., 56.

28. Dacosta, "New Miscegenation," 25.

29. Moiseev and Egorova, *Los rusos en Cuba*, 138.

30. Mistral, *Selected Poems*, 196–197.

31. "Destituyen a la directora del canal Televisión Camagüey por emitir un documental censurado," http://www.cubanet.org/CNews/y07/dico7/2007.htm.

32. Fowler Calzada, "Todas íbamos a ser reinas," http://www.eictv.co.cu/miradas/index.php?option=com_content&task=view&id=587&Itemid=86. (Link no longer works.)

33. Rodríguez, "Nostalgia," 38.

34. Boadle, "Russian Women," http://www.reuters.com/article/2007/09/05/us-cuba-russia-women-idUSN2135841320070905.

35. From the word "meringue" (the fluffy combination of beaten egg whites and sugar), *desmerengamiento* — literally, the collapse of a meringue — is used in Cuba to describe the gradual weakening the socialist system.

36. Calcines, "Matrioshkas cubanas," http://opushabana.ohc.cu/index.php?option=com_content&view=article&id=1590&catid=26&Itemid=44.

37. Ibid.


CHAPTER 2

1. "*La rusa*" (the Russian woman) is the term most frequently used to refer to women from the Soviet Union, including those who are not of Russian origin.

2. González Reinoso, *Vidas de Roxy*, 16.

3. Ibid., 31.

4. González Reinoso, "Roxy the Red," 58–59.

5. Rutland, *Politics of Economic Stagnation*, 117.

6. Sánchez, "Extinction of the Panda," http://www.desdecuba.com/generationy/?p=731.

7. González Reinoso, *Vidas de Roxy*, 26.

8. González Reinoso, "Roxy the Red," 56.

9. Díaz Gómez, *La calle de los oficios*, 118.

10. From Severo Sarduy's "El barroco y el neobarroco," quoted in Tierney-Tello, *Allegories of Transgression*, 98.

11. González Reinoso, *Vidas de Roxy*, 134.

12. Ibid., 97.

13. Ibid., 19.

14. Ibid., 51.

15. Rodríguez, "Palabras prologares," in Reinoso, *Vidas de Roxy*, 12.

16. Reinoso, *Vidas de Roxy*, 25.

17. González Reinoso, "Roxy the Red," 55.

18. Fountain-Stokes, "Trans/Bolero/Drag/Migration," 195.

19. The performers' profiles were once available on the Mejunje website at http://www.divascubanas.com, where I initially learned of them, but the website no longer exists.

20. Muñoz, *Disidentifications*, 108–109.

21. Díaz Gómez, *La calle de los oficios*, 118.

22. González Reinoso, *Vidas de Roxy*, 37.

23. González Reinoso, "Roxy the Red," 61. I have made some additions to the published translation.

24. González Reinoso, *Vidas de Roxy*, 65.

25. García Espinosa, "For an Imperfect Cinema," http://www.ejumpcut.org/archive/onlinessays/JC20folder/ImperfectCinema.html.

26. Fernández de Juan, "Clemencia bajo el sol," 78.

27. Ibid., 79–80.

28. Ibid., 80.

29. Ibid.

30. Ibid., 81.

31. Ibid.

32. Ibid.

33. Ibid., 82.

34. Ibid.

35. Ibid., 84.

36. Ibid.

37. Ibid., 85.

38. Miralles, "Fotos de boda," *Las voces del pantano*, 58.

39. Miralles, "Wedding Photos," 294.

40. Miralles, "Fotos de boda," 66.

41. Miralles, "Wedding Photos," 302.

42. Miralles, "Fotos de boda," 66.

43. Miralles, "Wedding Photos," 302.

44. This is Pérez Castillo's spelling.

45. Pérez Castillo, "Bajo la bandera rosa," 39.

46. Bakuradze, "Post-Pioneer Inferiority Complex."

47. Pérez Castillo, "Bajo la bandera rosa," 32.

48. Ibid., 40.

49. Pérez Castillo, *Haciendo las cosas mal*, 10–11.

50. Ibid., 72.

51. Ibid., 89.

52. Ibid., 39.

53. Ibid., 40.

54. Ibid., 123.

55. Rodríguez Febles, *Sputnik*, 206.

56. Ibid., 207.

57. Ibid., 208.

58. Ibid., 213.

59. Black, "Cuba: The Revolution," 378.

60. Rodríguez Febles, *Sputnik*, 215.

61. Dacosta, "New Miscegenation," 25.

62. Rodríguez Febles, *Sputnik*, 216.

63. Ibid., 222.

64. Ibid., 228.

65. Ibid., 229.

66. Ibid., 240.

67. Ibid., 245.

68. Ibid., 252.

69. Ibid., 249.

70. Ibid., 261.

71. Ibid., 263.


CHAPTER 3

1. Ferrer, "Around the Sun," 102.

2. Bermejo Santos, "*Islas* y las difusión del quehacer," 150.

3. Ibid., 153.

4. Feijóo, *Viaje a la Unión Soviética*, 162. Feijóo's fascination with Russian folk-lore is somewhat analogous to Alejo Carpentier's, as seen in many of Carpentier's *crónicas*, in *Concierto barroco* (1974), and in *Consagración de la primavera* (1978). In these novels, Carpentier identifies Igor Stravinsky as the key to transculturating American arts through a process comparable to the composer's embrace and invention of the indigenous within the modern idiom. See Loss, "Stravinsky," and Fernández Díaz, "Igor Stravinsky en Alejo Carpentier."

5. Feijóo, *Viaje a la Unión Soviética*, 108.

6. Bejel, *Gay Cuban Nation*, 100.

7. Quoted in Leiner, *Sexual Politics*, 25.

8. Ferrer, "Around the Sun."

9. See Carlos Espinosa Domínguez, "The Mammoth That Wouldn't Die."

10. Fidel Castro, "Discurso pronunciado a los estudiantes cubanos becarios en la Unión Soviética y al personal de la embajada de Cuba en la URSS," July 2, 1972, http://www.cuba.cu/gobierno/discursos/1972/esp/f020772e.html.

11. Díaz, *Siberiana*, 80.

12. Guillot Carvajal, review of *Siberiana*, 176.

13. Plasencia, review of *La sexta parte del mundo*, 30.

14. Díaz, *Siberiana*, 63–64.

15. In Luis Palés Matos's poem "Mulata Antilla," the poetic subject appears to be seduced by the mulatto's body odor, but as Alan West-Durán has observed, *catinga* denotes "the strong, read negative odor of either indigenous people or Africans" (West-Durán, "Puerto Rico," 57).

16. Two editions of this collection were released simultaneously, one selling for hard currency and the other for national pesos. They were differentiated only by their covers. The one sold in hard currency featured a matrioshka with a *guajiro's* sombrero on its head, a classic representation of the Soviet-Cuban alliance that reinforces the theme of odd juxtapositions that characterizes the volume. The cover of the edition sold in national currency was illustrated by the Cuban artist Hanna Chomenko and is

a more complex image of an Afro-Cuban face, reminiscent of Armenteros's, which is embraced by various arms and suspended above a field worked by a nondescript peasant. The image of a matrioshka with a sombrero is reminiscent of the movie poster for the 1962 Soviet documentary about the Bay of Pigs entitled *Isla en llamas* (Island in Flames), directed by Roman Karmen and featuring a Sovietized rectangular and militaristic Cuban face wearing a *guajiro*'s sombrero. A very similar image — *Patrioska,* by artist Carlos René Aguilera Tamayo — appears on the 2009 cover of the literary and cultural magazine *Sic,* in a special issue on the presence of Russia in Cuban culture.

17. Armenteros, "La fracasada inmortalidad," in *El país que no era,* 17.

18. Ibid., 20.

19. Ibid., 23.

20. Ibid., 75.

21. Ibid., 77.

22. Díaz, *Siberiana,* 81.

23. Ibid., 66.

24. Ibid., 139.

25. Prieto, *Enciclopedia,* 67.

26. Ibid., 116.

27. Ibid., 112.

28. Yulzari, "Discurso transnational," http://www.baquiana.com/Numero_XXVII -XXVIII/Ensayo_II.htm.

29. Díaz, *Siberiania,* 82.

30. Ibid., 101–102.

31. Ibid., 136.

32. Ibid., 138.

33. Bhabha, *Location of Culture,* 122.

34. Gates, *Signifying Monkey.*

35. Prieto, *Rex* (2007), 109.

36. Prieto, *Rex* (2009), 140.

37. Prieto, *Rex* (2007), 109.

38. Prieto, *Rex* (2009), 140.

39. Prieto, *Rex* (2007), 109.

40. Prieto, *Rex* (2009), 141.

41. Prieto, *Rex* (2007), 49.

42. Prieto, *Rex* (2009), 57.

43. Prieto, *Rex* (2007), 158–159.

44. Prieto, *Rex* (2009), 212.

45. Prieto, *Rex* (2007), 158.

46. Prieto, *Rex* (2009), 212–213.

47. Rojas, "Las dos mitades," 233.

48. Prieto, *Livadia,* 30.

49. Prieto, *Nocturnal Butterflies of the Russian Empire,* 22.

50. Prieto, *Treinta días,* 19.

51. Ibid., 83.

52. Ibid., 103–104.

53. Ibid., 105.

54. Ibid., 165.

55. Ibid., 101.

56. Ibid., 102. This phrase appears in English only.

57. Tanya Weimer elucidates this aspect of Prieto's work with regard to the protagonist of *Livadia*. "This foreigner that tries to insert himself in local life conforms to an example of mimetism in which the protagonist learns to re-create what the Russians consider natural. He does not achieve it, because his complexion and his attitude always call attention" (*La diáspora cubana*, 149). Translation mine.

58. Prieto, *Livadia*, 45.

59. Ibid., 21.

60. Prieto, *Nocturnal Butterflies*, 12.

61. Fernández Fé, "De lémures y economías," 349.

62. Prieto, *Enciclopedia*, 142.

63. Prieto, *Rex* (2007), 142.

64. Prieto, *Rex* (2009), 188–189.

65. Ibid., 318.

66. Laub, "Truth and Testimony," 63.

67. Díaz, *Las cuatro fugas*, 43.

68. Ibid., 85.

69. Ibid., 76.

70. Rojas, "*Souvenirs* de un Caribe soviético," 30.

71. García Montiel, "Cartas desde Rusia," in *Presentación del olvido*, 45.

72. Álvarez Gil, "Tres cerditos," in *Unos y otros*, 38.

73. Ibid., 40.

74. Ibid.

75. Ibid.

76. Álvarez Gil, "Una casa en medio del mar," in *Unos y otros*, 98.

77. Ibid., 100.

78. Ibid., 101.

79. Ibid., 105.

80. Ibid., 110.

81. Álvarez Gil's "¿Recuerdas, Natalia?" (Do You Remember, Natalia?) is a similarly naïve story about a young Cuban man who falls in love with a Russian woman but who ends the relationship abruptly, as "nunca he pensado casarme con una extranjera" (I have never thought of marrying a foreigner). His response to her invitation to *Carmen* at the Bolshoi is telling. Having initially refused on account of his homophobic opinion of ballet, he accepts, intrigued by imagining how "los rusos construirían un mundo que yo consideraba, de cierta manera, un poco mió también" (*Unos y otros*, 15; the Russians would construct a world that I considered, in a way, a little bit mine, too). The world that was already "by blood," "a little bit" Alvárez Gil's was Spain, the former empire, where *Carmen* is set—not the Soviet Union.

82. In the story after which the book is titled, a Cuban at a hotel bar in a small town

in Transylvania converses with Mercedes, a young lady whose jasmine perfume is reminiscent of someone he knew years before and whose eyes remind him of his mother's. The narrator then discovers the reason behind the young "Hungarian's" expertise in Spanish: "Cuando en el hotel de su novio anunciaron que realizarían aquí en Sovata una reunión de los países del CAME, y sabiendo que Cuba era miembro, se interesó si no vendría algún cubano" (12). (When in her boyfriend's hotel they announced that a meeting of the COMECON countries would take place here in Sovata, and knowing that Cuba was a member, she wondered if some Cuban might come.) The secret is divulged: Mercedes's father was actually Cuban and her parents met in Kiev, where the narrator then reveals he too had studied.

83. Wilson, "A Ten-Point U.S. Program," http://www.heritage.org/Research/Latin America/bg658.cfm.

84. Armenteros, "Miscélaneas," in *País que no era*, 80.

85. Hernández Salván, "Requiem for a Chimera," 166.

86. Armenteros, "Miscélaneas," 49.

87. Rojas, "Las dos mitades," 232.

88. Armenteros, "Misceláneas," 50.

89. Ibid., 52.

90. Ibid., 53.

91. The Polish woman felt her country to be oppressed by the Soviets. Similarly, in the 2005 novel *Casa de cambio*, by Alejandro Aguilar (born in 1958 in Camagüey, Cuba), Antonio is part of the last wave of students to head East, from Cuba to Hungary, to study engineering. He finds himself as both an observer of what the easterners do when their demarcations collapse and as a go-between between the distinct worlds that are collapsing before his eyes in 1989. In order to survive, he acts as a translator for the mafia, like Manuel from *Las cuatro fugas de Manuel*, and as a trafficker of their funds. Antonio regularly confronts Hungarians' antipathy toward the Soviets: first from Rojas, the functionary from the Cuban embassy who describes Hungarians' mistaken animosity toward the Soviets, and then from a lover named Agi, who before revealing her feelings about Russians to Antonio, tells him that she suspects he, as a Cuban, won't be able to understand. "Tal vez porque eres cubano no puedas entender cuánto odiamos a los rusos. Ellos no se contentan con ocupar nuestro país y someternos a sus costumbres" (53). (Maybe because you're Cuban you can't understand how much we hate the Russians. They're not satisfied with occupying our country and subjecting us to their customs.) This declaration is reminiscent not only of Armenteros's description of cultural hegemony, but also of Díaz's characters, who are unable to envision understanding the other.

92. The question of literary value is relative and generational, as the commentary of Eduardo Heras León (born in 1940) makes clear. A Cuban writer and director of the Centro Onelio Jorge Cardoso, Heras León notes the immense value of recently distributed Soviet war literature, such as *La carretera de Volokolamsk*, for Cubans who were about to go fight in the Bay of Pigs. Heras León's interview appears in Enrique Colina's fifty-two-minute documentary *Los rusos en Cuba* (produced in collaboration with RFO, Histoire, Canal Overseas Productions, Beau Comme Les Antilles, Beau Comme Une Image).

93. Armenteros, "Misceláneas," 74.

94. Rojas, "*Souvenirs* de un Caribe soviético," 23.

95. Ibid., 25.

96. Abreu, "Deuda," 10.

97. In a speech entitled "Los manuscritos no arden I: sobre tres poetas rusos y un poeta cubano," presented at the University of Connecticut on April 28, 2011, Reina María Rodríguez similarly focused on the impact of her readings of Soviet counter-memory (characterized by Anna Akhmatova, Marina Tsvetaeva, and Boris Pasternak) on her writing and on that of the Cuban poet Heberto Padilla.

98. "Asiste Raúl a la inauguración del Pabellón de Rusia en la Feria del Libro," *Vanguardia*, 2010, http://www.vanguardia.co.cu/index.php?tpl=design/secciones/lectura/portada.tpl.html&newsid_obj_id=18969. (This link no longer works.)

99. Armenteros, "Misceláneas," 59.

100. The narrator/protagonist explains to his friend, a fellow Cuban traveler, César, the reason behind his Russian companion's absence. She was off visiting her family who "tampoco me soportan, por extranjero creo y por mi piel" (don't put up with me either, because I'm a foreigner, I think, and because of my skin)—a statement which garners laughter from his friend, "un auténtico negro asfaltil o asfáltico" (62) (a true black, as dark as tar or asphalt). The two Cubans' desires around race continue to surface when César—known to be a womanizer—discusses all the women in the student work brigade: "¡Hembras, hembras de todas las nacionalidades hasta mongolas!" (63) (Females, females of all nationalities even Mongols!).

101. Armenteros, "Misceláneas," 70.

102. Ibid., 56.

103. "Siberiada" refers to Andrei Konchalovsky's 1979 four-part epic Soviet film representing Siberia in the twentieth century.

104. Díaz-Briquets, "Demographic and Related Determinants of Recent Cuban Emigration," 114.

105. Díaz, *Las cuatro fugas*, 21.

106. Of the many artistic figurations of such characters that come to mind is Sergio, the tortured protagonist of Tomás Gutiérrez Alea's *Memorias de subdesarrollo*, who struggles with the Sovietization of Havana, continually envisioning himself from the point of view of a foreigner and yet never leaving. A very important difference between Sergio and Manuel is that Díaz's protagonist was born in Holguín in 1970 and raised with the Revolution's values; he identifies with the Revolution's cause, yet by the novel's conclusion he pronounces his hatred for Castro.

107. Díaz, *Las cuatro fugas*, 34.

108. Guerrero, "Retrato del científico adolescente," http://www.letraslibres.com/revista/libros/las-cuatro-fugas-de-manuel-de-jesus-diaz.

109. Díaz, *Las cuatro fugas*, 48.

110. Ibid., 153.

111. Ibid., 157.

112. Ibid., 160.

113. Álvarez Gil, *Callejones de Arbat*, 20.

114. Ibid., 159.

115. Ibid.

116. See Jorge Ferrer, "La resistencia a la vulgaridad," April 29, 2009, http://www.eltonodelavoz.com/archivo/www.cubaencuentro.com/jorge-ferrer/blogs/el-tono-de-la-voz/la-resistencia-a-la-vulgaridadhtml.html.

117. Alvarez Gil, *Callejones de Arbat*, 144.

118. Álvarez Gil, *Callejones de Arbat*, 251. Original text is italic.

119. See Newman, "The Presence and Function of Russia," and Tanya N. Weimer's reading of Prieto's work as national allegory and as part of a more elaborate analysis of his work's cosmopolitanism in *La diáspora cubana en México*.

120. Fornet, *Los nuevos paradigmas*, 132.

121. Prieto, *El tartamudo y la rusa*, 77 and 80. The first edition of this book was published under the title *Nunca antes habías visto el rojo* in Havana in 1996.

122. Prieto, "You've Never Seen Red like This Before," trans. Esther Allen, ⟨wordswithoutborders.org/article/youve-never-seen-red-like-this-before⟩.

123. Prieto, *Enciclopedia de una vida*, 54.

124. "You, Petya, who Could easily write such a thing, a real book, a primary book, without commentary or citations in bold face, and without the dark gleam of his name, the Commentator's, contained within or casting its Light from any page of your book or any of the Fonds of your adult memory" (Prieto, *Rex* [2009], 307).

125. Birkenmaier, "Art of the Pastiche," 131.

126. Domínguez, "The Political Impact on Cuba of the Reform and Collapse," 110.

127. Newman, "Presence and Function," 12.

128. Prieto, *Treinta días en Moscú*, 22.

CHAPTER 4

1. During the 1960s, many cartoons shown on television in the United States, such as *Tom and Jerry*, *Popeye*, and *Krazy Kat*, were actually made in studios in Prague, on account of the expertise of the animators. See http://www.pbs.org/independentlens/animateddogs/animation1.html.

2. Masvidal Saavedra, "De *otakus* y *mangakas*," http://www.lajiribilla.co.cu/2008/n394_11/394_16.html.

3. For an account of how exiled Cubans felt robbed of their country by Soviets, see Néstor T. Carbonell's memoir *And the Russians Stayed: The Sovietization of Cuba*.

4. Díaz Infante, "Muñequitos rusos, nostalgia cubiche," http://www.duaneldiaz.blogspot.com/2007/04/muequitos-rusos-nostalgia-cubiche.html. (This link no longer works.)

5. Leyva Martínez, "Miami: Pequeñas nostalgias del castrismo," http://arch1.cubaencuentro.com/desde/20030320/6b1ffba34607b446bdb97b1561830eaa.html.

6. Rubio, "Material Culture," 304–305.

7. Prieto, *El humor de Misha*, 100.

8. Brennan, *At Home in the World*, 261.

9. Ibid., 305.

10. Generación Asere, "Sobre *Goodbye, Lolek!*" http://generacionasere.blogspot
.com/2008/05/sobre-goodbye-lolek.html. (This link now goes to a members-only
section.)

11. Jácome, "The Muñequitos Rusos Generation," 32.

12. See http://www.taringa.net/posts/animaciones/5681642/El-MegaPost-de
-Muñequitos-Rusos-(Dibujos-Animados-Rusos).html. This link now goes to a members-only section.

13. About this matter, Antón Vélez Bichkov remarked in his 2004 speech: "'Gracia',
que le valió una suspensión por un tiempo, por parte de la dirección del ICRT, obvia-
mente mucho más complacida con los animados que la audiencia misma" ("Humor,"
which earned him a temporary suspension by the authorities of the ICRT, who were
obviously much more pleased by the cartoons than the audience itself).

14. Ernesto René is Ernesto René Rodríguez's pen name.

15. The video can be seen at http://www.youtube.com/watch?v=lkqDDlUFPMo.

16. See information about Gorki Luis Aguila Carrasco's incarceration in 2003 at
http://www.freemuse.org/sw3956.asp. Also see Marco Werman, "Gorki," *PRI's The
World*, January 19, 2005, http://www.publicbroadcasting.net/wabe/.artsmain/article
/10/70/729763/Programs/Gorki/.

17. Many analogous phenomena can be found in the Soviet Bloc. In Russia, in 2000,
in fact, a new version of *The Bremen-Town Musicians* aired.

18. The Lenin school was founded by Fidel Castro and Leonid Brezhnev in 1974.
From the post-Soviet perspective, the following lines from Fidel Castro's "Dedication
of Lenin Vocation School of Calabazar" speech may seem difficult to believe:

> With eternal love and profound gratitude we dedicate this school to the memory
> of Vladimir Ilich Lenin, [applause] the genial revolutionary leader and founder
> of the first socialist state in the history of mankind. For the bright paths that he
> opened for man's future, for the outstanding services that he rendered the world,
> for the decisive assistance that the fraternal and internationalist state founded
> by him has given and for what his thought, his life and his example represent for
> revolutionaries on earth, this school, this pride of our people will bear his im-
> mortal name. [applause]
>
> Dear Comrade Brezhnev, during long months the teachers, workers, and stu-
> dents of this school and the construction, workers have made great efforts by day
> and night in order that not a single thing was lacking, not even a leaf on the trees
> in the greenery surrounding it, on the occasion of your visit and in order to receive
> you with the great love that you deserve as general secretary of the Central Com-
> mittee of the glorious Communist Party of the Soviet Union, [applause] for your
> courageous struggle for world peace, for your loyalty to the Leninist principles and
> for your feelings of friendship and affection for our revolutionary fatherland.
>
> It is a great honor and a grand occasion of happiness and pleasure for all of
> us that this school bearing the brilliant and honorable name of Lenin is dedi-

cated by you, who today holds Lenin's honorable post in the Communist Party of the Soviet Union [applause].

Eternal glory to Vladimir Ilich Lenin! Long live the inviolable friendship.

The speech is available at http://www.lanic.utexas.edu/project/castro/db/1974/1974 0131.html.

19. Israel, "Change Is Coming," http://www.reuters.com/article/globalNews/id USN1321778820080313?sp=true.

20. For more information on La Babosa Azul, see Cuba Underground's portal at http://cubaunderground.com/component/option,com_muscol/itemid,114/id,3/view ,album.

21. Guerra, "En Cuba es difícil guarder secretos," http://www.lanacion.cl/prontus_ noticias/site/artic/20061122/pags/20061122194534.html.

22. Sánchez, "Evoking the Bolos," June 5, 2008, http://www.desdecuba.com /generationy/?m=200806&paged=2.

23. Rodríguez, "Sobre Sovexportfilm," 23.

24. Ibid.

25. For more information about Katia Olevskaya, see "Historia de nuestras transmisiones: La voz de Rusia," http://spanish.ruvr.ru/historia, and the July 14, 2009, posting on the blog Escucha Chile, http://www.escuchachile1973.blogspot.com/2009_07_01 _archive.html.

26. Rodríguez, "Sobre Sovexportfilm," 23.

27. "Cheburashka" was first adapted to the screen in 1969 with the stop-motion film *Gena, the Crocodile*, directed by Roman Kachanov.

28. Rodríguez, "Sobre Sovexportfilm," 23.

29. Ibid.

30. Ibid., 26.

31. Ibid., 24.

32. Ibid.

33. Ibid.

34. Ibid., 25.

35. Ibid., 26.

36. Menchú, *Me llamo Rigoberta Menchú*, 1.

37. Menchú, *I, Rigoberta Menchú*, 1.

38. Guerra, *Nunca fui primera dama*, 9.

39. Guerra, *Todos se van*, 250.

40. Ibid.

41. Ibid.

42. Zardoya Loureda, "Ideología y revolución," 36.

43. Guerra, *Nunca fui primera dama*, 74.

44. Ibid., 76.

45. Ibid., 78.

46. Hernández, "Un diario," http://laparadadelosmangos.blogspot.com/2009/04 /un-diario-desde-el-pais-caribeno-criado.html. (This link no longer works.)

47. Guerra, *Nunca fui primera dama*, 13.

48. Ibid., 10.

49. Guerra, "De cómo los rusos se fueron despidiendo," in *Ropa Interior*, 68.

50. Hernández Busto, "La lección de Demonia," http://arch1.cubaencuentro.com /cultura/20050804/8ffddfcb196d249346a80a3731703b95/1.html.

51. Guerra, *Nunca fui primera dama*, 34.

52. Rivalta as quoted in Power, *Fnimaniev*, 19–20.

53. See Rivalta, "*Fnimaniev! Fnimaniev!*"

54. Bhabha, *Location of Culture*, 122.

55. Pérez, "Ferdinando Prenom," in *Trillos urbanos*, 16.

56. Ibid., 16–17.

57. Del Río, "Regresan los rusos," http://www.lajiribilla.cu/2008/n366_05/labutaca .html.

58. Acosta, "Cine en Cuba," http://www.periodistas-es.org/cine/cine-en-cuba-el -regreso-de-los-rusos.

59. Ibid.

60. Pérez, *Trillos urbanos*, 84.

61. Ibid., 63.

62. Flores, "El selenista," http://www.habanaelegante.com/SpringSummer2006 /AzoteaDos.html.

63. Flores, "Mea culpa por Tomás," http://www.habanaelegante.com/SpringSummer 2006/AzoteaDos.html.

64. Translated by Kristin Dykstra.

65. Rodríguez, "Solarística," http://www.cubaunderground.com/anonimo-literario -taller-no-1/solaristica.

66. Ibid.

67. Ibid.

68. Ibid.

69. Ibid.

70. Ibid.

71. Ibid.

72. Ibid.

73. Ibid.

74. Ibid.

75. *9550* was made on a small budget by the production company Por la Izquierda, and to my knowledge, has only been screened at the symposium I co-organized at the University of Connecticut entitled "Cuba-USSR and the Post-Soviet Experience" in February 2007.

CHAPTER 5

1. Nora, *Realms of Memory*, 14–15.

2. Ibid., 15.

3. Huyssen, *Present Pasts*, 1.

4. Although the website of Distribuciones Potemkin no longer functions, an announcement and description of it can be found at http://www.kaosenlared.net/noticia/distribuciones-potemkin.

5. Terdiman, *Present Past*, 13.

6. Pérez, "Cuba en el CAME," http://www.nuso.org/upload/articulos/1108_1.pdf.

7. Bain, *Russian-Cuban Relations since 1982*, 83.

8. See Rojas's *"Souvenirs* de un Caribe soviético."

9. Pereira, as quoted in Pereda, "Manuel Pereira presenta," http://www.elpais.com/articulo/cultura/PEREIRA/_MANUEL/Manuel/Pereira/presenta/Espana/Ruso/autobiografia/generacion/cubanos/elpepicul/19820526elpepicul_16/Tes.

10. Pereira, *El ruso*, 106.

11. See Fuentes, *Posición uno*, 163–166.

12. Regarding this commercial accord, Silvia Pérez remarked: "During his [Mikoyan's] time in Cuba, the first agreement of commercial exchange was signed, a product of the conversations sustained by Mikoyan with the direction of the Revolutionary Government. The agreement was established for the USSR to buy 425 thousand tons of sugar in 1960 and in the successive four years, a million tons annually. In addition, a credit of 100 million pesos was conceded with very low interest (2 and ½ percent) to use on the purchase of equipment, machinery and materials; and when it is needed, technical assistance for the construction of plants and factories . . . The relative weight of the Socialist countries and of the USSR in exterior commerce of Cuba was elevated from 1.4% and .9% respectively in 1958, to 21.6% and 15.3% in 1960. At the same time, economic relations with the rest of the socialist countries were also developing." From Pérez, "Cuba en el CAME," http://www.nuso.org/upload/articulos/1108_1.pdf.

13. Rodríguez, "Nostalgia."

14. Quoted in López, "Tres horas," 54–55.

15. Ibid., 55.

16. Miralles, "Una breve exposición."

17. Tonel studied at the Lenin school between grades 10 and 13.

18. Molina, "La marca de su cicatriz," 841.

19. Berman, "Bound to Outlast?" 164.

20. As Alejo Carpentier affirms, "Soviet literature had an early diffusion in Cuba. First the poets Yeset and Mayakowsky were known and already read by 1924." See Carpentier's "Publicaciones y libros cubanos," http://www.lajiribilla.co.cu/2001/n26_noviembre/762_26.html. In fact, the racial and monetary inequities in Cuba that are described in Mayakovsky's poem "Black and White" (1925) are often considered a reference for Yevgeny Yevtushenko's part in the script for Mikhail Kalatozov's 1964 film *Soy Cuba* (I Am Cuba). See *Mayakowsky's Cuban Poems*, translated by Langston Hughes. According to Desiderio Navarro, Tatiana Gorstko and he compiled and translated a collection of Mayakovsky's poems in the mid-1980s, the majority of which were previously unpublished in Spanish. While the editors were paid for their work by the Cuban publisher Arte y Literatura, the volume, *Poesía de crítica social de Vladímir Maiakovski* (Vladimir Mayakovsky's Poetry of Social Critique), has not yet been published.

21. Hernández, "Mayakovski en la Habana," 78.

22. Ibid., 80.

23. In 2010, photographs by Alberto Korda of Che Guevara and Fidel Castro playing golf were put up for auction in England, stirring much debate as to the year that the game took place and the reason behind their playing the game.

24. Sánchez, "El sabor de la galleta," 685.

25. Haacke and Bourdieu, *Free Exchange*, 21–22.

26. The critic Desiderio Navarro took the lead in this debate. Just one year later, in 2008, it was well contained and collected within a volume by multiple authors, several of whom were not central to the initial debate. The book was published in Havana by the Centro Teórico-Cultural, directed by Navarro, which speaks to the practices of critique and negotiation in Cuba today. Furthermore, the very title of the volume, *La política cultural del período revolucionario: Memoria y reflexión* (Cultural Politics of the Revolutionary Period: Memory and Reflection), places emphasis on the "pastness" of the event.

27. Pedro Pablo Oliva as quoted in Montero Méndez, "A propósito de la exposición," http://www.lajiribilla.co.cu/2007/n312_04/mirada.html.

28. Betancourt, "The Rebellious Children of the Cuban Revolution," 69.

29. Ibid, 69–70.

30. Ibid, 81.

31. Vives, "Timing Lacking Mixture," 911.

32. See Campins's images at http://bp1.blogger.com/_IWCt35YCtSU/Rwt9yUX f89I/AAAAAAAAAE0/DmvkeRVVmGs/s1600-h/Campins.jpg and at http://www .alejandrocampins.com/en/pintura/pinturas.html, from 2006 and 2007.

33. Prieto, "Halfway of a Hundred Roads, a Brief Voice," http://www.walter lippmann.com/docs1614.html.

34. Campins's work is also critical of other contemporary moments. His painting *Modern Democracy*, which has a similar orange, red, and white color scheme, depicts a kind of personified hybrid object with a sad-looking face that appears to be a cross between an airplane, a bus, and a ship. It does not appear as if the Soviets are the most guilty in this visual narrative. See http://tromponmetabiotico.blogspot.com/2008/10 /alejandro_campins.html.

35. See http://3.bp.blogspot.com/_IWCt35YCtSU/Rwt2PkXf81I/AAAAAAAADo /WQ6lF4XGNxw/s1600-h/Marrero.jpg.

36. Numerous reflections and resignifications of automobiles from the Soviet Bloc have occurred in recent years, including the satiric piece "Moskovich" by the comedy group "Punto y coma," which begins with the question of how to say "mierda" (shit) in Russian; the answer is "Moskovich," a commentary on Cubans' opinion about the automobile.

37. Grillo, "Vostok," http://www.cubancontemporaryart.com. Grillo's article is no longer accessible.

38. Erjavec, introduction to *Postmodernism and the Postsocialist Condition*, 3.

39. Ibid., 7.

40. Ibid.

41. The recollection of the Cold War in outer space is not confined to post-Socialist art in the post-Socialist world. Pablo Picasso's *Etude por Yuri Gagarin* (1961) is one of the first artistic homages to the first human in outer space. Eve Sussman and the Rufus Corporation's *White on White: The Pilot (just like being there)*, a 2009 exhibit at the Winkleman Gallery in New York City, is another example. As Jonathan T. D. Neil asserts in a review of the show, "The contents of the Cosmodrome are of particular importance for Sussman and Rufus. There, preserved like some eighteenth-century period room, lies the office of Yuri Gagarin, the world's first spaceman." See Neil, review of *White on White*, http://www.artreview.com/profiles/blog/show?id=1474022:BlogPost:760765. As Neil frames it, the intertextual reference to the Russian painter and theoretician Kasimir Malevich is more significant than the direct reference to extratextual reality, yet this contemporary encounter with Gagarin in New York City in 2009 cannot go unnoticed.

42. Fernández, *Cuba and the Politics of Passion*, 31.

43. Fernández Larrea, "Carta a Yuri Gagarin," http://arch.cubaencuentro.com /humor/2002/01/14/5351.html.

44. See the band's biography at http://www.unsigned.com/nacionalelectronica.

45. Like *9550* (2006), Colina's documentary implements Soviet film to illustrate the strange juxtaposition of Cuban and Soviet sentimental worlds, but it clearly has a much larger budget and greater access to archives.

46. With respect to his reasoning for making the film, the director stated in an interview with Sandra del Valle Casals: "Sentía la curiosidad de descubrir cómo ve un loco los temas relacionados con la sociedad cubana, qué piensa una persona desequilibrada del bloqueo, de las relaciones Cuba-Estados Unidos; como otra manera de otorgarle también voz y voto a esa gente que uno ve todos los días en las esquinas de este país y de las que uno se ríe — cosa que al menos a mí me resulta medio alarmante" (I was curious to discover how a madman sees topics related to Cuban society, what an unbalanced person thinks about the blockade, about relations between Cuba and the United States; as another way to grant vote and voice to these people that one sees everyday on the corners of this country and that one laughs at — something that, at least for me, is very alarming). See Casals, "Esteban Insausti," http://laventana.casa.cult.cu/modules.php ?name=News&file=article&sid=3057. I find it curious that the Soviets, the other pole in the Cold War, were not part of the initial conscious logic. We may speculate that the very discourse of the insane inspired the film's framing of the Soviet Exposition of 1960.

47. Ponte, "'Existen': ¿Nación que es locura?'" http://www.cubaencuentro.com /cultura/articulos/existen-nacion-que-es-locura-15315/.

48. This is the thesis of my article "*Skitalietz*: Traducciones y vestigios de un imperio caduco."

49. Ponte, *Corazón de skitalietz*, vii–viii. Reina del Mar publishing house decided that the epilogue was more like a prologue and printed it at the beginning of the book.

50. Ponte, "Corazón de skitalietz," in *Un arte de hacer ruinas y otros cuentos*, 184.

51. Ponte, "Heart of Skitalietz," in *In the Cold of the Malecón and Other Stories*, 118.

52. Ponte, "Corazón de skitalietz," 184.

53. Ponte, "Heart of Skitalietz," 118.

54. Ponte, "Corazón de skitalietz," 164.

55. Ponte, "Heart of Skitalietz," 91.

56. Ponte, "Corazón de skitalietz," 185.

57. Ponte, "Heart of Skitalietz," 119.

58. Ponte, "Corazón de skitalietz," 188.

59. Ponte, "Heart of Skitalietz," 122.

60. Ponte, "Corazón de skitalietz," 165.

61. Ponte, "Heart of Skitalietz," 93.

62. Ponte, " 'Existen': ¿Nación que es locura?' " http://www.cubaencuentro.com /cultura/articulos/existen-nacion-que-es-locura-15315/.

63. Loss, *Cosmopolitanisms*, 174.

64. *Madness, Colors Magazine* 47, 10. Some of the images from this issue of *Colors* minus the text are at the website for the magazine (http://www.colorsmagazine.com /issues/47).

65. See http://www.etymonline.com/index.php?term=schism.

66. Martínez Shvietsova, "Skizein," http://www.cubaliteraria.cu/revista/laletradel escriba/n72/articulo-3.html.

67. Cortázar, *La prosa del observatorio*, http://www.literatura.org/Cortazar/prosa .html.

68. Cortázar, from *Prose from the Observatory*, translated by Anne McLean, http:// www.guernicamag.com/poetry/2269/cortazar_1_15_11/.

69. Martínez Shvietsova, "Skizein."

CODA

1. See http://www.temas.cult.cu/debates/libro%204/050-069%20rusos.pdf for a transcript of the discussion. The topics covered by the *Temas* roundtable are worth noting. Diverse in their positions, the panelists—Zoia Barash, Dmitri Prieto Samsonov, the playwright Julio Cid, and Yoss—expounded upon the areas of Soviet inheritance that they know best. Barash discussed cinema; Prieto Samsonov discussed, among other issues, the establishment of an association of Russian immigrants on the island; Julio Cid addressed Soviet influence on artistic pedagogy; and Yoss, the discrepancies between what actually occurred and the language that was used to describe the occurrences, as well as the influence of the Soviets on the artists of his generation. Mervyn J. Bain informed me that in 2009 in Moscow a comparable roundtable took place, entitled "50 Years of the Cuban Revolution (roundtable at the Institute of Latin American Studies), "an event that points to the need to realize a comparative investigation on current Cuban and Russian memorialization. The transcript is published in *Latinskaya Amerika* 6 (2009), 4–31.

2. In 2007, prior to the 2008 accord, the Russian Mikhail Kosyrev-Nesterov directed the feature-length *Ocean* in Cuba, the first such co-production in twenty-five years, about the universal themes of betrayal and love. It premiered in 2008, to largely positive reviews. In 2010, Juan Padrón also brought back on stage the Cuban missile

crisis with the animated film *Nikita chama boom*, which takes a comedic stance toward the 1963 baby boom in Cuba.

3. Sergio, the protagonist of Tomás Gutiérrez Alea's film *Memorias del subdesarrollo* (Memories of Underdevelopment), reflects on this event early in the film. This by now classic 1968 movie is about Cuba's transition from a capitalist system to a revolutionary Socialist one.

4. León González, "Feliz camagüeyano," http://www.pprincipe.cult.cu/articulos/feliz-camagueyano-por-premio-internacional-con-texto-sobre-marti.htm. (This link no longer works.)

5. Álvarez Álvarez, *La cultura rusa*, 107.

6. Travieso, *Cuentos de grandes escritores rusos*, 19.

7. Ibid., 18.

8. Cuban-Russian military collaborations prior to the Cuban and October Revolutions were already under way at the height of the Gray Period. One instance of this is a 1970 cartoon in *Bohemia* entitled "Episodios olvidados de nuestra gesta de independencia" (Forgotten Episodes from Our Fight for Independence) that features three Russians who fight in Cuba's war for independence.

9. Although the twentieth International Book Fair of Cuba in 2011 was dedicated to Cuba's new allies, the ALBA countries, the Russian Pavilion returned once again.

10. For a chronicle on this unusual encounter, see Mir, "Lo que nos dijo el lacónico papá de Cheburashka," February 15, 2010, http://www.esquife.cult.cu/primeraepoca/agendaesquife/2010/Feria/03.html.

11. As did many components of the Havana book fair, this exhibition traveled to many provinces. The cover of the catalogue, along with a handful of the paintings, can be seen at http://www.lajiribilla.cu/2010/n458_02/458_140.html.

12. *Veselye Kartinki*, edition undertaken for the program "Rusia, país invitado de honor de la XIX Feria Internacional del Libro de la Habana" Cuba 2010.

13. "Huellas culturales rusas," http://www.temas.cult.cu/debates/libro%204/050-069%20rusos.pdf.

14. Boym, *Future of Nostalgia*, 49.

15. I am quoting what Yoss said at the roundtable, as opposed to the published roundtable transcript at http://www.temas.cult.cu/debates/libro%204/050-069%20rusos.pdf, since the transcript has been edited.

16. Like many other journals in 2010, *El cuentero*'s March 2010 issue paid tribute to the new proximity between Russia and Cuba by publishing, among other pieces, an essay on Chekhov, an excerpt of Virginia Woolf's "The Russian Point of View," and a short story by contemporary Russian-American writer Gary Shteyngart.

17. Yoss, "Ivana Ivanovna," 25.

18. Ibid., 30.

19. Ibid., 31.

20. Iván de la Nuez, "De la tempestad a la intemperie," 167. Ponte, *La fiesta vigilada*, 67.

# Works Cited

Abreu, Juan. "Deuda." Speech delivered at Kosmopolis: Fiesta Internacional de la Literatura, held at the Centro de Cultura Contemporánea de Barcelona, September 19, 2004. http://www.cccb.org/rcs_gene/juan_abreu_cast.pdf.

Acanda, Jorge Luis. "Racapitular la Cuba de los 90." *La Gaceta de Cuba* no. 3 (2000). http://biblioteca.filosofia.cu/php/export.php?format=htm&id=34&view=1.

Acosta, Dalia. "Cine en Cuba: El regreso de los rusos." *Periodistas en Español*, October 30, 2009. http://www.periodistas-es.org/cine/cine-en-cuba-el-regreso-de-los-rusos.

Aguilar, Alejandro. *Casa de cambio.* Dover, N.H.: Cursack Books, 2005.

Allatson, Paul. *Key Terms in Latino/a Cultural and Literary Studies.* Malden, Mass.: Blackwell, 2007.

Álvarez Álvarez, Luis. *La cultura rusa en José Martí.* Camagüey, Cuba: Acana, 2010.

Álvarez Gil, Antonio. *Callejones de Arbat.* San Juan, Puerto Rico: Terranova Editores, 2012.

———. *Del tiempo y las cosas.* Havana: Unión, 1993.

———. *Naufragios.* Seville: Algaida Editores, 2002.

———. *Nunca es tarde.* Seville: Fundación José Manuel Lara, 2005.

———. *Unos y otros.* Havana: Unión, 1990.

Appiah, Kwame Anthony. "Is the Post- in Postmodernism the Post- in Postcolonial?" *Critical Inquiry* 17, no. 2 (Winter 1991): 336–357.

Armengol, Alejandro. "Unas 24,000 víctimas de Chernobil atendidas en Cuba en 19 años." *Cuaderno de Cuba.* http://armengol.blogspot.com/2009/04/unas-24000-victimas-de-chernobil.html.

Armenteros, Antonio. *El país que no era.* Havana: Letras Cubanas, 2005.

Arreola, Gerardo. "Debaten en Cuba la renovación del socialismo." *Buscando camino* 4, no. 81 (April 2005). http://www.nodo50.org/caminoalternativo/boletin/81-9.htm.

"Asiste Raúl a la inauguración del Pabellón de Rusia en la Feria del Libro." *Vanguardia*, February 12, 2010. http://www.vanguardia.co.cu/index.php?tpl=design/secciones/lectura/portada.tpl.html&newsid_obj_id=18969. This link no longer works.

Bain, Mervyn J. "Gorbachev's Legacy for Russian-Cuban Relations in the 1990s." In *Re-*

*defining Cuban Foreign Policy: The Impact of the "Special Period,"* edited by H. Michael Erisman and John M. Kirk, 212–232. Gainesville: University Press of Florida, 2006.

———. *Russian-Cuban Relations since 1992: Continuing Camaraderie in a Post-Soviet World.* Lanham, Md.: Lexington Books, 2008.

Bakuradze, Nadya. "The Post-Pioneer Inferiority Complex." Speech delivered at the Cuba-USSR and the Post-Soviet Experience Conference, University of Connecticut, Storrs, February 5, 2007.

Bejel, Emilio. *Gay Cuban Nation.* Chicago: University of Chicago Press, 2001.

Benchoam, Ricardo. ¡*Llegamos al futuro!* Videoclip for Nacional Electrónica. http://www.youtube.com/watch?v=8OLwmR2sa6M&feature=related.

Berman, Salomon. "Bound to Outlast? Education for Socialism." In *Changing Cuba/Changing World,* compiled by Mauricio A. Font, 137–175. New York: Bildner Center for Western Hemispheric Studies, 2008. http://web.gc.cuny.edu/dept/bildn/publications/documents/FrontMatter2_001.pdf.

Bermejo Santos, Antonio. "Islas y la difusión del quehacer de las ciencias sociales." *Islas* 45, no. 135 (January–March 2003): 145–158.

Betancourt, Juan Carlos. "The Rebellious Children of the Cuban Revolution: Notes on the History of Cuban Sots Art." Translated by Antonio Garza. In *Caviar with Rum: Cuba-USSR and the Post-Soviet Experience,* edited by Jacqueline Loss and José Manuel Prieto, 69–84. New York: Palgrave, 2012.

Bhabha, Homi K. *The Location of Culture.* New York: Routledge Classics, 2005.

Birkenmaier, Anke. "Art of the Pastiche: José Manuel Prieto's *Rex* and Cuban Literature of the 1990s." *Revista de estudios hispánicos* 43 (2009): 123–147.

Black, George. "Cuba: The Revolution: Toward Victory Always, but When?" *Nation* 373, no. 12 (October 24, 1988): 373–385.

Boadle, Anthony. "Russian Women Stranded in Cuba since USSR Fall." September 5, 2007. http://www.reuters.com/article/2007/09/05/us-cuba-russia-women-idUSN2135841320070905.

Boym, Svetlana. *The Future of Nostalgia.* New York: Basic Books, 2001.

Brennan, Timothy. *At Home in the World: Cosmopolitanism Now.* Cambridge, Mass.: Harvard University Press, 1997.

Brown, Francisco, Ariel Dacal, Julio A. Díaz Vázquez, et al. "¿Por qué cayó el socialismo en Europa oriental?" *Temas* 39–40 (October–December 2004): 92–111.

Buck-Morss, Susan. *Dreamworld and Catastrophe: The Passing of Mass Utopia in East and West.* Cambridge, Mass.: MIT Press, 2000.

Calcines, Argel. "Matrioshkas cubanas." *Opus Habana,* March 31, 2009. http://opushabana.ohc.cu/index.php?option=com_content&view=article&id=1590&catid=26&Itemid=44.

Carbonell, Nestor T. *And the Russians Stayed: The Sovietization of Cuba: A Personal Portrait.* New York: Williams Morrow, 1989.

Carpentier, Alejo. "Publicaciones y libros cubanos después del triunfo de la revolución." *La Jiribilla* 26 (November 2001). http://www.lajiribilla.co.cu/2001/n26_noviembre/762_26.html.

Castro Ruz, Fidel. "Dedication of Lenin Vocational School of Calabazar." Speech deliv-

ered at Calabazar, Havana, January 31, 1974. http://lanic.utexas.edu/project/castro
/db/1974/19740131.html.

―――. "Discurso pronunciado a los estudiantes cubanos becarios en la Unión Soviética y al personal de la embajada de Cuba en la URSS." Speech delivered at the Cuban
Embassy, Moscow, July 2, 1972. http://www.cuba.cu/gobierno/discursos/1972
/esp/f020772e.html.

―――. "Palabras a los intelectuales." Speech delivered at the National Library, Havana,
June, 16, 23, and 30, 1961. http://www.cuba.cu/gobierno/discursos/1961/esp/f30061e
.html.

―――. "Words to the Intellectuals." Speech delivered at the National Library, Havana,
June 16, 23, and 30, 1961. http://lanic.utexas.edu/project/castro/db/1961/19610630
.html.

Cortázar, Julio. La prosa del observatorio. Buenos Aires: Lumen, 1972.

Cuba mi amor. Directed by Penda Houzangbe. Thesis, Escuela Internacional de Cine y
Televisión de San Antonio de los Baños, 2004.

Dacosta, Zeta. "The New Miscegenation: Las Polovinas." Islas, September 2009, 23–28.
http://www.angelfire.com/planet/islas/English/Islas4-13.htm.

de la Nuez, Iván. "De la tempestad a la intemperie." In Paisajes después del muro, edited
by Iván de la Nuez, 163–179. Barcelona: Ediciones Península, 1999.

―――. "Llega el 'eastern.'" El País. May 8, 2010. http://www.elpais.com/articulo
/portada/Llega/eastern/elpepuculbab/20100508elpbabpor_3/Tes.

del Río, Joel. "Regresan los rusos a la Cinemateca." La Jiribilla 366 (May 10–16, 2008).
http://www.lajiribilla.cu/2008/n366_05/labutaca.html.

del Valle Casals, Sandra. "Esteban Insausti: 'Con el cine no se juega.'" La Ventana, February 27, 2006. http://laventana.casa.cult.cu/modules.php?name=News&file=article
&sid=3057.

Desde lejos. Directed by Guillermo Centeno. Havana: ICAIC, 1989.

"Destituyen a la directora del Canal Televisión Camagüey por emitir un documental
censurado." CubaNet, December 20, 2007. http://www.cubanet.org/CNews/y07
/dic07/2007.htm.

Díaz, Jesús. Las cuatro fugas de Manuel. Madrid: Espasa, 2002.

―――. Siberiana. Madrid: Espasa Calpe, 2000.

Díaz-Briquets, Sergio. "Demographic and Related Determinants of Recent Cuban Emigration." International Migration Review 17, no. 1 (Spring 1983): 95–119.

Díaz Gómez, Yamil. La calle de los oficios. Havana: Centro Cultural Pablo de la Torriente
Brau, 2007.

Díaz Infante, Duanel. "Muñequitos rusos, nostalgia cubiche." Cuba: La memoria incon-
solable: Apuntes sobre cultura, historia e ideología, April 6, 2007. http://www.duanel
diaz.blogspot.com/2007/04/muequitos-rusos-nostalgia-cubiche.html.

Díaz Torres, Daniel. Lisanka. Madrid: Ibermedia. Havana: ICAIC. Moscow: Mosfilm
Studios, 2009.

Domínguez, Jorge I. "The Political Impact on Cuba of the Reform and Collapse of
Communist Regimes." In Cuba after the Cold War, edited by Carmelo Mesa-Lago,
99–132. Pittsburgh: University of Pittsburgh Press, 1993.

Erjavec, Aleš. Introduction to *Postmodernism and the Postsocialist Condition: Politicized Art under Late Socialism*, edited by Aleš Erjavec, 1–55. Berkeley: University of California Press, 2003.

Espinosa Domínguez, Carlos. "The Mammoth That Wouldn't Die." Translated by Elizabeth Bell. In *Caviar with Rum: Cuba-USSR and the Post-Soviet Experience*, edited by Jacqueline Loss and José Manuel Prieto, 109–117. New York: Palgrave, 2012.

*Existen*. Directed by Esteban García Insausti. Havana: Producciones Sincover, 2005.

Feijóo, Samuel. "Viaje a la Unión Soviética." *Islas* 9, no. 2 (1967): 83–307.

Feijóo, Samuel, and Bulgakova, Nina, eds. *Poetas rusos y soviéticos*. Havana: Universidad Central de las Villas, 1966.

Fernández, Damián J. *Cuba and the Politics of Passion*. Austin: University of Texas Press, 2000.

Fernández de Juan, Adelaida. "Clemencia bajo el sol." In *Nuevos narradores cubanos*, edited by Michi Strausfeld, 77–87. Madrid: Siruela, 2000.

Fernández Delgado, Kevin. "Gallina." *El cuentero*. El Dinosaurio Prize, 2008. http://www.centronelio.cult.cu/index.php?option=com-content&task=view&id=678&itemid=147.

Fernández Díaz, Verónica. "Igor Stravinsky en Alejo Carpentier." *SiC: Revista literaria y cultural* 44 (October–December 2009): 27–31.

Fernández Fé, Gerardo. "De lémures y economías." *Encuentro* 20 (2001): 348–349.

Fernández Larrea, Ramón. "Carta a Yuri Gagarin." *Encuentro en la red* 279, January 14, 2002. http://arch.cubaencuentro.com/humor/2002/01/14/5351.html.

Fernández Retamar, Roberto. *Calibán: Apuntes sobre nuestra cultura en América*. Mexico City: Diogenes, 1971.

Ferrer, Jorge. "Around the Sun: The Adventures of a Wayward Satellite." Translated by Anna Kushner. In *Caviar with Rum: Cuba-USSR and the Post-Soviet Experience*, edited by Jacqueline Loss and José Manuel Prieto, 95–107. New York: Palgrave, 2012.

———. "Una aventura de Roberto Fandiño en Moscú." *El tono de la voz*, July 27, 2009. http://www.eltonodelavoz.com/archivo/www.cubaencuentro.com/jorge-ferrer/blogs/el-tono-de-la-voz/una-aventura-de-roberto-fandino-en-moscu.html.

Fornet, Jorge. *Los nuevos paradigmas: Prólogo narrativo al siglo XXI*. Havana: Letras Cubanas, 2006.

Fowler Calzada, Víctor. "Todas íbamos a ser reinas." *Miradas: revista del audiovisual*. http://www.eictv.co.cu/miradas/index.php?option=com_content&task=view&id=587&Itemid=86. (Link no longer works.)

Fuentes, Norberto. *Posición uno*. Havana: Unión, 1982.

García Espinosa, Julio. "For an Imperfect Cinema." Translated by Julianne Burton. *Jump Cut*, no. 20 (1979): 24–26. http://www.ejumpcut.org/archive/onlinessays/JC20folder/ImperfectCinema.html.

García Montiel, Emilio. *Presentación del olvido*. Miami: Linkgua, 2010.

García-Zarza, Isabel. "Cuba aún guarda huellas de la era soviética." *El Nuevo Herald*, December 11, 2000, 21A (3).

Gates, Henry Louis, Jr. *The Signifying Monkey: A Theory of Afro-American Literary Criticism*. Oxford: Oxford University Press, 1988.

Generación Asere. "Sobre *Goodbye, Lolek!*" May 14, 2008. http://generacionasere
.blogspot.com/2008/05/sobre-goodbye-lolek.html.

*Gente de Moscú.* Directed by Roberto Fandiño. 1963.

González Reinoso, Pedro. *Vidas de Roxy o el aplatanamiento de una rusa en Cuba.* Bogotá:
San Librario Books, 2010.

———. "Roxy the Red." Translated by Dick Cluster. In *Caviar with Rum: Cuba-USSR
and the Post-Soviet Experience,* edited by Jacqueline Loss and José Manuel Prieto,
55–65. New York: Palgrave, 2012.

*Good Bye, Lenin!* Directed by Wolfgang Becker. Berlin: X-Filme Creative Pool. Cologne:
Westdeutscher Rundfunk, 2003.

*Good Bye, Lolek.* Directed by Asori Soto. Havana: Havana Producciones Aguaje, 2005.

Grillo, Rafael. "Vostok: The Cuban-Soviet Paradox." Contemporary Cuban Art, November 2007. http://www.cubancontemporaryart.com. Accessed November 30, 2007
(site now discontinued).

Guerra, Wendy. "En Cuba es difícil guardar secretos." Interview by Mili Rodríguez
Villouta. *La Nación* (Santiago de Chile), November 26, 2006. http://www.lanacion
.cl/prontus_noticias/site/artic/20061122/pags/20061122194534.html.

———. *Nunca fui primera dama.* Barcelona: Bruguera, 2008.

———. *Ropa interior.* Barcelona: Bruguera, 2008.

———. *Todos se van.* Barcelona: Bruguera, 2006.

Guerrero, Gustavo. "Retrato del científico adolescente." Review of *Las cuatro fugas
de Manuel,* by Jesús Díaz. *Letras Libres,* April 2002. http://www.letraslibres.com
/revista/libros/las-cuatro-fugas-de-marvel-de-jesus-diaz.

Guillot Carvajal, Mario L. Review of *Siberiana. Revista Hispano Cubana* 8 (Fall 2000):
174–176.

Haacke, Hans, and Pierre Bourdieu. *Free Exchange.* Cambridge, Mass.: Polity Press in
association with Blackwell, 1995.

Hart, Celia. "La bandera de Coyoacan." In *Apuntes revolucionarios: Cuba, Venezuela y el
socialismo internacional,* by Celia Hart, 27–33. Madrid: Fundación Federico Engels,
2006. http://www.lahaine.org/b2-img/celia_apuntes.pdf.

Hernández, Ihosvany. "Un diario desde el país caribeño criado con códigos soviéticos."
Review of *Nunca fui primera dama,* by Wendy Guerra. April 13, 2009. http://www
.laparadadelosmangos.blogspot.com/2009/04/un-diario-desde-el-pais-caribeno
-criado.html. (This link no longer works.)

Hernández, Juan. "Mayakovski en la Habana." *Islas* 9, no. 2 (1967): 77–83.

Hernández, Rafael. "The Cuban Transition: Imagined and Actual." Speech delivered at
the University of Chicago, October 7, 2009. http://news.uchicago.edu/multimedia
/latin-american-briefing-series-cuban-transition-imagined-and-actual-rafael
-hernandez.

Hernández Busto, Ernesto. "La lección de Demonia." *Cuba Encuentro,* August 4, 2005.
http://arch1.cubaencuentro.com/cultura/20050804/8ffddfcb196d249346a80a37317
03b95/1.html.

Hernández Salván, Marta. "Requiem for a Chimera." *Revista de Estudios Hispánicos* 43,
no. 1 (January 2009): 149–171.

Houzangbe, Penda. *Cuba mi amor.* Thesis, Escuela Internacional de Cine y Televisión de San Antonio de los Baños, 2004.

"Huellas culturales rusas y de Europa del Este en Cuba." Roundtable discussion with panelists Rafael Hernández, Zoia Barash, Julio Cid, Dmitri Prieto Samsonov, and Yoss. Instituto Cubano del Arte e Industrias Cinematográficos (ICAIC), May 28, 2009. http://www.temas.cult.cu/debates/libro%204/050-069%20rusos.pdf.

Huyssen, Andreas. *Present Pasts: Urban Palimpsests and the Politics of Memory.* Palo Alto, Calif.: Stanford University Press, 2003.

*I Am Cuba: The Siberian Mammoth.* Directed by Vicente Ferraz. Rio de Janeiro: Três Mundos Produções, 2005.

Israel, Esteban. "Change Is Coming to Cuba, on Chinese Wheels." Reuters, March 13, 2008. http://www.reuters.com/article/2008/03/13/us-cuba-transport-idUSN13217 78820080313?sp=true.

Jácome, Aurora. "The *Muñequitos Rusos* Generation." Translated by Katherine M. Hedeen. In *Caviar with Rum: Cuba-USSR and the Post-Soviet Experience,* edited by Jacqueline Loss and José Manuel Prieto, 27–35. New York: Palgrave, 2012.

———. *Muñequitos rusos . . . y otros: Para los cubanos que como yo, los siguen recordando con añoranza.* http://www.munequitosrusos.blogspot.com/.

La Fountain-Stokes, Lawrence. "Trans/Bolero/Drag/Migration: Music, Cultural Translation, and Diasporic Puerto Rican Theatricalities." *WSQ: Women's Studies Quarterly* 36, nos. 3 and 4 (Fall/Winter 2008): 190–209.

Laub, Dori. "Truth and Testimony: The Process and the Struggle." In *Trauma: Explorations in Memory,* edited by Cathy Caruth, 61–76. Baltimore: Johns Hopkins University Press, 1995.

Leiner, Marvin. *Sexual Politics in Cuba: Machismo, Homosexuality, and AIDS.* Boulder, Colo.: Westview Press, 1994.

León González, Yanetsy. "Feliz camagüeyano por premio internacional con texto sobre Martí." *Príncipe: Portal de la cultura de Camagüey, Cuba,* November 16, 2010. http://www.pprincipe.cult.cu/articulos/feliz-camagueyano-por-premio-internacional-con-texto-sobre-marti.htm. This link no longer works.

Leyva Martínez, Ivette. "Miami: Pequeñas nostalgias del castrismo." *Cubaencuentro.* March 20, 2003. http://arch1.cubaencuentro.com/desde/20030320/6b1ffba34607b446bdb97b1561830eaa.html.

*The Lives of Others.* Directed by Florian Henckel von Donnersmarck. Burbank, Calif.: Walt Disney Studios Motion Pictures International, 2006.

López, Luis. "Tres horas en la URSS." *Verde Olivo* 17, no. 30 (July 1976): 54–55.

López-Cabrales, María del Mar. *Arenas cálidas en alta mar: Entrevistas a escritoras contemporáneas en Cuba.* Santiago: Editorial Cuarto Propio, 2007.

Loss, Jacqueline. *Cosmopolitanisms and Latin America: Against the Destiny of Place.* New York and London: Palgrave, 2005.

———. "*Skitalietz*: Traducciones y vestigios de un imperio caduco." In *La vigilia cubana: Sobre Antonio José Ponte,* edited by Teresa Basile, 95–109. Rosario, Argentina: Beatriz Viterbo, 2009.

———. "Stravinsky: His Times and His Travels in Alejo Carpentier's *Concierto barroco*." Master's thesis, University of Texas, 1995.

Martínez Shvietsova, Polina. "17 abstractos de una agenda." *El cuentero*. http://www.centronelio.cult.cu/index.php?option=com_content&task=view&id=241&Itemid=90.

———. "Skizein (Decálogo del año cero)." In *Skizein (decálogo del año cero), y otros cuentos* (Premio Iberoamericano de Cuento Julio Cortázar, 2008), 13–25. Havana: Letras Cubanas, 2008.

Martínez Shvietsova, Polina, and Dmitri Prieto Samsonov. ". . . So, Borscht Doesn't Mix into the *Ajiaco*? An Essay of Self-Ethnography on the Young Post-Soviet Diaspora in Cuba." Translated by Kristina Cordero. In *Caviar with Rum: Cuba-USSR and the Post-Soviet Experience*, edited by Jacqueline Loss and José Manuel Prieto, 133–159. New York: Palgrave, 2012.

Masvidal Saavedra, Mario. "De *otakus* y *mangakas* en el Caribe." *La Jiribilla* 394 (November 22–28, 2008). http://www.lajiribilla.co.cu/2008/n394_11/394_16.html.

Mayakovsky, Vladimir. *Mayakowsky's Cuban Poems*. Translated by Langston Hughes. Moscow, 1933.

*Memorias del subdesarrollo*. Directed by Tomás Gutiérrez Alea. Havana: ICAIC, 1968.

Menchú, Rigoberta, and Elisabeth Burgos-Debray. *I, Rigoberta Menchú: An Indian Woman in Guatemala*. Translated by Ann Wright. New York: Verso, 1984.

———. *Me llamo Rigoberta Menchú y así me nació la conciencia*. Mexico City: Siglo Veintiuno, 1983.

Mir, Andrés. "Lo que nos dijo el lacónico papá de Cheburashka." *Revista electrónica esquife*, February 15, 2010. http://www.esquife.cult.cu/primeraepoca/agendaesquife/2010/Feria/03.html.

Miralles, Jorge. "Una breve exposición: . . . *fruto de la fantasía*." Speech read in absentia at the Cuba-USSR and the Post-Soviet Experience Conference, University of Connecticut, Storrs, February 6, 2007.

———. "Fotos de boda." *Las voces del pantano*. Havana: Unión, 2001.

———. "Wedding Photos." Translated by Jacqueline Loss. *Mandorla: Nueva Escritura de las Américas* 9 (2006): 299–310.

Mistral, Gabriela. *Selected Poems of Gabriela Mistral*. Translated by Ursula K. Le Guin. Albuquerque: University of New Mexico Press, 2003.

Moiseev, Alexander, and Olga Egorova. *Los rusos en Cuba*. Havana: Abril, 2010.

Molina, Juan Antonio. "La marca de su cicatriz. Historia y metáfora en la fotografía cubana contemporánea." In *Nosotros, los más infieles: Narraciones críticas del arte cubano, 1993–2005*, edited by Andrés Isaac Santana, 835–845. Murcia, Spain: CENDEAC, 2007.

Montero Méndez, Hortensia. "A propósito de la exposición 'Puente para las rupturas: Pensar los 70.'" *La Jiribilla* 312 (April 28–May 4, 2007). http://www.lajiribilla.co.cu/2007/n312_04/mirada.html.

Moore, David Chioni. "Is the Post- in Postcolonial the Post- in Post-Soviet? Toward a Global Postcolonial Critique?" *PMLA* 116, no. 1 (January 2001): 111–128.

Morales Catá, Guillermo. "Invaden balseros aéreos cubanos aeropuerto internacional de Madrid-Barajas y solicitan asilo politico." *Cubanet*, March 12, 2002. http://www.cubanet.org/CNews/y02/mar02/1202.htm.

Muñoz, José Esteban. *Disidentifications: Queers of Color and the performance of politics.* Minneapolis: University of Minnesota Press, 1999.

*Los músicos de Bremen.* Music video directed by Ernesto René, 2001. http://www.youtube.com/watch?v=lkqDDlUFPMo.

"Nacional Electrónica." *Unsigned Entertainment.* http://www.unsigned.com/nacional electronica.

Navarro, Desiderio, ed. *La política cultural del período revolucionario: Memoria y reflexión.* Havana: Centro Teórico-Cultural, Criterios, 2008.

Neil, Jonathan T. D. Review of *White on White: The Pilot (just like being there)*, by Eve Sussman and the Rufus Corporation. *Artreview.com*, May 22, 2009. http://www.artreview.com/profiles/blog/show?id=1474022:BlogPost:760765.

Newman, Britton. "The Presence and Function of Russia in the Fiction of José Manuel Prieto." Master's thesis, University of North Carolina, 2008.

*9550.* Directed by Jorge E. Betancourt and Ernesto René. Havana: Producciones por la Izquierda, 2006.

Nora, Pierre. *Realms of Memory: Rethinking the French Past.* Translated by Arthur Goldhammer. New York: Columbia University Press, 1996.

Padilla, Heberto. *Fuera del juego.* Havana: Unión, 1968.

Pereda, Rosa María. "Manuel Pereira presenta en España 'El Ruso,' su 'autobiografía de una generación de cubanos.'" *El País*, May 26, 1982. http://www.elpais.com /articulo/cultura/PEREIRA/_MANUEL/Manuel/Pereira/presenta/Espana /Ruso/autobiografia/generacion/cubanos/elpepicul/19820526elpepicul_16/Tes.

Pereira, Manuel. *El ruso.* Havana: Unión, 1980.

Pérez, Ricardo Alberto. *Trillos urbanos.* Havana: Letras Cubanas, 2003.

Pérez, Silvia. "Cuba en el CAME. Una integración extracontinental." *Nueva Sociedad* 68 (September–October 1983): 131–139. http://www.nuso.org/upload/articulos /1108_1.pdf.

Pérez Castillo, Ernesto. "Bajo la bandera rosa." In *Los que cuentan: Una antología*, edited by Ernesto Pérez Castillo, 31–49. Havana: Ediciones Cajachina, 2007.

———. "Escribir no es una carrera." Interview by Leopoldo Luis. *Caimán barbudo* 350 (2008). http://www.centronelio.cult.cu/index.php?option=com_content&task =view&id=518&Itemid=62.

———. *Haciendo las cosas mal.* Havana: Unión, 2009.

Plasencia, Azucena. Review of *La sexte parte del mundo. Bohemia* 69, no. 48 (December 2, 1977): 30.

Ponte, Antonio José. *Un arte de hacer ruinas y otros cuentos.* Mexico City: Fonda de Cultura Económica, 2005.

———. *Corazón de skitalietz.* Cienfuegos, Cuba: Reina del Mar, 1998.

———. "'Existen': ¿Nación que es locura?" *Encuentro en la Red*, April 18, 2006. http:// www.cubaencuentro.com/cultura/articulos/existen-nacion-que-es-locura-15315/.

————. *La fiesta vigilada*. Madrid: Anagrama, 2007.

————. *In the Cold of the Malecón and Other Stories*. Translated by Cola Franzen and Dick Cluster. San Francisco: City Lights, 2000.

Prieto, Abel. "Halfway of a Hundred Roads, a Brief Voice." Interview by Elizabeth Mirabal Llorens and Carlos Velazco Fernández. Translated by Ana Portela. *Juventud Rebelde*, October 14, 2007. http://www.walterlippmann.com/docs1614.html.

————. *El humor de Misha: La crisis del "socialismo real" en el chiste político*. Buenos Aires: Colihue, 1997.

Power, Kevin. *Fnimaniev*. 2004. Published in conjunction with the exhibition Fnimaniev!! shown at Galería Aural, Alicante, Spain.

Prieto, José Manuel. *Enciclopedia de una vida en Rusia*. Mexico City: Consejo Nacional para la Cultura y las Artes, 1998.

————. *Encyclopedia of a Life in Russia*. Translated by Esther Allen. New York: Grove Press, forthcoming.

————. "Heberto Padilla, the First Dissident." Translated by Jorge Castillo. In *Caviar with Rum: Cuba-USSR and the Post-Soviet Experience*, edited by Jacqueline Loss and José Manuel Prieto, 119–130. New York: Palgrave, 2012.

————. *Livadia*. Barcelona: Mondadori, 1999.

————. *Nocturnal Butterflies of the Russian Empire*. Translated by Carol Christensen and Thomas Christensen. New York: Grove Press, 2000.

————. *Nunca antes habías visto el rojo*. Havana: Letras Cubanas, 1996.

————. *Rex*. Madrid: Anagrama, 2007.

————. *Rex*. Translated by Esther Allen. New York: Grove Press, 2009.

————. *El tartamudo y la rusa*. Mexico City: Tusquets, 2002.

————. *Treinta días en Moscú*. Barcelona: Mondadori, 2001.

Prieto Samsonov, Dmitri. "Descubrir 'el agua tibia': La identidad cubano-(post)-soviética como horizonte polémico." *Reviste electrónica esquife* 56 (April–May 2007). http://www.esquife.cult.cu/primeraepoca/revista/56/13.htm.

————. "Jurel en Pesos." In *Ternura entre milenios*. Edited by Polina Martínez Shvietsova and Dmitri Prieto Samsonov. Havana: Unicornio, 2004.

————. "Military Bases in 'Our America.'" *Havana Times*, August 18, 2009. http://www.havanatimes.org/?p=12727.

————. "The Moon Landing and Woodstock Anniversaries." *Havana Times*, August 19, 2009. http://www.havanatimes.org/?p=12782.

————. "The Pravda of Reggaetón." *Havana Times*, May 9, 2009. http://www.havanatimes.org/?p=8363.

————. "Trotsky in Havana." *Havana Times*, March 26, 2009. http://www.havanatimes.org/?p=6621.

Quiroga, José. *Cuban Palimpsests*. Minneapolis: University of Minnesota Press, 2005.

Rodríguez, Ernesto René. "Solarística." *Cuba Underground* (Anónimo Literario, Taller 1), February 3, 2005. http://www.cubaunderground.com/anonimo-literario-taller-no-1/solaristica.

Rivalta, Gertrudis. "*Fnimaniev! Fnimaniev!* The Tortoise and the Hare: The Black *Moña*."

Translated by Jacqueline Loss. In *Caviar with Rum: Cuba-USSR and the Post-Soviet Experience*, edited by Jacqueline Loss and José Manuel Prieto, 171–181. New York: Palgrave, 2012.

Rodríguez, Reina María. "Carta para no ser un espíritu prisionero." *Cuba Encuentro*. January 15, 2007. http://www.cubaencuentro.com/cultura/articulos/carta-para-no -ser-un-espiritu-prisionero-29675.

———. "Nostalgia." Translated by Kristin Dykstra. In *Caviar with Rum: Cuba-USSR and the Post-Soviet Experience*, edited by Jacqueline Loss and José Manuel Prieto, 37–53. New York: Palgrave, 2012.

Rodríguez, Rubén. "Sobre Sovexportfilm." *La gaceta de Cuba* 3 (2007): 23–26.

Rodríguez Febles, Ulises. *Sputnik*. In *El concierto y otras obras*. Havana: Letras Cubanas, 2007.

Rojas, Fernando. "De lo efímero, lo temporal y lo permanente." In *Vivir y pensar en Cuba*, edited by Enrique Ubieta Gómez, 13–33. Havana: Centro de Estudios Martianos, 2002.

———. "El triunfo de Stalin." *El caimán barbudo* 321 (April 2004). http://www .caimanbarbudo.cu/caiman321/especial1.htm. Accessed July 6, 2005 (site now discontinued).

Rojas, Rafael. "Las dos mitades del viajero." *Encuentro de la cultura cubana* 15 (1999–2000): 231–234.

———. "*Souvenirs* de un Caribe soviético," *Encuentro de la cultura cubana* 48/49 (Spring/Summer 2008): 18–33. http://www.cubaencuentro.com/revista/revista -encuentro/archivo/48-49-primavera-verano-de-2008/souvenirs-de-un-caribe -sovietico-97168. (This link no longer works.)

Rosales Catá, Guillermo. "De la Habana a Moscú en patera aérea." March 3, 2002. http:// www.canalsolidari.org/noticia/de-la-habana-a-moscu-en-patera-aerea/13165.

Rossi, Jacques. *The Gulag Handbook: An Encyclopedia Dictionary of Soviet Penitentiary Institutions and Terms Related to the Forced Labor Camps*. New York: Paragon House Publishers, 1989.

Rubio, Raúl. "Material Culture across Revolutions." In *Cuba: In Transition? Pathways to Renewal, Long-Term Development, and Global Reintegration*, edited by Mauricio A. Font with the assistance of Scott Larson, 293–309. New York: Bildner Graduate Center, 2006.

*Los rusos en Cuba*. Directed by Enrique Colina. Malakoff: RFO, 2008.

Rutland, Peter. *The Politics of Economic Stagnation in the Soviet Union: The Role of Local Party Organs in Economic Management*. Cambridge, England: Cambridge University Press, 1993.

Sánchez, Suset. "El sabor de la galleta olvidada sobre la mesa." In *Nosotros, los más infieles: Narraciones críticas del arte cubano, 1993–2005*, edited by Andrés Isaac Santana, 681–691. Murcia, Spain: CENDEAC, 2007.

Sánchez, Yoani. "Evoking the Bolos." *Generation Y*, June 27, 2009. http://www.desde cuba.com/generationy/?m=200806&paged=2.

———. "The Extinction of the Panda." *Generation Y*, June 27, 2009. http://www.desde cuba.com/generationy/?p=731.

*La sexta parte del mundo.* Directed by Jesús Díaz, Julio García Espinosa, Tomás Gutiérrez Alea, et al. Havana: ICAIC, 1977.

*Sin Embargo.* Directed by Judith Grey. New York: Leaf Productions, 2003.

Smith, Martin Cruz. *Havana Bay.* New York: Random House, 1999.

*Soy Cuba.* Directed by Mikhail Kalatozov. Havana/Moscow: ICAIC/Mosfilm, 1964.

Terdiman, Richard. *Present Past: Modernity and the Memory Crisis.* Ithaca: Cornell University Press, 1993.

Tierney-Tello, Mary Beth. *Allegories of Transgression and Transformation: Experimental Fiction by Women Writing under Dictatorship.* Albany: State University of New York Press, 1996.

*Todas iban a ser reinas.* Directed by Gustavo Pérez. Camagüey, Cuba: TV Camagüey Productions, 2006.

Travieso, Julio. *Cuentos de grandes escritores rusos.* Havana: Editorial Arte y Literatura, 2009.

Ubieta Gómez, Enrique. "Prólogo." *Vivir y pensar en Cuba,* edited by Enrique Ubieta Gómez, 5–10. Havana: Centro de Estudios Martianos. 2002.

*Un rey en la Habana.* Directed by Alexis Valdés. Culver City, Calif.: Columbia Tri-Star, 2005 [distributor].

Vega Serova, Anna Lidia. *Ánima fatua.* Havana: Letras Cubanas, 2007.

———. *Limpiando ventanas y espejos.* Havana: Unión, 2001.

Vélez Bichkov, Antón. "¿Son rusos los muñequitos?" Speech delivered at Koniec Conference of the Soviet Diaspora in Cuba, Biblioteca l de Sancti Spriritus Cuba, March 4, 2004.

Vives, Cristina. "Timing Lacking Mixture (Raúl Cordero en los espacios incompletos)." In *Nosotros, los más infieles: Narraciones críticas del arte cubano, 1993–2005,* edited by Andrés Isaac Santana, 907–912. Murcia, Spain: CENDEAC, 2007.

Weimer, Tanya N. *La diáspora cubana en México: Terceros espacios y miradas excéntricas.* New York: Peter Lang, 2008.

Werman, Marco. "Gorki." *PRI's The World,* January 19, 2005. http://www.publicbroad casting.net/wabe/.artsmain/article/10/70/729763/Programs/Gorki/.

West-Durán, Alan. "Puerto Rico: The Pleasures and Traumas of Race." *Centro Journal* 17, no. 1 (2005): 46–69.

Whitfield, Esther. *Cuban Currency: The Dollar and "Special Period" Fiction.* Minneapolis: University of Minnesota Press, 2008.

Wilson, Michael G. "A Ten-Point U.S. Program to Block Soviet Advances in South America." Heritage Foundation Report, June 22, 1988. http://www.heritage.org /Research/LatinAmerica/bg658.cfm.

"Yanelima te da la bienvenida." http://www.taringa.net/posts/animaciones/5681642 /MegaPost-de-Munequitos-Rusos-_Dibujos-Animados-Sovieticos.html. (This link now goes to a members-only section.)

Yoss. "Ivana Ivanovna y la peste a grajo." *El cuentero* (March 2010): 24–31.

———. "Lo que dejaron los rusos." *Temas* 37–38 (2004): 138–144.

Young, Robert J. C. *Colonial Desire: Hybridity in Theory, Culture and Race.* New York: Routledge, 1995.

Yulzari, Emilia. "Discurso transnacional en *Siberiana y las cuatro fugas de Manuel* de Jesús Díaz." *Revista literaria baquiana* 5, nos. 27–28 (2004). http://www.baquiana .com/Numero_XXVII-XXVIII/Ensayo_II.htm.

Zardoya Loureda, Rubén. "Ideología y revolución: Notas sobre el impacto del derrumbe soviético y el socialism europeo en Cuba." In *Vivir y pensar en Cuba*, edited by Enrique Ubieta Gómez, 34–55. Havana: Centro de Estudios Martianos, 2002.

# Index